Contemporary Analysis in Education Series

Parents and Schools: The Contemporary Challenge

Edited by
Flora Macleod

The Falmer Press
(A member of the Taylor & Francis Group)
London • New York • Philadelphia

UK The Falmer Press, Falmer House, Barcombe, Lewes, East Sussex, BN8 5DL

USA The Falmer Press, Taylor & Francis Inc., 242 Cherry Street, Philadelphia, PA 19106-1906

First published 1989

British Library Cataloguing in Publication Data

Parents and schools: the contemporary challenge.—
(Contemporary analysis in education series)
1. Great Britain. Schools. Relations with parents.
I. Macleod, Flora. II. Series
371.1′03′0941
ISBN 1-85000-498-6
ISBN 1-85000-499-4 (pbk.)

Library of Congress Cataloging-in-Publication Data

Parents and schools: the contemporary challenge / edited by Flora Macleod
p. cm. — (Contemporary analysis in education series)
Bibliography: p.
Includes index.
ISBN 1-85000-498-6 —ISBN 1-85000-499-4 (pbk.)
1. Home and school—Great Britain. 2. Education—Great Britain—Parent participation. 3. Education accountability—Great Britain. 4. Educational equalization—Great Britain.
I. Macleod, Flora (Flora J.). II. Series.
LC225.33.G7P37. 1989 370.19′31′—dc19 89-30792

Typeset in 11/13pt Bembo by
Photo·graphics, Honiton, Devon

Jacket design by Caroline Archer

Printed in Great Britain by Taylor & Francis (Printers) Ltd, Basingstoke

Parents and Schoo
The Contemporary C … ng

CONTEMPORARY ANALYSIS IN EDUCATION SERIES
General Editor: Philip Taylor

6 *Education and Cultural Pluralism*
Edited by Maurice Craft

7 *Language and Learning: An Interactional Perspective*
Edited by Gordon Wells and John Nicholls

8 *Educational Research: Principles, Policies and Practices*
Edited by Marten Shipman

9 *Schooling and Welfare*
Edited by Peter Ribbins

10 *Assessing Educational Achievement*
Edited by Desmond L. Nuttall

11 *Education, Recession and the World Village*
Edited by Frederick M. Wirt and Grant Harman

12 *Social Education: Principles and Practice*
Edited by Chris Brown, Clive Harber and Janet Strivens

13 *Education and Society Today*
Edited by Anthony Hartnett and Michael Naish

14 *Education and Youth*
Edited by David Marsland

15 *Economics and the Management of Education: Emerging Themes*
Edited by Hywel Thomas and Tim Simkins

16 *The Changing Primary School*
Edited by Roy Lowe

17 *Mathematics in Primary Education*
Edited by Michael Preston

18 *The Primary School Teacher*
Edited by Sara Delamont

19 *Educating Teachers: Changing the Nature of Pedagogical Knowledge*
Edited by John Smyth

20 *Political Education in Britain*
Edited by Clive Harber

21 *Informal Primary Education Today: Essays and Studies*
Edited by Alan Blyth

22 *Language and Literacy in the Primary School*
Edited by Margaret Meek and Colin Mills

23 *Development and Dilemmas in Science Education*
Edited by Peter Fensham

Contents

General Editor's Preface

'Teacher power' and 'pupil power' have been matters for contention and concern in times past and may well be again. Now it is 'parent power': a power recognized in Acts of Parliament but not yet fully realized in practice.

It is the purpose of this book, ably edited by Flora Macleod, to provide a framework within which 'parent power' can be examined and explored not only as a political phenomenon but also as a social and educational one.

The several authors who contribute to this book juxtapose education's possibilities and limitations, its value and personal dimensions, with the political realities in which it must make its way and in doing so raise many timely questions; questions to which answers will be sought over the next decade. Whether satisfactory answers will be found remains to be seen. What is certain is that although the debate about 'parent power' has begun, it has not yet tackled some of the central issues: the millenial nature of education and the genuine differences of view about where schooling should lead a nation's children, at least in a democracy.

It is the virtue of this book that it opens out much that needs to be debated as 'parent power' bears down on the schools and what they seek to do and can achieve. Its many contributors should be pleased at this.

Philip Taylor
Birmingham, 1989

Overview

Flora Macleod

Introduction

This book aims to identify and examine the central issues underlying the current interest in parental involvement in schooling. Its content and organization are based on a view that the contemporary interest in home–school relations rests on two major concerns. First there is a desire to equalize educational opportunities in the face of discriminatory forces thought to operate in both schools and the broader community. The main dimensions of these forces are conceived to relate to: (i) social class; (ii) ethnic sub-culture; (iii) gender. Secondly there is the evident desire to increase the accountability of schools to parents. This desire is manifest in legislation on parent governors, in machinery for parental choices both between and within schools and is strongly featured in the Education Reform Act, 1988.

With this in mind, the book is divided into two major sections, one on issues pertaining to equalizing opportunity and the other on issues pertaining to accountability. Within each section authors were invited to tease out issues of value, policy and practice as appropriate to their main brief and particular expertise.

Education and Equity

The Social Class Dimension

In the 1960s and 1970s compensatory education programmes were mounted on the assumption that schooling (and particularly early schooling) could compensate for social class differences in opportunities. Implicit in these programmes were conceptions of extant forms of home–school relations and the need to change them. In chapter 1 of this volume, Jim Murphy re-examines the aims and assumptions behind such interventionist ventures. He contends that the way educational reformers treat the finding of class differences in representation in higher education and differences in outcome of formal schooling is ill-conceived — their conclusion that working class groups are being discriminated against does not follow from their analysis of the data. Instead Jim Murphy, through a reanalysis of the data, cites evidence which suggests that these differences in outcome and representation are due to a working class value system which does not give high priority to education. He asserts that egalitarian interventionist policies are based on an assumption that education is intrinsically good and those without it are somehow diminished. This assumption in turn is based on a value system not necessarily upheld by all strata of society. Hence such policies no matter how well intended have benefited the academically more inclined and have threatened to make the uneducated the unemployed.

Working class indifference to education was something to be eradicated. This, according to Murphy, is a sentiment which has changed little even since the demise of compensatory education. Since school cannot eradicate this alone, parents, it was argued, must be brought to the realization that education is important. Hence an emphasis was placed on changing parental attitudes via parental involvement programmes. Jim Murphy firmly believes that this situation will only be resolved when working class indifference to education is taken seriously. Then, and only then will a more equitable set of political policies emerge aimed at reducing the occupational impact of the academically more inclined over those indifferent to education.

The Cultural Dimension

Jim Murphy's approach is to deal with the whole issue of discrimination and equality. In chapter 1 he uses social class as a vehicle and in chapter 2 he uses race. He does not accept the close link between racial discrimination and racial underachievement often referred to in the literature. In his view the data contradict this link. The evidence, he argues, seems to suggest that different racial groups have different attitudes to education and the acquisition of qualifications. He also believes that other interpretations of the data are equally valid, for example, short stay at school, lack of language support within schools and so on. He maintains that the emphasis on the racial discrimination explanation detracts from proper analysis of the causes of underachievement among certain racial and ethnic groups and therefore inhibits the search for appropriate solutions.

He argues that the situation will only be resolved by an honest analysis of the findings and conclusions which follow from the data — an analysis not blinded by the 'official' view that underachievement is due to racial discrimination.

The Gender Dimension

This is an area that has received little or no attention in the family/schooling debate and yet, as Beverly Anderson points out in chapter 3, it is a matter of considerable importance as the family and the school both promote and hinder girls' and boys' development. In a review of the literature she cites evidence which strongly implies that, despite historical changes which have affected women's position in British society, the family is still on the whole very conservative. The family is a powerful socializing agent whose evolution within a predominantly patriarchal system has resulted in doubling the pressures on liberated women who choose to work outside of it. The family is thus seen as an arena in which women's oppression is at its greatest and a source of ambivalence for many women.

Most schools at best preserve the status quo and at worst actively perpetuate the stereotype. Examples of good practices are few and far between. Yet much of the impetus for change has also come from within schools, often from the energy and commitment of individual teachers. Beverly Anderson believes a concerted effort is needed. If schools fail to work in partnership with families and the broader community on this issue then children are likely to continue to grow up with many of the old stereotyped views, expectations and aspirations whatever the ethos and practice of the school. With this in mind, she draws implications for the newly formed governing bodies and other groups and individuals in a position of influence in home–school–community relations.

Values

Like Jim Murphy, John Raven (chapter 4) believes that there are many difficulties posed by: (a) the need to cater for people who have very different priorities and tastes; and (b) the commonly held belief that justice involves treating people equally. Before issues associated with parent power and school quality can be properly thought through, policy makers, he argues, must: (a) face the fact that people will try to extend their values to other people's children in the assumption that they are appropriate for all children; and (b) find a way of coming to terms with values in public education. Like Jim Murphy, he too sees the origin of values as being partly social class based although admits that the transmission process is far from understood and extremely complex.

In John Raven's opinion schools must do what good parents do. That is, they must identify, respect and nurture the types of behaviours their children value in order to foster their competencies and talents. Thus the key development needed to improve the quality of education is to increase the range of distinctively different options on offer. Children, he maintains, are born with predispositions to develop very different concerns and talents and likewise society needs people with very different interests and competencies. However, the provision of choice as it appears in recent legislation is in itself neither appropriate nor effective for improving the quality of educational provision or for enabling families to influence what happens in schools. With this in mind, the final part of his chapter is taken up with discussing the expectations, tools and structures which are required to perform these functions while keeping education within the public sector.

Accountability to Parents and the Community

Towards an Independent Education for All

Antony Flew (chapter 5) maintains that while ostensibly comprehensivization was to raise standards at all levels by making an academic education available to all, it was in reality an integral part of the socialist vision — the pursuit of an egalitarian society irrespective of its effect on standards. Accountability to individual parents for standards achieved and to the tax payer for money spent did not feature; comprehensivization was seen by its initiators and supporters to be an 'intrinsic good' — that is, something to be pursued for its own sake as opposed to being judged for its actual consequences.

The present educational reforms are viewed as being too little too late — a belated response that does not go far enough down the road towards giving parents more power to choose their children's education. Antony Flew argues for a radical reform in British schools which emphasizes competition among the providers of the education service (the schools) for scarce resources (the pupils and the fees they bring). This competition he believes is the key to improving the overall quality of the schooling delivered.

Parent Power

Ted Wragg (in chapter 6) presents a brief overview of the evolution of greater accountability to parents. He distinguishes between parental rights and parental power and between actual and perceived power. These are then discussed in the context of the rights parents ought to have within a democratic society.

The key to increased parental influence he believes is via collectively formed pressure groups. He is also all too aware of the inevitable unequal distribution of this power with the knowledgeable, articulate and persistent benefiting most. He sees no role for parental influence on the quality of schooling through teacher appraisal. This he regards as purely a professional matter while admitting that the professional/lay demarcation line is unclear.

Parent Governors

Michael Golby begins the next chapter (chapter 7) on a similar theme by stating that the limits of parental involvement need to be identified and tested. He contends that the needs of parents in relation to other interested people must be worked out and negotiated. With this and recent legislation in mind he takes the school governing body as a case study of one particular approach to involving parents in order to shed light on some of the broader issues.

He asserts that a social Darwinian ideology lies behind the present government's enthusiasm for the parental cause. That is, the belief that quality in education, as in species, is ensured through competition in an environment of scarce resources. Although these political motives are at odds with his own ideological stance, Michael Golby is cautiously optimistic from his research findings that school governing bodies may present a last opportunity for the rebirth of citizen participation in a public concern. Thus whatever the motives the effects may satisfy more liberal and democratic ideals.

The Politics of Parental Involvement

It would seem that despite the present government's drive for increased parent power and influence there is no real mechanism whereby this can be achieved effectively and equitably. In practice this shift in the balance of power could mean increased power for central government and a decreased role for intervening bodies such as trade unions and local education authorities. In chapter 8 Ian Morgan, a former president of the National Union of Teachers takes up this controversy.

Like Ted Wragg he is concerned about the uneven distribution of individual and group influence that increased parent power will inevitably bring and looks forward to the day when all schools are so equally well resourced that 'parental choice' and 'parent power' will become redundant concepts. He regrets education being perceived as a commodity and subjected to market forces with the parents, as opposed to the child, being viewed as the consumer. He does not accept that the division of parents and schools is as real as this approach implies.

He goes on to outline the NUT's position vis-à-vis parental involvement and the recent legislation on increased parent power. Like Michael Golby he is keen on public as opposed to parental participation in education but unlike Michael Golby he is pessimistic about the potential of school governing bodies to increase local democracy and community influence. Rather he perceives the government's motives to be more sinister and the outcome to be the consolidation of control and power at the centre.

Parents and the Left: Rethinking the Relationship

Antony Flew's views (chapter 5) are not shared by all right wing thinkers, but, David Reynolds (chapter 9) opines that this lack of ideological homogeneity is offset by a shared distrust of teachers, trade union officials and left wing local authority politicians. This unites them in legislating for the transference of power from the providers of the education service to its consumers (the parents). Like Ian Morgan, David Reynolds sees this as an empty gesture whereby parents are only given the freedom to determine the means toward goals predetermined by the state. The rhetoric is devolution of power to the parents in the interest of greater accountability and higher standards. The reality is increased power and control at governmental level in the interests of political advancement.

An analysis is offered as to why the traditional socialist approach distrusts accountability and holds a lack of regard for parental influences. He accepts that the variability in the quality of schooling since comprehensivization has probably greatly increased but sees this as due to selection by catchment area as opposed to ability which was the case in the tripartite system. Nevertheless quality and excellence in schooling have become issues which have been effectively exploited by the right. Hence he argues that until Labour can generate an alternative non-market based solution to deal with the issue of school quality, the Tory approach is likely to continue to be favoured by those concerned about educational standards. He speculates that the skilled working class as a group may have been particularly swayed by market based remedies to low quality schooling.

The way forward he believes is by ensuring rights while still respecting the educational rights of others. He contrasts this approach with the Tory plight to self-determination via parental rights. The remaining part of the chapter is taken up with how this policy can be effectively implemented and made politically attractive.

Community Education and Parental Involvement

Community education aims to decentralize educational power. It aspires to give people greater say in the decisions which affect them directly. Thus emerging issues within community education were considered germane to the theme of this volume and especially within the context of the Education Reform Act 1988. In chapter 10 Joyce Watt argues that the contribution of community education is vital to a productive relationship between families and schools. However its effectiveness has been reduced by an unsuccessful quest for coherent theories which in turn has left all sorts of issues unresolved. Parental involvement, she maintains, is only one of many dimensions of schooling which has suffered because of this.

In particular she regrets the fact that there was not a sufficiently strong 'community school' voice at national level to anticipate and react to the recent governmental proposals which led to the Education Reform Act 1988. She fears that the changes which will inevitably result from this new radical legislation on parent governors and managers of schools are built on such fragile foundations that they will have powerful and traumatic consequences for all concerned.

Parental Views on TVEI

Major and minor organizational and curriculum changes in British schools up until now have always first and foremost been political matters. Apart from the ballot box parents' views were rarely consulted directly. But what is the parental frame of mind? Richard Pring and Jill Christie (chapter 11) attempted to shed light on this question by talking to parents about the Technical and Vocational Educational Initiative (TVEI) — a recent radical curriculum change in secondary schools. Their data provide considerable information on parents' perceptions of education as far as their children are concerned, on their aspirations for their children and on the degree to which they had been taken into partnership by the schools. Several important questions about parent participation in major curriculum innovations are raised.

Part 1: Education and Equity

1 *Does Inequality Matter — Educationally?*

Jim Murphy

Introduction

Like the uneven distribution of wealth, the uneven consumption of education has long been regarded in liberal circles, as blatantly unfair and patently unjust. Indeed such is the certitude of the educational establishment on this matter that researchers and reformers alike have, for the last thirty years, openly defined class, racial, and sexual differences in education as quite unacceptable in terms of justice.

It is thus ironic that the single most cited determinant of class difference in educational representation is not class discrimination in treatment but class difference in aspiration.

Though not always advanced on its own, the fact that the working class have never regarded education with quite the same urgency as the middle class, has figured in all but a handful of commentaries.[1]

In one respect, of course, explaining difference in representation in terms of difference in aspiration is not in the least surprising; after class difference in representation, class difference in aspiration is the second most recorded fact in educational research. That said however, it is an explanation which in this context has one evident shortcoming, for whilst it explains working class underrepresentation in a parsimonious manner — it is difficult indeed to see how any group, rich or poor, could prosper educationally without some enduring commitment to their studies — it is an explanation which falls well short of confirming that belief which has, for the last hundred years, confidently taken working class underrepresentation to be unfair.

Not only does appealing to aspiration explain working class

underrepresentation without any reference to inequality — a not inconsequential limitation in the circumstances — but such an appeal introduces into the analysis, an explanation which is very different from and on the face of it, quite incompatible with the traditional explanation.

At its least significant, appealing to aspiration seriously compromises the conventional view which has over the years confidently attributed working class underrepresentation to inequalities in access, provision, selection and treatment. True, this near unilateral appeal to aspiration does not deny the existence of such inequalities, merely their relevance in explaining working class underrepresentation. On this view, the determinants of working class underrepresentation, to put it bluntly, are seen as residing not in the way the educational system treats the working class — be it fair or otherwise — as in the general indifference of the working class to protracting their education.

However if appealing to working class indifference casts doubt over the traditional explanation, it has another and in this context, very much more threatening implication: it calls into question not merely the standard attribution of such underrepresentation to inequality, but in so doing, the standard view of such underrepresentation as unfair and unjust.

The reason is simple and is simply this: in appealing to class difference in aspiration to explain class difference in representation, the researcher has conceded not just the fact that the different classes regard education differently, but more importantly the possibility suggested by such a fact, namely that the working class are perhaps not after all quite as interested as the middle class in passing into adulthood, passing examinations.

True, appealing to class difference in aspiration does not in any sense, finally resolve the question of whether class difference is unfair — it does however greatly complicate the matter for before class difference in representation can now be dismissed as unfair, the research establishment must show clearly and unequivocally that such indifference has its origins in inequality and injustice. The reason is not merely because it is good academic practice to corroborate claims; it is that in the absence of such an empirical requirement, dismissing class difference as unfair, parochially precludes the possibility that the working class might see the world and the place of education in that world differently, to the middle class.

As will be shown the cost of such parochialism has, in egalitarian terms been high, for instead of promoting greater educational equality, such intellectual prejudice has fostered even greater social inequality.

The Unpredictable Consequences of Educational Inequality

As every school boy knows, the rings on the trunk of a tree say something about its age. A similarly simple 'rule' has long influenced discussions on education. On this rule the more the class, racial and sexual complexion of higher education resembles that of the population at large, the fairer the educational system. It is a measure used by political and educational commentators alike. In 1950, this handy measure became, with approval of the *Yearbook of Education* the 'official index' of educational inequality: a decade later it was enshrined in the 'official definition' of educational equality. Unlike assessing the age of trees however, measuring educational inequality in this manner has yielded results which are not always easily explained by appealing to inequalities. Quite why this should be is not, as yet, clear — whether it is because no relationship exists between the fairness of the system and the social composition of higher education, or whether the relationship is far more complicated than was first imagined, remains to be seen. What is clear, however, is that on those countless occasions when researchers, and reformers, have used this device, its findings have never been easily reconciled with reality.

One of the first researchers to use this device was the otherwise sceptical researcher C.A. Anderson[2] in an influential study of higher education 'in two dozen populations'. His study uncovered stark differentials between the manual sections of the communities concerned. It was a discovery which, applying the index, Anderson understandably took as indicating '. . . definite inequality in opportunities for higher education'.[3] It was a 'reading' however which Anderson had some difficulty sustaining for when he came to account for such *inequality* his explanation spoke not of inequality and its educationally damaging effects but more neutrally, if no less plausibly, of difference and difference in educational aspiration. Not only did Anderson explain such underrepresentation of the labouring classes in terms of their cultural dispositions, but somewhat surprisingly given his evaluation, he actually discounted the one inequality traditionally regarded as responsible for such difference, namely the high cost of higher education. According to Anderson this long standing 'cause' did not appear to be an especially significant factor at all. Many commentators he conceded did attribute such differentials to '. . . the inability of such groups to defray the cost of higher education', but his own data he insists '. . . demonstrate equally clearly a penchant for parents in certain groups to overlook existing opportunities well within their children's grasp, because of their own traditional preconceptions'.[4] Though there is little doubt on this explanation that the reason for such underrepresentation was the reluctance or as Anderson loads it, the 'lack of perspective' on the part of the labouring classes to take advantage of the existing opportunities, it was a discovery that did little to dent Anderson's confidence in the much vaunted index of inequality: ironically the fact that his explanation made no reference to inequality except to dismiss it, was of little consequence: that the labouring classes failed to take advantage of available opportunities mattered even less. For Anderson, as his conclusion makes very clear '. . . the present results certainly demonstrate that inequality of opportunity for higher education is a widespread and stubborn characteristic of these societies'.[5]

It was a contradiction however that was in the event to perturb the research community no more than it did Anderson, — calculating the equity of an educational system was after all, likely to be more complicated than gauging the age of trees. The possibility that there might be little or no relationship between educational inequality and educational disparity was not considered, even though when this index was applied to such reforms as the 1944 Act and comprehensivization, it showed rather paradoxically that the eradication of such inequalities as 'fees' and the '11+' had not made the system fairer.

What was rather more ironic perhaps was that the research establishment, though freely conceding that such egalitarian initiatives had rid the educational system of these not inconsiderable inequalities, proceeded nonetheless to write off such initiatives as egalitarian failures.[6]

Indeed some ardent advocates of this index felt compelled, given the stability of the participation rates to go one step further to enquire whether such policies could be regarded as egalitarian at all. 'In sum' asks Gray '. . . if egalitarian policies have failed to have egalitarian consequences, it seems reasonable to ask in what sense they were egalitarian'.[7] The fact that fees were a memory and the '11+' a fast-fading reality was evidently, if somewhat surprisingly, of little consequence. The research establishment was, it seemed, more concerned to get rid of class difference in representation than it was with getting rid of class discrimination in access. On this 'index', levelling educational representation, not eradicating educational discrimination, was evidently the acid test of an egalitarian reform, even though as the achievement of Asian pupils now makes very clear, it is quite possible for a grossly discriminated group to match in performance the white majority. Nevertheless despite such a limitation, the 'index' lost none of its appeal. Indeed some commentators were intent on revealing the disequalizing factors and forces which were responsible for such persisting disparity and on this index, inequality.

Bowles' ostensively radical thesis on schooling in American capitalism was one such account. His analysis revealed that the link between class attainment and class inequality was indeed very much more complicated than had been imagined. As his two-step explanation made clear, part of this disparity between the classes was a function of educational inequality and part was a consequence of social inequality. As the first step in his analysis reveals '. . . class differences in schooling are maintained in large measure through the capacity of the upper class to control the basic principles of school finance', through 'inequalities in financial resources', through 'class inequalities in school socialization', 'through tracking and in the attitudes of teachers and particularly guidance personnel who expect working class children to do poorly'.[9]

Though Bowles offers little in the way of evidence to justify linking these inequalities to working class underrepresentation, — like most commentators Bowles for some reason simply assumes that educational inequality adversely impacts on academic performance — he proceeds nonetheless to his central thesis declaring that '. . . social class inequalities in our school system and the role they play in the reproduction of the school division of labour are too evident to be denied'.[10]

Significant though the link between educational inequality and class difference in representation is, it is evident from the second phase of his analysis that it is in fact quite simply irrelevant. 'Class differences in schooling' he now insists '. . . are due primarily to what I have called class sub-culture'.[11] Moreover lest there be any doubt on this point, Bowles bluntly insists that, far from being all-powerful, '. . . the ability of the school to change a child's personality, values, and expectation is severely limited'[12] and that, in any event '. . . inequalities in school resources may not be of crucial importance in maintaining inequalities in the effects of education'.[13]

Though such concessions put a considerable hole in his central thesis concerning the importance of schooling in reproducing capitalist inequality, they have, in this context, a no less significant effect — they leave Bowles in much the same predicament as Anderson a decade earlier, with an explanation for this 'inequality' which makes no reference to educational or social equality.

It is a limitation which, if lost on Anderson, was quickly spotted by Bowles, for having insisted that class difference in representation was the upshot of class difference in aspiration, Bowles proceeds to pre-empt such an objection by insisting that such difference is, in fact, 'an adaptation' in his words, to capitalist inequality. 'Such sub-cultural differences' he now surmises, '. . . stem from the everyday experience of workers in the structure of production characteristic of capitalist societies'.[14]

Though such an assumption was perhaps inevitable, if Bowles was not to end up like Anderson with an explanation which went in the opposite direction to his evaluation of such differences, as unfair, it does have one rather awkward implication; it leaves Bowles with a scenario which turns at base on nothing more compulsive than Bowles' assurance that such sub-cultural differences are not differences, but inequalities.

Though assuming class differences in aspirations to be unfair, it is precisely the one assumption the researcher, as researcher, cannot make, if he is not to beg the question under investigation, it is an assumption which the research establishment has routinely deployed to 'head off' the tendency for explanations of class differences in representation to end up pointing to nothing more 'inegalitarian' than class differences in taste for education. Whilst such an assumption is perhaps inevitable, if the research establishment is not to abandon once and for all, the 'index', which it has so uncritically 'accepted', the consequence of such blind faith has been the proliferation of scenarios which are neither empirical, radical or sceptical.

Typical in this regard is the hugely influential and hugely abstract tract of Bourdieu and Passeron. Like Bowles, Bourdieu and Passeron take the essential function of education to be the perpetuation of social inequality. Unlike Bowles, however, who took the role of school in 'conserving power and privileges' to be self-evident, Bourdieu and Passeron feel it is necessary to give some account of how the educational system manages to 'conceal' this 'transformation' '. . . without either those who carry it out (teachers) or who undergo it, (pupils) ever ceasing to misrecognize its objective truth'.[15] According to the authors, the school fulfils this function by quietly 'excluding', 'dispossessing' and 'disinheriting' the working class in 'producing and attesting capacities'. Though Bourdieu and Passeron are rather vague as to how the educational system actually effects such exclusion — they conveniently beg this crucial question by taking the existence of class difference in education to be, as the French version of the index must have it, '. . . the most accurate formulation of the order of magnitude of the inequality of social conditioned educational opportunity'[16] — it is an explanation which, were it supported, would no doubt go some way towards sustaining their view of schools in structuring class divisions.

However, having explained working class underrepresentation one way, Bourdieu and Passeron proceed like Bowles to explain it quite another. True the second like the first still sees working class underrepresentation as unfair, but instead of explaining such underrepresentation in terms of working class exclusion, Bourdieu and Passeron appeal this time to the general indifference of the working class. It seems that the French working class, like their American and British counterparts, are not actually all that enamoured of education. As Bourdieu and Passeron explain, 'they eliminate themselves before being examined'.[17]

However, unlike Anderson who saw nothing untoward in attributing working class underrepresentation to 'difference in aspiration' and claiming inequality, Bourdieu and Passeron try to avoid this looming contradiction by pointing to the inegalitarian underpinnings of such indifference. Indeed it is the containment of this contradiction which provides 'Reproduction' with its central theme. Despite its distressing language, it is an account which has come to stand as one of the definitive statements on the inegalitarian causation of working class indifference, even though, as with Bowles, not a single scrap of evidence is advanced to show that inequality spawns indifference.

As Bourdieu and Passeron see it, explanations of working class underrepresentation which appeal to working class aspirations miss the point by not, as they see it, 'going beyond negative explanation in terms of lack of motivation'.[18] Such indifference, the authors warn, is not what it seems: it is, they insist, quite the contrary, for by a felicitous coincidence, it seems that 'every act of choice by which a child excludes himself from access to a stage of education or resigns himself to a devalorized type of course takes account of the ensemble of the objective relation . . . between his social class and the educational system'.[19]

Though it is, of course, crucial to Bourdieu and Passeron's view of class difference as unfair, that they sustain such a claim, it is a claim which surprisingly is never once corroborated. True, it is a suggestion which Bourdieu and Passeron reiterate and expand, '. . . objective conditions determine both aspirations and the degree to which they can be satisfied'.[20] Nevertheless, critical though evidence of some link between cultural difference and structural inequality is, none is presented. Though establishing such a link is no doubt a daunting, perhaps even an impossible task[21] the stark fact of the matter is that without some tangible evidence of such a link, Bourdieu and Passeron are left with a scenario which conveniently, if somewhat parochially precludes the one possibility that most threatens their speculative edifice, the possibility that the French working class, like their British, American and Russian counterparts, are little interested in 'staying on' at school longer than is strictly necessary.

For some reason, it is a possibility which neither Bourdieu nor Passeron feel warrants taking seriously. As their homily to those who 'refuse' to accept their uncorroborated view of the matter makes very clear, such a reasonable possibility is born only of innocence. 'Blessed then are modest folk who when all is said and done aspire in their modesty to nothing but what they have: and praise be to the social order which refuses to hurt them by calling them to over-ambitious destinies'.[22]

Evidently in the parochial world of Bourdieu and Passeron, no-one, still less no group would willingly forgo a protracted education at public expense.

Whatever the ultimate explanation for working class underrepresentation, whether it be another manifestation of difference in a differentiated society or another manifestation of inequality in an unfair society, it is clear from the work of Coleman that the present certitude regarding the unfairness of class difference in education does not derive from statistical analyses of the matter. True the Coleman Report had few doubts that class and racial differences in schooling were unfair. Indeed so convinced was Coleman of the inherent unfairness of such difference that he went so far as to 'promote' the official index of inequality to a definition. Such confidence was not, however, borne out by the report. Not only did the report fail to find any significant link between inequalities in funding and difference in performance, but the main sources of such underrepresentation were, it observed, actually cultural. As

Coleman put it 'the sources of inequality of educational opportunity appear to lie first in the home itself and the cultural influences immediately surrounding the home'.[23]

However, though Coleman's discovery at best patently failed to support the prevailing wisdom on the unfairness of class differences, it was nonetheless taken by Coleman and the research community as confirming the collective wisdom. The fact that the groups in question were found to be less well disposed to education was ironically, not a reason for considering the soundness of a making 'educational equality', and so, 'social equality', contingent on the eradication of such differences, but as a reason, even for radical thinkers like Bowles '. . . for changing student attitudes towards schooling'.[24] For some reason, the only egalitarian response to working class indifference was not its endorsement as difference, but its unconditional abolition.

Fortunately not all attempts to show that class difference in representation is unfair, are quite so confused. Most indeed are quite straightforward and avoid the contradiction posed by explaining such difference, in terms of aspiration, by loudly insisting that such aspiration is itself unfair.

Despite having all the hallmarks of expediency, this not inconvenient view of class difference in aspiration has come to enjoy considerable support in educational circles. Indeed such has been its appeal over the years that few commentators have ever doubted, even for a moment its essential veracity. For most commentators such difference between the classes or more exactly, such indifference on the part of the working class admits only of one interpretation: it is for most, as it was for Bourdieu and Passeron, the inevitable, if regrettable consequence of structural inequality. Though not always presented in quite such a trenchant manner, it is a view nonetheless which has always slipped easily from the lips of the researcher and reformer alike.

In this regard Bruner's uncompromising view of such indifference as '. . . a reaction to defeat'[25] is nothing if not typical. It differed little from the characterization of such indifference as was advanced a decade earlier by Plowden and a decade later by Essen and Wedge. In each case the general indifference of the poor was seen as directly related to the fact that they were beset by disadvantage and deprivation.

For Plowden such a lack of parental interest was, as she saw it, one of the more elemental handicaps of being 'born the child of an unskilled worker'.[26] In a similar vein Essen and Wedge, on being faced with much the same class discrepancies in aspiration came to much the same view, taking such indifference to be an 'adaptation' on the part of the poor to adverse social circumstances.[27]

However, by far the most significant manifestation of this view and of the enduring appeal of this view is to be detected in the so-called 'strong' definition of educational equality; a definition which since the mid-1960s has not merely assumed that class difference in aspiration is unfair, but has precluded it could be otherwise, by defining class difference in representation to be unfair.

On this definition, it matters little whether the different classes hold different views on education for on this definition, '. . . inequality in outcome' was, Halsey confidently opined, 'a measure of *de facto* inequality of access'.[28] Or as another advocate put it somewhat earlier, '. . . even in a system where everybody starts under exactly the same conditions, they may still end up differently and if they do so, the system will produce educational inequality'.[29]

On this definition, the otherwise difficult task of showing that working class indifference was indeed the product of inequality and injustice, was neatly avoided. On this view, the indifference of the working class was indisputable evidence of inequality. There was thus no contradiction in seeing class difference in aspiration as did Glass in the 1950s as the main reason for the 'discrepancies in educational opportunity',[30] or as did Floud in the 1960s as the 'prime source so to speak of "unnatural" inequalities in education', [31] or as did Husen in the 1970s as a 'hindrance to the achievement of equality'.[32] or as did Ball in the 1980s an enduring indicator of 'the unequal resources available to pupils'.[33] On this definition, class difference in aspiration could be the cause of inequality, for on this definition such difference was merely a proxy for social and economic inequality.

Nor indeed was there, on this definition, any contradiction in taking such indifference, as did the *educational reformers* to be pathological. Despite the strident objections of *educational researchers* at the time to the ethnocentricity of such appraisals,[34] the reform establishment were merely making explicit what the research establishment had insisted all along; that working class indifference was quite unacceptable in a fair and equitable society.

True, the researcher was typically a little more dispassionate than the reformer. Few were prepared to juxtapose, as did Carlson, working class indifference with real misfortunes such as 'brain-damage, protein deficiency and sickness'. Few however could, given their commitment to the 'strong' notion of equality, disagree with his declaration that 'to equalize opportunity means to offset these disadvantages — more appropriately it means to prevent them'.[35] The presentation was perhaps different but the diagnosis was the same: working class indifference was something to be eradicated, a sentiment that has changed little, even with the demise of compensatory education. The school may no longer be seen as capable of remediating such indifference but remediating such indifference remains the unquestioned goal of equality, even when, as with Widlake, it requires 'bring(ing) parents to the realization of their role in the education of their children',[36] or when as with Little it insists on 'parental support in their efforts to teach their own children more effectively at home',[37] or when, as with Cox and Jones, it requires 'programmes to improve . . . parental attitudes to education',[38] or when as with Ekstrom *et al.*, it demands 'policies . . . to help parents increase their interest in . . . their children's school progress'.[39]

Such an unremittingly dismal and patronizing view of working class indifference is not of course, exclusive to the liberal left: the radical right have never had much time either, for those not inclined on fifteen years of cerebral activity. Bantock's sermonizing about 'the fool' not seeing 'the same tree as the wise man'[40] is merely another manifestation of the same incapacity to take seriously working class indifference, as led more liberal commentators to contemplate compulsion as a way to remediating such indifference. As Robinson saw it '. . . children from disadvantaged homes must be led to the dominant curriculum'[41] whilst for Blackstone there is, it seems a need for 'effective, even statutory, parent involvement in schools'.[42] In each case, the critical question of whether such indifference is a matter requiring rectification is ironically taken as read. True, given that the prevailing definition of educational equality deems such indifference unfair, there is strictly speaking no requirement for individual commentators to 'show' that on each and every occasion such indifference actually has its origins in deprivation and disadvantage.

The main difficulty here however is that the definition which has allowed a generation of researchers and reformers to write off working class indifference as unfair, has not itself ever been shown to be valid.

Some commentators indeed are quite forthcoming on this matter and freely concede like Essen and Wedge that this 'critical' assumption is based not on evidence, but on belief — in Essen and Wedge's case on the belief of Gans that '. . . the only proper research perspective, I believe, is to look at the poor as an economically and politically deprived population whose behaviour, values and pathologies are adaptations to their existential situation'.[43] Others are not quite so candid, but their advocacy of this definition has no greater purchase on reality than that of Essen and Wedge. Strangely neither Coleman nor Plowden, who did so much to promote this notion, appear to have seen it as necessary. In each case, the strong notion was commended not because there was conclusive evidence — a necessary precondition for a definition — that such indifference was unfair, but merely because the strong notion was seen to be better than the weak notion, which sought only the eradication of discrimination, bias and unfairness.

For Coleman, the critical limitation of the weak notion was that in its concern with 'equal inputs', it failed to make due allowance for the fact that, as he puts it 'families differ sharply in what they are able to give to their children educationally'.[44] As he and others had well documented some years previously the distribution of 'educationally strong families' split extensively but not exclusively along class lines.

Though such a discovery, viewed dispassionately, attested to little more than the incidence in the population of different attitudes, it was clear that, for Coleman at least, these differences were not all that they appeared. In fact they were indicative of something very different, not cultural difference but structural inequality, or as he put it '. . . massively unequal influences in the environment of different children'.[45] Indeed so confident was Coleman on the matter, that instead of showing, as this claim implied, that such differences in disposition were the result of social inequality, Coleman proceeded to take this speculative proposition to be not only true, but self-evident. Indeed he defined it to be so. Whilst in other contexts such ignorance, as to the causation of class different attitudes, would have been a compulsive reason for not defining class differences in representation as unfair, Coleman proceeds nonetheless to do just that by committing 'public schooling to reduce handicaps that children face as a function of their early environment'.[46] If not easily defended, such shift was felicitous, for without such a parochial assumption, Coleman would have been left with an explanation for class difference in achievement which provided no support whatsoever for seeing such differences as unfair. True the general indifference of the working class might in reality be very much more than just another innocuous difference in a differentiated society, the difficulty here is that in the absence of evidence or of a definition which showed beyond reasonable doubt that such difference was the result of inequality, the equity or otherwise of such indifference remains just so much speculation, and in egalitarian terms, dangerous speculation, at that.

This point can be developed by looking at Plowden's justification for this 'strong' definition of equality. As with Coleman, Plowden's advocacy of this definition turned not on demonstrating its validity in a culturally diverse society, but rather on berating the weak notion for its incapacity to 'explicitly and sufficiently allow for handicaps imposed by the environment'.[47] Though it is, of course, arguable whether a definition of educational equality should concern itself with matters which fall under the domain of social equality, Plowden was evidently in no doubt, insisting that 'equality was not enough'. Equality she felt needed a 'new cutting edge', declaring that:

> . . . schools in deprived areas should be given priority in many respects. The first step must be to raise the schools with low standards to the national average: the second quite deliberately to make them better. The justification is that the homes and neighbourhoods from which many of their children come, provide little support and stimulus for learning.[48]

'Closing the gap' in achievement for Plowden, as for Coleman became the new goal of 'equality'; what was not quite so clear however, was why Plowden took such an unflattering view of differences in attainment, particularly when, as her justification reveals, the groups concerned had evidently some difficulty containing their indifference to school.

Plowden has an answer, 'it is time the nation came to their aid'.[49] However, lost in the rhetoric, was any indication that not being interested in education was, as Plowden saw it, a matter requiring compensation, for instead of showing that the general indifference of the disadvantaged was in some sense a consequence of impoverishment, Plowden like Coleman merely assumed it to be so and in so doing, clearly and quite unambiguously made 'closing the gap' in attainment between the classes the ultimate objective of educational equality.

The main difficulty with such a definition, however, is not that it is strong, but that it is blind, for in failing to allow for the possibility that the working class might actually regard education as did Plowden's gypsies, 'as a waste of time',[50] the research establishment now finds itself with a definition which simply leaves no room for working class indifference as a legitimate response to education. It is not that the assumption is implausible — though there are indicators which suggest the influence of disadvantage is neither as predictable nor as total as this assumption suggests — from the college boys in Whyte's *Street Corner Society*[51] to the high achievers in Essen and Wedge's survey: it is, that once made, such an assumption simply precludes the other, not implausible interpretation suggested by such indifference, namely that the working classes are just not interested.

A tedious scholastic point, it is in this instance of rather more than passing academic interest, for not only does this definition rule out of the academic debate any possibility of ever taking seriously working class indifference, as indifference, but more importantly, it rules out of the political debate any possibility of ever treating such indifference as indifference.

The second consequence is, more important than the first, for whilst the first says more about the preferences and prejudices of the research establishment who observing working class indifference, spontaneously assume it to be pathological, the second effectively ensures that the educationally indifferent remain at the behest of the academically inclined.

True such a pejorative view of working class indifference is typically masked by a well meaning if patronizing liberalism as the following remarks of Glennerster makes clear, 'the egalitarian would want to put considerable emphasis on both the wider perspectives that education can offer and the pleasure it can bring to children living in a cramped environment'.[52] However, for all the no doubt genuine concern of the research establishment, the impact of such intellectual prejudice on those children living in a cramped environment has been neither liberal nor equitable.

A Degree of Inequality

It is an objection which derives initially from nothing more controversial than the observation that post-war reform, apart from making the educational system somewhat fairer, by eradicating, for example, fees and the 11+, made it considerably bigger. In this context, it is this massive expansion of education, especially of higher education, which is here crucial, for notwithstanding its egalitarian presentation, it is a measure which, since its inception, has served only to strengthen further what Young once described as 'the tyranny of the clever.'[53] Not only has such a costly expansion done nothing to foster the interests of the 'least advantaged' — a not unpredictable consequence given the historic indifference of the working class to protracting their education beyond the statutory minimum but it has more importantly, set in train developments which now threaten to take the work from the working class.

Not the least of these developments is that as a direct consequence of such expansion, Britain has, for the last ten years been producing more graduates than there are jobs for graduates.[54] Though Britain is by no means unique in this regard, such overproduction of graduates has left Britain as it has other industrialized nations, in the invidious position of seeing most of its expensively educated labour being recruited into jobs which, as Pearson indicated, have little or no direct link with their graduate specialism.[55]

At first sight of course, it is the economic not the egalitarian justification for higher education which is most directly damaged by such overproduction. With graduate unemployment over the last decade rarely dropping below double figures, it is now apparent that in investment terms, Britain is spending more than is warranted by the traditional economic argument. However despite its evident economic significance, such overproduction is not without its egalitarian implications, for it has been clear since 1983, that not only do most graduates go into jobs which make no demand on their graduate qualifications, but an increasing minority of all graduates now enter directly or retrain for jobs which as Tarsh recently observes 'would not be seen as graduate level or at least traditionally so'.[56] It is a development which is presently most clearly evident in the colleges where some 29 per cent of their 1983 output went directly into work variously described as 'secretarial/creative/entertainment and artistic.'[57] In the same year, however, it also became clear that much the same trend beset the universities and polytechnics. As Tarsh observed of the polytechnic sector, some 13 per cent of its graduate output went into work so described, a figure which increased to 20 per cent if the rather ambiguous category of 'management services' was included.[58] For the universities, the same categories were the first destinations of 16 per cent of all female graduates, and 14 per cent of male graduates.

In addition to graduate unemployment and under employment, a not inconsiderable minority of graduates were involved in 'other training' courses (for the polytechnics, 15 per cent: for the universities

10 per cent); a category which on closer scrutiny revealed for example that as many as 40 per cent of such graduates were engaged in study leading to secretarial and clerical qualifications.[59]

Though such a downward drift of graduates is, as Meadows and Cox well argued, an understandable consequence of previous expansionist policies,[60] it is a development which for all its intelligibility is not easily defended, at least in egalitarian terms. With graduates increasingly foraging lower down the occupational ladder, it is hard indeed not to get the impression, that having long subsidized the undergraduate in his studies, the non-graduate is now poised to pay an even higher price. Indeed it is a price which they are in the event unlikely to avoid, given that employers, it seems, still prefer graduates over non-graduates even when, as the Standing Conference of the Employers of Graduates indicated, they are looking for skills (such as leadership) which are not generally taught at university and for abilities (such as intelligence and adaptability) which are not exclusive attributes of graduates.[61]

Of course there is little, given such preferences, that the egalitarian reformer can do to stop the clever, or more exactly, the educated, from colonizing the market place. Nevertheless, the egalitarian is quite well-placed to reduce, if only by a little, the occupational impact of the academically inclined over the educationally indifferent. To do so, however, would require that the egalitarian reformer take seriously working class indifference and reconsider the equity of the Robbins principle, that fine sounding piece of special pleading which has since 1966 ensured that if those of academic disposition are able and willing to spend three years in college or university then the government should provide it. Though such a reconsideration would have the evident merit of being even-handed, if a little painful — in that it would reduce for rich and poor alike the chance of a higher education — it might, more importantly put a question mark behind that mentality which has for so long indulged the academically inclined at the expense of the educationally indifferent. At a time when even hi-tech societies cannot utilize, still less exploit, the annual outpouring of expensively educated labour, contracting higher education would be a gesture towards redressing a reform which now threatens to make the uneducated, the unemployed.

Notes

1 For example, in alphabetical order:
ANDERSON, C.A. (1961) 'Access to higher education and economic development', in HALSEY, A.H., FLOUD, J. and ANDERSON, R.A. (Eds) *Education, Economy and Society*, New York, The Free Press.
BALL, S. (1986) 'Streaming and Mixed Ability and Social Class', in ROGERS, R. (Ed) *Education and Social Class*, Lewes, Falmer Press.
BOUDON, R. (1974) *Education, Opportunity and Social Inequality*, Wiley, New York.
BOURDIEU, P. AND PASSERON, J. (1977) *Reproduction in Education, Society and Culture*, London, Sage.
BOWLES, S. (Ed) (1969) 'Towards equality of educational opportunity?' in *Harvard Educational Review*, Equal Educational Opportunity, pp. 115–25, Massachusetts, Harvard University Press.
BOWLES, S. (1977) 'Unequal education and the reproduction of the social division of labour' in KARABEL, J. and HALSEY, A.H. (Eds) *Power and Ideology in Education*, London, Macmillan.
BRUNER, J. (1977) 'Poverty and childhood', *Oxford Review of Education*, vol. 1, pp. 71–87.
CARLSON, K. (1972) 'Equalizing educational opportunity', in GORDON, E. and MILLER, L. (Eds) *Equality of Educational Oportunity*, New York AMS.
COLEMAN, J.S. *et al.* (1966) *Equality of Educational Opportunity*, Washington, US Government Printing Office.
COLEMAN, J.S. (1975) 'Equal educational opportunity: A definition', *Oxford Review of Education*, vol. 1, pp. 27–9.
COX, T. and JONES, C. (1983) *Disadvantaged 11 Year Olds*, Oxford, Pergamon.
DOBSON, R. (1977) 'Social status and inequality of access to higher education in the USSR', in KARABEL, J. and HALSEY, A.H. (Eds) *Power and Ideology in Education*, London, Macmillan.
DOUGLAS, J.W.B. *et al.* (1971) *All our Future*, London, Panther.
EKSTROM, R. (1987) 'Who drops out of high school and why?' *Teacher College Record*, pp. 356–73.
ESSEN, J. and WEDGE, P. (1982) *Continuities in Childhood Disadvantage*, London, Heinemann.
EVETTS, J. (1973) *The Sociology of Educational Ideas*, London, Routledge and Kegan Paul.
FINCH, J. and RUSTIN, M. (Eds) (1986) *A Degree of Choice?*, Middlesex, Penguin.
FLOUD, J. (1961) 'Social class factors in educational achievement' in HALSEY, A.H. (Ed) Ability and Educational Opportunity, Paris, OECD.
FLUDE, M. (1974) 'Sociological accounts of differential attainment' in FLUDE, M. and AHIER, J. (Eds), *Educability, Schools and Ideology*, London, Croom Helm.
GLASS, D.V. (Ed) (1954) *Social Mobility in Britain*, London, Routledge and Kegan Paul.

HALSEY, A.H. (1972) *Educational Priority*, London, HMSO.
HALSEY, A. H., HEATH, A.F. and RIDGE, J.M. (1980) *Origins and Destinations*, Oxford, Clarendon Press.
HARGREAVES, D. (1982) *The Challenge for the Comprehensive School*, London, Routledge and Kegan Paul.
HUSEN, T. (1975) *Social Influences on Educational Attainment*, Paris, OECD.
JACKSON, B. and MARSDEN, D. (1968) *Education and the Working Class*, Middlesex, Penguin.
JENCKS, C. *et al.* (1973) *Inequality*, London, Allen Lane.
LITTLE, A. (1986) 'Educational inequalities: Race and class', in ROGERS, R. (Ed) *Education and Social Class*, Lewes, Falmer Press.
MORTIMORE, J. AND BLACKSTONE, T. (1982) *Disadvantage and Education*, London, Heinemann Educational Books.
CENTRAL ADVISORY COUNCIL FOR EDUCATION, *Children and Their Primary Schools: the Plowden Report*, London, HMSO.

2 ANDERSON, C.A. (1961), *op. cit.*, p. 261.
3 *Ibid*, p. 262
4 *Ibid*, p. 263.
5 *Ibid*, p. 263.
6 For example, as regards educational reform in general, see:
HALSEY, A.H. (1972), *op. cit.*
HALSEY, A.H. *et al* (1980), *op. cit.*
HALSEY, A.H. and SYLVA, K. (1987), 'Plowden: History and prospect.' *Oxford Review of Education*, Vol. 13, No. 1.
WILLIAMSON, W. (1986), 'Who has access?' in Finch, J. and Rustin, M. *op. cit.*, pp. 67–91.
As regards the 1944 Act, see:
BALL, S. (1981) *Beachside Comprehensive*, Cambridge, University Press.
BELLABY, P. (1976) *The Sociology of the Comprehensive School*, London, Methuen.
DOUGLAS, J.W.B. *et al.* (1971), *op. cit.*
FLOUD, J, (1961), *op. cit.*
FORD, J. (1969). *Social Class and Comprehensive School*, London, Routledge and Kegan Paul.
GLASS, D.V. (1954), *op. cit.*
WESTERGAARD, J. and LITTLE, A. (1964) 'The trend of class differentials in educational opportunity', *British Journal of Sociology*, vol. 15, pp. 301–16.
7 GRAY, J. (1981) 'From policy to practice – some problems and paradoxes of egalitarian reform', in SIMON, B. AND TAYLOR, W. (Eds). *Education in the Eighties*, London, Batsford.
8 SWANN, M. (1985) *Education for All*. London, HMSO.
9 BOWLES, S. (1977), *op. cit.*, pp. 143–46.
10 *Ibid*, p. 144.
11 *Ibid*, p. 147.
12 *Ibid*, p. 147.
13 *Ibid*, p. 149.
14 *Ibid*, p. 149.

15 BOURDIEU, P. and PASSERON (1977), *op. cit.*, p. 67.
16 *Ibid*, p. 223.
17 *Ibid*, p. 153.
18 *Ibid*, p. 154.
19 *Ibid*, p. 155.
20 *Ibid*, p. 207.
21 MAHON, E. (1985) 'When is a difference not a difference?' *British Journal of Sociology*, Vol. 36, No. 1, pp. 73–6.
22 BOURDIEU, P. and PASSERON (1977) *op. cit.*, p. 207.
23 COLEMAN, J.S. (1966) *op. cit.*, p. 73–4.
24 BOWLES, S. (1969) *op. cit.*, p. 123.
25 BRUNER, J.S. (1975) *op. cit.*, p. 42.
26 PLOWDEN, B. (1967) *op. cit.*, p. 31.
27 ESSEN and WEDGE (1982) *op. cit.*, p. 11.
28 HALSEY, A.H. (1979) 'Social mobility and education', in RUBENSTEIN, D. (Ed). *Education and Equality*, pp. 57–78. Middlesex, Penguin.
29 GALTUNG, J. *et al.* (1974) *Educational Growth and Educational Disparity*, Paris, UNESCO.
30 GLASS, D.V. (1954) *op. cit.*, p. 16.
31 FLOUD, J. (1961) *op. cit.*, p. 94.
32 HUSEN, T. (1975) *op. cit.* p. 20.
33 BALL, S. (1986) 'Streaming and mixed ability and social class' in ROGERS, R. (Ed). *Education and Social Class*, Lewes, Falmer Press, p. 96.
34 KEDDIE,N. (1973) *The Myth of Cultural Deprivation*, London, Penguin. FLUDE, M. (1974) *op. cit.*, p. 22.
35 CARLSON, K. (1972) *op. cit.*, pp. 118–121.
36 WIDLAKE, P. (1986) *Reducing Educational Disadvantage*, Milton Keynes, Open University.
37 LITTLE, A. (1986) *op. cit.*, p. 37.
38 COX, T. and JONES, C. (1983) *op. cit.*, p. 38.
39 EKSTROM, R. (1987) *op. cit.*, p. 371.
40 BANTOCK, G.H. (1981) *The Parochialism of the Present*, London, Routledge and Kegan Paul.
41 ROBINSON, P. (1976) *Education and Poverty*, London, Methuen.
42 MORTIMORE, J. and BLACKSTONE, T. (1982) *op. cit.*, p. 177.
43 ESSEN, J. and WEDGE, P. (1982) *op. cit.*, p. 11.
44 COLEMAN, J.S. (1975) *op. cit.*, p. 27.
45 *Ibid*, p. 27.
46 *Ibid*, p. 28.
47 PLOWDEN REPORT (1967) *op. cit.*, p. 57.
48 *Ibid*, p. 56.
49 *Ibid*, p. 57.
50 *Ibid*, p. 598.
51 WHYTE, W.B. (1955) *Street Corner Society*, Chicago, Chicago University Press.
52 GLENNERSTER, H. (1979) 'Education and inequality', in RUBENSTEIN, D. (Ed.) *Education and Equality*, Middlesex, Penguin.
53 YOUNG, M. (1958) *The Rise and Fall of the Meritocracy*, London, Thames and Hudson.

54 University Grants Committee (1986) *University Statistics 1984–1985: First Destinations of Graduates*, Vol. 2, Cheltenham.
55 Pearson, R. (1984) *Improving Job Prospects Ahead?* Nature, March.
56 Tarsh, J. (1985) 'Trends in the graduate labour market' *Employment Gazette*, pp. 193–201.
57 *Ibid*, p. 200.
58 *Ibid*, p. 196.
59 *Ibid*, p. 198.
60 Meadows, P. and Cox, R. (1987) 'Employment of graduates 1975–1990'. *Employment Gazette*, pp. 191–200.
61 Dean, T.E. (1985) Response from the Standing Conference of Employers of Graduates to the Green Paper on the Development of Higher Education into the 1990s (Mimeograph).
62 Tarsh, J. (1987) 'What happens to New Graduates?' in Clarke, A. and Tarsh, J. (Eds) *UK Education and Training 1987*, Policy Journals, Berks.

2 *Race, Education and Intellectual Prejudice*

Jim Murphy

Introduction

For most commentators the fact that the different races, in a racialist society, have very different educational profiles, speaks for itself. As with the historic disparity between the rich and the poor, the differential in achievement between black and white pupils has long been regarded as pathological, as the predictable but undesirable consequence of what the Swann Report described as 'racism in general and racism in school especially.'[1] It is a view which in research circles at least, finds few dissenters for like Swann, most commentators are convinced that racism is as educationally damaging as it is morally indefensible. Indeed so widely accepted is this view in educational research that it is now difficult to find any form of racism, whether in school or out of school which has not at some time been seen as having an adverse effect on minority achievement. In addition to what the Swann Report recently described as 'the extra level' of social and economic deprivation endured by ethnic minorities, the racial barriers now identified as limiting black achievement range from prejudice on the part of teachers to discrimination on the part of employers, from hostility on the part of pupils to indifference on the part of governments, from inadequacies in pre-school provision to irregularities in housing, from bias in text-books to the absence in school of appropriate black role models. Though such research, as Swann readily concedes, cannot as yet specify 'which factors are the most important',[2] there is little doubt amongst educational commentators as to the cumulative effect of such prejudice on performance. As the predecessor of the Swann Report put it when explaining the relatively poor attainment of West Indian children, '. . . we are convinced from the evidence . . . that racism, both intentional and unintentional has a direct and important bearing on performance.'[3]

Given such a view of the matter, it is perhaps small wonder that racism, in its many guises, has come to be seen as critical in explaining the stark variation in attainment that exists between children of different racial origin. For all its appeal, however, it is a view which, like its class based predecessor, is not easily reconciled with reality or more precisely with what is currently known of that reality.

True, there can be little doubt that many of these cited barriers to racial performance are racialist, nevertheless there is little on present statistics to suggest that such grim discrimination is as educationally damaging as Rampton, Swann and others confidently assert.

The Evidence Assessed

Though the first warning, against so closely linking racial discrimination and racial underachievement, was sounded some twenty years ago by Coleman,[4] it was not ironically until the Rampton Committee collected such data as there was on minority performance that the wisdom of so tightly linking discrimination and underrepresentation became suspect in Britain. Though there were, to be precise, some reasons, even before Rampton, for 'doubting' the perceived significance of discrimination on minority performance, many commentators regarded such factors as poor language acquisition, and length of stay as critical. It was patently clear, however, with the publication of Rampton that rather too much had been made of racial discrimination in this regard.

Not only was there, given the perceived significance of discrimination, a rather surprising degree of variation in the attainment of different racial groups, but more ominously for the explanation endorsed by the report, Asian pupils were, depending on the statistics chosen, performing as well as, or better than the white majority. Instead of underachieving relative to white children, as the thesis suggested, Asian pupils were, if anything, overachieving. As the Rampton Report observed, some 13 per cent of Asian pupils compared with 12 per cent of others left school with one or more 'A' levels, whilst 5 per cent of Asians compared with 4 per cent of others went on to higher education.[5] What, on Rampton's thesis, ought never to have happened, was, as Rampton's statistics confirmed, very much a reality: as in America, with Coleman and Jencks,[6] what conventional wisdom predicted, the data contradicted.

As in America, however, it was a discovery which was to have few implications, for the much perceived, if as yet unsubstantiated link between discrimination and underachievement. For some reason, the fact that Asian pupils happened on inspection to be overachieving instead of underachieving mattered little. Minority performance was still regarded as it was when the data 'allowed' for such an interpretation, as a pattern of failure, which according to Kuya '. . . is imposed on minority groups.'[7] For most commentators the fact that *most* minority groups were underachieving was evidence, if evidence was required, of the depressing effect of discrimination on achievement.

It would be difficult though, given such certitude, to know what in Popper's terms would refute this view of discrimination — Asians after all, overachieve in spite of considerable discrimination — most commentators, nevertheless, still portray discrimination as crucial in limiting attainment of minority groups. True, most commentators in an attempt to accommodate this awkward fact, not unwisely, restricted their claims about the effects of discrimination to those minorities who were actually underachieving relative to whites. Others however, have been rather less circumspect.

A case in point is the widely published investigation by Eggleston, Dunn and Anjali.[8] The investigation, in keeping with convention, claimed that racial discrimination especially on the part of teachers, adversely affected the performance of minority pupils. 'If racial prejudice operates among teachers the consequences', they warn in their conclusions, 'are likely to be detrimental to the attainments of most if not all pupils of that group.'[9] Despite its solemnity, it was a claim which was not borne out by their study, for whilst there was evidence in their study of prejudice on the part of teachers, there was little sign, on their own data, that it was having the effects they claimed. As is evident from their data on 'O' level, GCE and 16+ entries,[10] white pupils were not, ironically, overselected relative to children of different racial background. Indeed not only were white boys outnumbered in the highest category 'nine or more entries' by Asian boys, by a factor of almost 2 : 1, but with the exception of this category, they were underselected relative to Afro-Caribbean pupils. Not only were as large a percentage of Afro-Caribbean boys entered for '6–8' examinations but a larger proportion were entered for '1–5' examinations. In addition, a smaller percentage of Afro-Caribbean pupils than white pupils found themselves in the position of being entered for no examinations.

Likewise with their data on girls; again apart from the fact that Afro-Caribbean girls were 'slightly less likely to be entered for nine or more examinations'[11] non-whites compared well with whites. Indeed when the percentage of girls taking more than six examinations were considered, all three groupings showed a remarkable similarity, given the perceived effects of discrimination. For Asian, Afro-Caribbean and white girls respectively, the percentages taking six or more examinations were 73 per cent, 71 per cent and 72 per cent. Again, in the highest category, Asian girls matched white girls.

Whatever the wisdom of using examination entries as a measure of discrimination, Eggleston must now explain on this data, not only why Asian pupils fare as well as or better than whites, but why, given government statistics on racial abuse, Asian pupils fare better than West Indian pupils.

As he observes in his review of the literature, Asians are much more likely to suffer racial abuse than any other racial groups. 'People of South Asian origin' he concedes 'are fifty times more likely to be subjected to racial attack than are white Britons — and are more likely to be so attacked than are West Indians.'[12] Nevertheless, even if such dissonant data is set aside, Eggleston is still left attributing to racial discrimination, an effect which, on his own evidence, appears not to have materialized. Most commentators however are typically a little more circumspect and have in general avoided claims about the effects of racial discrimination which are quite so patently at odds with their data on racial performance. Rarely however, have the resulting explanations been any the more convincing.

Rampton is not atypical in this regard, for though his claim about the effects of discrimination is confined only to West Indian pupils — the awkward overachievement of Asians is conveniently set aside — none of the explanations he advances actually supports his claim. Indeed, if anything, Rampton's various explanations of West Indian underachievement, serve only to contradict such a claim, for by a perverse irony, those arguments which go some way to explaining such underachievement, make little or no reference to discrimination, whilst those that appeal to discrimination transpire on closer scrutiny, to have little or nothing to do with educational achievement. Some indeed appear quite unrelated to both racial discrimination and educational achievement. One such factor is what Rampton describes as inadequate pre-school provision, a factor which the Report sees as contributing to West Indian underachievement, in that with more West Indian mothers 'forced' to work, it makes the relaxed care of their children hard to achieve.[13]

The main difficulty however with such an elaborate explanation is that, apart from its questionable assumption about importance of 'relaxed care' in facilitating educational achievement and its patronizing inference about the inability of West Indian parents to provide such care, Rampton advances little in the way of evidence, in support of this central supposition; the supposition that pre-school facilities foster educational achievement. Indeed notwithstanding the historical failure of the Headstart programme to materially affect long term performance, Rampton simply assumes that such a deficiency matters. Nevertheless, despite such a convenient assumption, it is soon evident from Rampton's account that even were such a supposition valid, it would not explain West Indian attainment, for as he makes clear inadequate pre-school provision is a deficiency which affects most of the population. Somewhat awkwardly, given that Rampton is concerned with racial discrimination, it seems that West Indians, as a group, are not notably less well provided for in this regard, than are other groups. As his Report makes clear, 'like most parents, West Indians are unlikely to be able to obtain places for their children in day nurseries.'[14]

Though it is not easy on this explanation to detect any link, educational or racial, between this deficiency and West Indian underachievement, Rampton's second explanation does, at least, go some way to explaining West Indian underachievement. Unfortunately for Rampton, it is an explanation which makes little reference to racial discrimination.

The factor in question is the relatively poor reading attainment of West Indian children, a characteristic which Rampton not implausibly regards as a serious handicap in the way of their educational progress. As Rampton put it '. . . if reading is not learnt quickly, the child will inevitably have difficulty keeping pace with the demands of our education system.'[15]

Though it is difficult, educationally speaking, to fault Rampton's view on the matter — it is hard indeed to see how any group, black or white, could compete given such an educational handicap — such an explanation, were it to be taken at face value, contradicted rather than endorsed Rampton's earlier declaration about the critical impact of race. Instead of appealing to racial discrimination to explain West Indian underachievement, this explanation assigns priority to a factor which, however debilitating educationally, is not easily attributed to racial discrimination.

Indeed, even when Rampton comes to speculate as to the 'causes' of such a handicap, the causes, like the handicap have, it seems, little to do with racial discrimination. It is, as his account makes clear, variously attributed to social deprivation, linguistic handicap, self-image, length of stay and again, somewhat patronizingly, to the lack of understanding amongst West Indian parents of the developmental significance of play. As Rampton opines 'each of these factors plays some part in the overall picture of underachievement'.[16] Although this view is not without its difficulties, Asian pupils for example, achieve despite being not unfamiliar with such conditions, its verification would not in any event sustain his original claim regarding the centrality of racism in depressing West Indian attainment. Indeed were such a view to be verified, Rampton would have succeeded only in introducing into his analysis a 'rival' interpretation for West Indian performance — an interpretation which in this instance points not to racism, but to other factors as responsible.

However, amongst the many accounts advanced by Rampton, there is one which attributes West Indian underachievement to factors which are clearly and unmistakably racist. The explanation in question focuses on teachers, and like Eggleston's explanation sees prejudice on the part of teachers as crucial. There are, he observes, some within the teaching profession who 'hold explicitly racist views' and rather more who '. . . have negative patronizing or stereotyped views about ethnic minority groups.'[17] As Rampton sees it, the effects of such prejudice hardly needs labouring. Such 'prejudice' he observes 'can and does . . . have a detrimental effect on all children whom they encounter.'[18]

However, despite such confidence when Rampton comes to examine the most popular variant of this view — the variant which holds such prejudice as responsible for unfairly channelling West Indian pupils into CSE, rather than GCE examinations — Rampton's initial confidence about the depressing effects of teacher prejudice rapidly gives way to ambivalence and doubt.

Whilst he observes, for example, that West Indians do indeed seem to be disproportionately represented in CSE streams, he is not as he subsequently admits, convinced that such overrepresentation in low streams is the upshot of teacher prejudice. As he puts it '. . . further evidence is required in order to decide whether such overrepresentation in CSE streams is the result of low teacher expectations or simply a consequence of the overall underachievement of West Indian pupils.'[19] Given the various and essentially non-racist explanations already advanced by Rampton for such overall underachievement, it is hard not to get the impression that, for Rampton as for Eggleston, sentiment not evidence was the factor informing this claim about the adverse effects of racism on West Indian performance.

However if Rampton failed to sustain his central claim about the debilitating effects of race on West Indian attainment, the follow-up study under the chairmanship of Lord Swann fared little better in this regard. Though Swann's central declaration was little different to that advanced by Rampton — for Swann '. . . a substantial part of ethnic minority underachievement, where it occurs, is the result of racial prejudice and discrimination on the part of society at large'[20] — his justification for such a claim was considerably more complicated. As Swann saw it the critical and inescapable fact was that ethnic minorities were '. . . on average more socially and economically deprived than the white majority'.[21]

Though Swann's scenario is very much more complicated than that advanced by Rampton, it is, for all its complexity no easier to reconcile with reality than that of Rampton. As with Rampton, Swann's view of deprivation and discrimination, as critically retarding minority progress, is simply not borne out by his own data. Indeed, in Swann's case, so evident is the contradiction between what his scenario predicts and what his data indicates, that even Swann concedes that his scenario does 'not easily explain the close resemblance in performance between Asians and whites.'[22] With Asians beset on the one hand by racial discrimination and on the other by social deprivation, 'one might expect', he rightly infers 'to find Asian performance to be poorer than white performance.'[23] However, as he freely concedes, 'in general, it is not.'[24]

Though such an admission, in other less politically charged contexts, might have resulted in the modification, if not the abandonment of his scenario, Swann is quite unperturbed. The fact that his scenario taken seriously, categorically precluded such an eventuality was for Swann of little consequence. 'We need not' he suggests, 'be surprised, for we are dealing with a very complex interaction between social class, ethnicity and race'. However, as soon becomes clear, Swann is not entirely convinced by his own argument, for instead of elaborating on how, in the case of Asian pupils, the interaction of two negative factors comes to exert a strong positive influence on their performance, Swann makes do with a rather more conventional explanation. As he sees it, there are two possible reasons for why Asians do better than his scenario suggests. The first being that the different racial groups 'react differently' to discrimination and deprivation, the second that they have 'different attitudes to education and the acquisition of qualifications.'[25]

Unfortunately for Swann, however, though these two explanations might well go some way towards explaining why Asians do better than other similarly deprived and similarly discriminated groups, neither explanation however, does so, in a manner which is even remotely compatible with his original scenario. Instead of confirming Swann's central claim about the adverse effect of discrimination on performance, the first simply contradicts it by suggesting that the effects of discrimination are not always adverse; the second, perversely, rivals it by explaining racial attainment in terms of cultural disposition towards education rather than in terms of racial discrimination or social deprivation. As is clear from Swann's concluding remarks on the difference in achievement between West Indian and Asian pupils, the critical determinant now is not racial discrimination as his official view asserted, but more awkwardly cultural difference. As he puts it, '. . . the reason for the very different school performance of Asians and West Indians seems likely to lie deep within their respective cultures.'[26]

Such a discrepancy between his 'official' view and his 'actual' explanation, flaws also Swann's analysis of Bangladeshi and Chinese pupils. In terms of his statistics, the Bangladeshi pupils were as Swann points out, 'the one Asian sub-group whose achievement was very low indeed.'[27] Once again, it is an observation which is easily explained. As Swann put it, 'their degree of social and economic deprivation not to mention racial harassment, is so high that we are not surprised at their marked level of underachievement.'[28] Once again, however, as is evident from the Appendix, where the performance of Bangladeshi children is considered in more detail, this magisterial verdict is somewhat at variance with the actual explanation advanced.

As the Appendix makes clear the factors that are seen as responsible for the stark underachievement of Bangladeshi children vis-à-vis other Asians have, ironically, little to do with discrimination or deprivation. Like Rampton's explanation of West Indian underachievement, educational handicap not racial discrimination is the chosen explanation. As the Appendix notes the length of time spent in school by pupils from Bangladesh is often quite short and even those pupils, who have been in pre-school before transferring to secondary school, have often had their schooling considerably disrupted by extended holidays in Bangladesh. In addition, the Report observes, 'many new arrivals have had no formal schooling whatsoever',[29] a deficiency which the Appendix regards as exacerbated by the fact that 'some 20 per cent of all the pupils . . . were either at the beginner or intermediate stage in their mastery of English.'[30] In stark opposition to Swann's official explanation, with its emphasis on racial discrimination and social deprivation, the Appendix ironically looks elsewhere for the determinants of Bangladeshi performance.

Much the same ambivalence flaws Swann's analysis of the academic attainment of Chinese children in British schools. In this instance, as in the case of Bangladeshi children, the actual explanation advanced by Swann to account for the achievement levels of such children ironically leaves little room for the view officially endorsed by the Report. Instead of appealing to discrimination to explain the perceived underachievement of Chinese pupils, Swann settles again for a more conventional explanation, attributing such underachievement to 'a lack of necessary language support.'[31] Once again those factors which the Report publicly insists are critical, notably discrimination and deprivation, are conspicuously absent in his analysis of Chinese performance, even though as Swann observes, the Chinese community have endured over the years a 'level of racism', which was 'both overt and covert.'[32]

Though the actual explanations Swann offers for Asian, Bangladeshi and Chinese performance are somewhat at variance with his official view which emphasizes deprivation and discrimination, it is ironically, his explanation of West Indian performance which most compromises his official view. Arguably the most significant aspect of Swann's data on West Indian performance is that it has improved dramatically and rapidly. In the short time between the interim report of Rampton and the final report of Swann, the percentage of West Indian leavers '. . . obtaining five or more higher grades at CSE and GCE 'O' level increased from 3 per cent to 6 per cent.' For English language 'the percentage obtaining higher grades . . . increased from 9 per cent to 15 per cent, whilst at 'A' level, 'the percentage obtaining at least one 'A' level pass has increased from 2 per cent to 5 per cent.[33]

Though there can be little doubt on these figures that West Indians have as Swann puts it 'closed the gap', Swann conspicuously fails to draw the one inference that his official view, taken seriously, dictates, namely that, as it beset West Indians deprivation and discrimination has declined somewhat in recent years. Though there is admittedly, little sign of such a felicitous change, it is an inference which, given his strictures on the critical effect of discrimination Swann cannot logically avoid.

It is, however, an inference which Swann understandably, if somewhat inconsistently chooses not to draw. Instead he prefers on this occasion to attribute the improvement in West Indian performance to their length of stay and 'their length of schooling in Britain'.[34] The main difficulty however with this otherwise convenient explanation is that, taken in conjunction with his official explanation, it leaves Swann with an account which predicts a deterioration rather than an improvement in West Indian performance. If discrimination and deprivation, as Swann insists, account for 'a substantial part of school underachievement', one might have expected West Indian performance to deteriorate as their exposure to discrimination and their habituation with deprivation increased. In the event however, as Swann's data reveals, the performance of West Indians like most minority groups, appears to improve, rather than deteriorate, with length of stay.

As it besets Swann, the difficulty with appealing to these factors is not that they do not explain West Indian progress, but that coupled to his central claim about the debilitating educational consequences of discrimination, it leaves Swann with an explanation for what is not happening, not for what is.

Nevertheless for Swann as for Parekh whom he quotes voluminously such a mismatch, great though it is, is of limited significance, for such is the complexity and sensitivity of this issue that it is all too easy, according to Parekh 'to demand impossible standards of proof and conceptual rigour'.[35]

Though not an unhelpful suggestion, when Swann is left as here struggling with an evaluation which goes in a very different direction to his various explanations, it is a suggestion which is, however, more convenient than compulsive. As Swann's analysis reveals, it is quite reasonable, on this accommodating rubric to take racial discrimination as responsible, even when, as in the case of Asian and West Indian pupils, it would have to be conceded that such discrimination had both a positive as well as a negative impact on educational performance. Indeed such an emigma is, as Swann is at pains to point out, not in the least surprising. 'We would' Swann warns the reader in bold print, '. . . remind anyone who thinks that racial prejudice and discrimination must have identical effects on every minority of Parekh's perceptive comment . . . that (such) an assumption is invalid because it wrongly assumes that the same factor must always produce the same results'.[36]

Unfortunately for Swann and Parekh the stark fact of the matter is that since both insist from the outset that discrimination is a crucial determinant of underrepresentation, underrepresentation is precisely what one would expect. Of course, had Swann and Parekh[37] not attributed underrepresentation to discrimination in the first instance, then there might be some merit in their reminding the world of what the world knows already, namely that different groups faced with the same evil, react differently. Such a reminder, however, does have the effect of casting as critical the differences as mark off one racial group from another, not the similarities which, as a consequence of discrimination, they jointly suffer.

Conclusion

In one sense, the failure of Swann and others to show that racial variation in attainment has its origins in racial discrimination is not particularly surprising: previous attempts to establish the same link between class discrimination and working class underrepresentation met with much the same fate. As the 1944 Act and Crosland's audacious experiment made very clear, making the system fairer made little difference, in the event, to class difference in representation.

In another sense, however, the failure of Swann and others to show that racial variations are rooted in racial discrimination matters and matters consequentially, for whilst it is unlikely, on past experience, to dent the appeal of this now widespread belief, it does, if nothing else, indicate the essentially speculative nature of an assumption, which for the last thirty years, has led one commentator after another to define first class difference, and now racial difference in attainment as quite unacceptable in terms of social justice.

Though it is admittedly not all that clear why, in the absence of some tangible link between discrimination and underrepresentation the research establishment has consistently taken such a dismal view of such underrepresentation, the fact of the matter is that in so doing, the research establishment has not only prejudged the equity or otherwise of such underrepresentation, but has done so in a manner which says rather more about researchers' own educational preferences and prejudices than it does about the preferences and prejudices of those he studies. True it is not merely, or solely, the liberal left who have taken such an uncompromising and unflattering view of the poor performance of the poor, be they black or white. As is evident from the excoriations of the radical right on falling standards, here too, the same uncompromising and uncorroborated view of such underachievement is enthusiastically endorsed. The resulting analysis is, of course, very different. What the left takes to be the consequence of bias on the part of teachers and discrimination on the part of the school, is for the right the result of incompetence on the part of teachers and ineffectiveness on the part of the school. For both, however, the poor performance of the poor admits of the same bleak evaluation — it is as unacceptable to the left, as it is to the right, and its removal is for both a precondition for their rather different visions of a better world.

Though it is not clear in either case how the removal of such underrepresentation can be effected by an institution which as Jencks and Rutter both discovered was, in the event, responsible for about two per cent of such variation, it is however not all that clear how enhancing the attainment of the poor, apart from making yet another imposition on the poor, would make for these 'better' worlds. Indeed, as far as it besets the liberal vision of a better world, this collective preoccupation with education and with closing the educational gap between the rich and the poor, between blacks and whites threatens, if anything, to usher in an even less equitable version of what already exists.

Apart from the fact that there is nothing in equality which demands that all groups, black and white, have comparable educational performances, and apart also from the not inconsiderable fact that even when ethnic minorities overachieve relative to whites, they still suffer twice the unemployment rate of whites, it is not at all clear in what sense the attainment of such parity would materially reduce even educational inequality.

The reason is this, for on this 'version' of equality, equality demands not, as one might expect, the eradication of racial discrimination in treatment but merely the abolition of difference in attainment. Of course were there some indication that discrimination was the only determinant of such variation in attainment, then Swann and others would be on strong ground: attaining parity would under such circumstances be reasonable surety of equality — or at least of educational equality.

The difficulty here however is that not only are there, as these commentators freely concede, other causes for such variation, but more importantly, as is well indicated by the statistics on Asian pupils and increasingly West Indian girls, it is evident that a considerable degree of attainment is not incompatible with a considerable degree of discrimination. Of course none of this makes racial discrimination any more defensible. It does however call into the question the wisdom of defining equality in a manner which were it realized, would provide no assurance that discrimination had indeed been eradicated.

True it is not the intention of the research establishment to trade-off parity in attainment for discrimination in treatment. Like Swann and countless others since Tawney, such commentators are concerned to see justice done. However, it is just that given such a version of justice, with its quite uncompromising disdain for educational profiles, which fails to match those of the white middle class, it is a trade-off which these commentators simply cannot avoid. As with the radical right the liberal left, it seems can see no reason and so, no defence for not attaining educationally.

Sadly for those, black or white, who for whatever reason fail to match in attainment the group norm, the future looks grim. For them, it seems, there is no refuge in either the brave new world of the left or the rejuvenated old world of the right.

It is perhaps no accident that the architects of these ostensibly very different utopias are the educated, and that for all their obvious differences both parties share the same parochial view of the world, which since Victorian times has come to regard a lack of education as a personal debility and a national liability.[38]

Notes

1 HMSO (1985) *Education for All: The Swann Report*. London, HMSO.
2 *Ibid*, p. 88.
3 Department of Education and Science (1981) *West Indian Children in Our Schools: The Rampton Report*, London, HMSO.
4 Coleman, J.S. *et al* (1966) *Equality of Educational Opportunity*, Washington, US Government Printing Office.
5 The Rampton Report (1981) *op. cit.*, pp. 8–9, tables D and F.
6 Jencks, C. *et al* (1972) *Inequality*, London, Allen Lane.
7 Kuya, D. (1979) 'The black child in Britain', in Rubinstein, D. *Education and Equality*, Harmondsworth, Penguin.
8 Eggleston, J., Dunn, D., and Anjali, M. (1986) *Education for Some*, Trentham, Trentham Books.
9 *Ibid*, p. 281.

10 *Ibid*, p. 208, Table 2.
11 *Ibid*, p. 207.
12 *Ibid*, p. 60.
13 The Rampton Report (1981) *op. cit.*, p. 15.
14 *Ibid*, p. 16.
15 *Ibid*, p. 19.
16 *Ibid*, p. 20.
17 *Ibid*, pp. 12–13.
18 *Ibid*, p. 12.
19 *Ibid*, p. 39.
20 The Swann Report (1985) *op. cit.*, p. 89.
21 *Ibid*, pp. 75–6.
22 *Ibid*, p. 85.
23 *Ibid*, p. 85.
24 *Ibid*, p. 85.
25 *Ibid*, p. 86.
26 *Ibid*, p. 87.
27 *Ibid*, p. 87.
28 *Ibid*, p. 87.
29 *Ibid*, p. 125.
30 *Ibid*, p. 120.
31 *Ibid*, p. 666.
32 *Ibid*, p. 668.
33 *Ibid*, p. 63.
34 *Ibid*, p. 63.
35 *Ibid*, p. 70.
36 *Ibid*, p. 86.
37 PAREKH, B. (1983) 'Educational opportunity in multi-ethnic Britain' in GLAZER, N. and YOUNG, K. (Eds) *Ethnic Pluralism and Public Policy*, London, Heinemann.
38 JENCKS, C. (1972) *op. cit*, p. 159
RUTTER, M. *et al* (1980) Fifteen thousand hours: A reply, *Oxford Review of Education*, Vol. 6. No. 3 p. 297. For a fuller consideration of this strange alliance, see MURPHY, J. (1985) 'Does the difference schools make, make a difference?' *British Journal of Sociology*, Vol. 36. No. 1, pp. 106–16.

3 *The Gender Dimension of Home–School Relations*

Beverly Anderson

Introduction

In 1989 British girls receive, in theory, exactly the same education as British boys. British women have had the vote for more than sixty years and the present Prime Minister is a woman. But what is the social and political context surrounding these facts? Is it one which enhances the confidence of girls and provides them with equal opportunities to those available for boys?

Since the passing of the Sex Discrimination Act in 1976 women in the UK have been entitled to equal treatment in employment, education and training.[1] Yet men continue to dominate politics, education and paid employment, and most women who earn money, do so in jobs with less security, lower status and poorer pay than men.[2] Even in education, which could be described as a women's industry since most people in it are female, the senior levels are dominated by men. Most primary and secondary school headteachers are male, and in higher education there is only one female head of a polytechnic, Pauline Perry at South Bank Polytechnic, whose precedent-breaking appointment in 1987 aroused considerable excitement in the press. Within the university sector the movement towards mixed colleges at Oxford and Cambridge shows how difficult it is to alter the gender balance in a manner which is fair to women. Although most former male colleges now admit female undergraduates and vice versa, this has not been matched by a similar new balance at the teaching and management levels. None of the old male colleges have chosen women to be their Wardens, Masters or Principals. But at least one former women's college at Oxford, Lady Margaret Hall, appointed a man to be its head when the vacancy occurred shortly after it became mixed. Nor have a large number of female academics become dons at the previously all-male colleges to balance the number of men being chosen for posts at the newly mixed female colleges.

It was awareness of this unwelcome trend, observed earlier in the United States, when single-sex colleges became mixed, which caused two distinguished Ivy League women's colleges, Mount Holyoke and Wellesley, to reject the idea of co-education and to opt in favour of remaining single-sex at the student level, though they have always had men on the teaching staff. In Britain too the value of segregated education for girls, either in separate institutions, or in single-sex classes, is being reassessed, spurred by research which reveals how unequally girls are treated, by teachers as well as by boys, in many mixed classes.[3]

But before examining the role of schools in promoting sexual equality it is important to consider gender relations in the home and what bearing, if any, these may have on the aspirations and achievements of boys and girls. While educators may accept the domestic context as an important element in all the major contemporary educational issues, what goes on at home is particularly relevant to the gender debate.

The problems of equality for women in the public spheres of politics, education and employment are compounded by the fact that they continue to do most of the work involved in running homes and rearing the young, whether they live in partnerships with men or alone.[4] Furthermore this part of their double load is, by and large, unacknowledged as well as unpaid, despite the publicity given to Rosalind Hines, identified as the 'average housewife' by Legal and General, the investment and insurance firm, in 1987, which calculated her replacement cost as wife and mother at £19,250 per year. The fact that this may have been done to persuade people to take out large insurance policies does not invalidate the figures. The hidden subsidy to the economy provided by the 'supported' wife is considerable. Yet the tax and benefits system does little to support or reward child-rearing. Although the cost of a resident housekeeper, for example, can be set against tax, childcare payments cannot. Workplace nurseries are regarded as fringe benefits and taxed accordingly by the Inland Revenue and it seems likely that child benefit, a hard-won fiscal reform which since the 1970s has paid money direct to mothers, will be phased out before the end of the current Parliament.[5]

On the face of it, it seems strange that women, who can, after all, only produce children in conjunction with men, should nevertheless continue to accept total responsibility for rearing the young, even when it is clear that, like men, they can earn money and operate effectively in the public domain. Could this disparity in power and prestige be due to some inherent genetic difference between the sexes?

So far, scientific enquiry has failed to establish any credible deficiencies in the female.[6] How then can the continuing imbalance be accounted for? An explanation was offered by feminist writers such as Elizabeth Janeway, Kate Millet and Shulamith Firestone, who have pointed out how recently the notion of the nuclear family, with women limited to private domestic roles, has developed, dating from the onset of industrialization when production shifted from home to factory.

Legislative reforms in the nineteenth century undoubtedly ended some of the worst exploitation of female factory workers, but ironically, as women retreated into the home they became invisible, since domestic labour has never been regarded as 'real' work. Hester Eisenstein records how the reversal of this trend began during World War Two, gathered pace during the 1950s, and was 'doubtless one of the major factors in the revival of the feminist movement in the 1960s'.[7]

But why was it that, as women moved back into the wage-earning domain alongside men, they failed to transfer an equivalent share of the domestic responsibility to their male partners, and received, on the whole, jobs with less security, lower status and poorer pay? In her seminal book, *Sexual Politics*, Millett concluded that the basic problems clustered round a set of expectations which society foisted upon women, often, as she and others noted, with their active cooperation.[8] The term gender was used to distinguish this group of attributes produced by psychological, cultural and social pressures from essentially physiological sexual traits which were inborn. In contemporary Western societies, called patriarchies by Millett, women were expected to be passive complements to males, whose 'instrumental', active roles encouraged traits which allowed them to dominate the worlds of employment and power. Women's power, such as it was, was confined to the domestic sphere and social pressures ensured that they operated solely within that sphere in cheerful and conformist obedience, without challenging male dominance. Patriarchy, wrote Millett, was so deeply embedded, 'that the character structure it creates in both sexes is perhaps even more a habit of mind and a way of life than a political system.'

Janeway saw the root of the problem as deriving from a 'social mythology' which persuaded women, on behalf of men, that theirs was a distinct role, focused on homemaking and child-rearing. As a result, though women were defined by a particular role, men were free to take on identities related to their occupations, not merely their sex, and could lay claim to a greater degree of autonomy and power. Sex roles, argued feminists, were used to oppress women and limit their capacity to control their own lives. Even the act of sexual intercourse had a political dimension for Millett, symbolizing the control all men exerted over women in our patriarchal systems. Shulamith Firestone went further, suspecting that even falling in love was, for men, a way of coping with their shame at wanting to consort with an essentially inferior class of beings. 'The biological family is an inherently unequal power distribution' she concluded. Only if women were freed from the obligation to bear and rear children could they gain equality with men. Although Juliet Mitchell took issue with much of this, she too referred to the 'social cult of maternity' which delegated child-bearing and rearing solely to women. These substitutes for paid work made a child the woman's product 'in the same way as a commodity is created by a worker'.[9]

At the heart of women's political inferiority, then, lay society's insistence on assigning to them exclusively the responsibility for child-care. Furthermore the damaging fact was that this role, seen as inferior to those men played, allowed men the freedom to choose powerful, 'instrumental' activities in the world outside the family.

In a significant passage Roaldo wrote that societies which:

> place positive value on the conjugal relationship and on the involvement of both men and women in the home seem to be most egalitarian in terms of sex roles.
> When a man is involved in domestic labour, in child-care and cooking, he cannot establish an aura of authority and distance. And when public decisions are made in the household women may have a legitimate public role.[10]

Ortner believed that women would have to free themselves from a false set of assumptions if their subordination was to end. Since all cultures cast women as the mediators between culture and nature and men as the definers of what culture was, as opposed to nature, men were able to benefit by controlling and manipulating the culture, to their advantage.[11]

The hostility with which these challenging ideas have been met is not surprising. As a number of academics have noted, during the last decade there has been a growing tendency on the part of the British government and its apologists to counter the egalitarian tendency inherent in feminism by exhorting women to return to their traditional family roles and responsibilities.[12] In 1979 Patrick Jenkin, then the newly appointed Secretary of State for Social Services, declared on television: 'Quite frankly, I don't think that mothers have the same right to work as fathers do. If the Good Lord had intended us to have equal rights to go out to work, he wouldn't have created men and women. These are biological facts.'[13] His comments aroused considerable derision in some quarters, since the version of the family being celebrated was peculiarly outdated even then.

It is clear from the statistics that the traditional two-parent family with a single breadwinner is no longer the norm. Women now make up 42 per cent of the employed. Sixty per cent of married women are wage-earners, though most women who work do so part-time and there is a direct correlation between the age of dependent children and the number of women who earn money through part-time jobs.[14] Most vulnerable are families consisting of a lone female breadwinner with dependent offspring. Yet Mr Jenkin's views were shared by considerable numbers of women as well as men. This is a crucial point to grasp, for it has important implications for educators and for links between home and school.

In the course of her research into women and shift work Charles found that, not only did male trade unionists believe that paid employment should fit in with a woman's 'prior domestic commitments', but that women themselves accepted what she calls a 'familial' rather than 'egalitarian ideology' to the extent that 'several felt strongly that men ought to earn more than women'.[15]

So the common pattern in families today is still one in which wage-earning women not only accept a double load of responsibilities, but often agree with the male view that men should earn more than women, particularly if the woman in question is married. Moreover, even in families where the men believe that they are doing their share of the domestic work, research shows that, in most cases, this is not the case.[16] And female teachers are as likely to be caught in this sort of gender trap as the mothers of their pupils.

Clarricoates has described how married women who teach in primary schools expect to stay home when their husband or child is ill, whatever their job. Since they do not require a similar commitment from their husbands they dread the consequences of becoming ill themselves. 'Rather', she says, 'than entertaining the possibility that social arrangements could be made for the care of sick children when their parents are in the work force, women teachers frequently seem to internalize the contradictory demands which society makes upon them.' Most of the men interviewed had no such problems. Far from recognizing any duty to share domestic work and responsibility for the children with their wage-earning wives, they saw the conflict between being a teacher and a parent in professional, not domestic terms. What concerned them were issues such as behaving like a teacher at home, instead of a father.

Clarricoates suggests that the guilt that female teachers customarily bear has another significant result. It erodes their self-confidence to the point where they doubt their capacity to fulfil the demands of positions of responsibility, even when they can summon up the courage to consider applying.[17] As Sharpe has shown, this guilt is shared by most other female workers.[18] Nevertheless there has undoubtedly been a perceptible shift in the attitudes and behaviour of many people since the days when press derision of 'bra-burners' and 'women's libbers' was countered with aphorisms like 'A woman without a man is like a fish without a bicycle'. But the pressure on women to conform to the old stereotypes is still immense.

Evidence that the familial lobby has not given up its fight to preserve the status quo is given by a new book, linked to a television series, written by former sociology lecturer, Bob Mullan. He asks, are mothers really necessary? His answer, unsurprisingly, is 'Yes'.

Summoning up the powerful authority of Dr. John Bowlby, whose famous research in the 1950s described maternal deprivation and its effects on evacuees, Mullan insists that 'only mothers can mother'. The alternatives, from shared parenting, through au pairs, child-minders, day nurseries or nursery schools are all dismissed as inadequate. 'On the whole women expect to be more closely tied to the home', he writes, and are 'resigned to the fact that men view themselves predominantly as breadwinners and playmates and act accordingly'. He doubts that the situation will ever change since 'Men take advantage in life in general, so why not in the matter of childcare'.[19]

While it would be foolish to take this careless and confused book too seriously, the fact that its author can not only find a publisher in 1987 but also a television series to promote his views is an indication that the gender debate has not yet moved much beyond the extremist polemics identified by Kirp, Yudorf and Franks as 'the politics of Armageddon', a verbal war between 'social movements that do not know the language of compromise'.[20]

Although in one sense, the traditional family is politically fashionable at present, as David has pointed out, the dominant political faction Mrs. Thatcher represents is seeking to transfer the costs and expenses of children back onto individual families. This, she notes, is in stark contrast to the Post-War bipartisan policies of 'welfare capitalism' culminating in the Labour government's notion of a social wage, whereby the state shared with families the costs of their responsibilities. And, as she rightly adds, 'Mothers will bear the burden of these costs'.[21]

It is ironical, in my view, that some feminists have inadvertently made the situation worse. By concentrating their demands on improving access to the work-place through campaigns for more crèches, nursery schools, better maternity leave provisions and so on, they have, while perhaps improving the prospects for single mothers in particular, diverted attention from fathers' responsibilities for their children's care. As a result their campaigns have left the basic inequities in the majority of households untouched and provide no moral support for the women caught up in them. The onus of child-care is still left on the mother or other women whom she pays to be her substitute. Yet, as David says in her article, what we need is 'a public commitment to children, to their care and education' which gives family responsibilities rather than 'work and the work ethic . . . pride of place'.

There is clearly room for more research into shared parenting and the ways in which it could be supported by public policy, for, as David reminds us, Lady Howe in an article in 1984, called for a 'renegotiation' of work and family', since 'once there is general acceptance that caring and domestic life are the equal practical responsibilities of men and women, then work patterns and policy and much else will fall into place'.[22] In the meantime, the reality is that though in some unskilled households women may well find it easier to get paid work than their husbands, their expectations have not kept pace with this economic change.

Nor is the younger generation necessarily going to look at things differently. In her longitudinal study of young people on the Isle of Sheppey in the early 1980s, Claire Wallace found that, although they no longer expect to live in a society offering full employment, their aspirations 'reflected traditional occupational roles and gender stereotypes'.[23] While many of the girls at 16 regarded marriage with 'critical ambiguity' their long-term expectations were as conservative as those of the boys in the sample. Both groups expected the male to be the breadwinner, and for the boys in particular, becoming head of a household was as important a sign of adult status as a steady job. Wallace noted 'some tension between work roles and domestic roles' on the part of the girls, but found that they too expected to marry someone with a full-time job, which would be more important than any job they themselves might have in the future.[24] British children today then, are being born into and brought up in households with very traditional power relationships, and the culture starts to define them in gender terms straight away. Baby girls and boys are handled differently, according to what sex the adult thinks they are.[25] Fathers working on puzzles with their sons and daughters encourage the boys to get it right, but try to 'shield' the girls by emphasizing the context of play. A look at television commercials for children's toys reveals the different techniques used in aiming at the two sexes. Advertising toys for boys use high action, fast cutting techniques, with martial music and hearty voice-overs. 'Girls toys' are displayed amid slow dissolves and soft fades, with harps and sweet soft voices on the soundtracks.

Nor is this the end of it. Furlong has shown how recent studies reinforce Sharpe's view, first expressed in 1976, that young women tend to be influenced in their occupational aspirations primarily by their mothers and female friends or relations.[26] Wallace describes the many studies which reveal a class difference in the relationship between gender and the decision to have children. Middle class children can count on parental support for their educational ambitions for a relatively long time. They expect to embark on careers before establishing families and have different definitions about what is sexually attractive to their working-class schoolmates.[27]

So while the family gender context is still, on the whole, very conservative, it is complicated by class considerations. This may seem a depressing account of present-day domestic reality, but since parents are the first educators, teachers need to understand and liaise with them if any progress is to be made. What is more, change is unlikely to take place if we underestimate the extent of the challenge ahead.

What roles, then, do schools play in gender equality and can they influence the situation in a positive way? Before we look at how schools can help, it is important to admit that, like homes, schools can sometimes be part of the problem, not the solution. Although children often arrive at school with gender expectations established, stereotypes can be reinforced by their teachers, often unwittingly, as a number of studies have made clear.

There is now substantial evidence about the ways in which children can be discouraged from stepping outside conventional roles and attitudes, starting at nursery school, and continuing through primary school via reading schemes and classroom practices to teaching techniques, curricula and teacher expectations in secondary schools.[28] As Kessler *et al* have shown in their study of Australian schools, schools are 'actively involved in constructing gender' through a range of practices which confer power and prestige on staff and students according to their gender. The academic curriculum too, 'expresses the perspective of the dominant group in the dominant sex.'[29]

And if girls, as Licht and Dweck have found, are inclined to blame themselves for their academic failures more readily than boys, in a way which affects their performance and career choices at a crucial stage,[30] it is no wonder that as adult working mothers they readily feel guilty when in fact they are trying to carry a double load as workers and parents. Peer group pressure is also significant. Lees has revealed how active girls are called 'slags' by boys, as a punishment for challenging traditional notions of female behaviour. So schools can, in a variety of ways, reinforce gender stereotypes through the hidden as well as the explicit curriculum, and through the actions and expectations of teachers as well as pupils.

Yet much of the impetus for change has also come from within schools. It is practising teachers who have joined together to challenge conventional stereotypes and to show how the ethos and curriculum can be altered to encourage equality. Kessler *et al* have shown how in one girls' school in Australia, Auburn College, there was a substantial change in staff and curriculum brought about by a change in the career expectations of the girls, as well as feminist ideas among its staff.[31] In Britain too there has been substantial movement. Organizations such as the Equal Opportunities Commission and the National Union of Teachers have produced reports and booklets challenging stereotypes and offering models of better practice.[32] At local authority level groups of teachers have pressed successfully for policy statements and in-service training to promote gender equality.[33]

Books and articles have been published disseminating the results of research into anti-sexist teaching strategies and curriculum development.[34] Publishers too have begun to offer a range of books showing less stereotyped role models in novels, poetry and non-fiction. There are booklists and checklists available now for teachers who want to provide more appropriate material in their classrooms.[35]

One thing that is missing so far is a frontal attack, through the curriculum, on gender roles within the family, although many teachers believe that both boys and girls should be prepared for parenthood and domestic responsibilities. But although Whitfield, among others, has described in detail what a compulsory course in family education would involve,[36] the new core curriculum is disappointingly silent on the subject. Despite this, and pressures from the centre to standardize provision, I believe that schools can, if they choose, introduce courses along these lines. Much of the work involved can be assigned to the traditional subject areas within the formal curriculum. What is needed is a coordinated approach to planning and syllabus development.

In her analysis of the Girls into Science and Technology (GIST) project, Kelly describes how a mixture of problem solving and research and development approaches were used to encourage girls to take optional science classes although even there many teachers, she says, found it hard to accept 'the links between their own assumptions and girls' underachievement'.[37] With hindsight she believes that the creation of a GIST committee within the school would have provided useful publicity and backing for the initiatives of individual teachers.

It is certainly the case that single teachers working without encouragement from other staff, and particularly the headteacher, are unlikely to make much headway in promoting equal opportunities within a school. They may persuade boys to listen to girls with respect, and to cooperate rather than compete in mixed groups. They may set special single-sex sessions for particular subjects or succeed in expanding the curriculum to include a feminist perspective. But if the rest of the school remains unchanged the impact of their efforts will at best be temporary.

Where a school does decide as a whole to intervene in what is taught and how it is delivered in order to enhance the opportunities available for girls, it is just as important to involve the whole community it serves. Governing bodies and parent-teacher associations need to be consulted at an early stage, a point worth emphasizing since in the past, some schools have tended to overlook this vital constituency. Yet their support is crucial. Parents who hear by accident about non-sexist strategies may well misunderstand what is happening if they are unfamiliar with the arguments. Some may feel threatened when they do begin to understand, if their traditional attitudes are challenged. But it is important to make the effort. For even if parents do not resist change overtly, unless the home reinforces the school's notions of gender equality, children, under the pressures outlined at the beginning, are likely to grow up with many of the old stereotyped views and expectations, whatever the ethos and practice of the school.

Although some schools have been reluctant to make links with homes, in others partnership with parents has long been a priority. This is just as well, since the new Education Act will bring about a considerable shift in the powers of parents and governors and may change the relationships between them and the staff. Schools which have been able to ignore parents up to now may find themselves in considerable difficulties if they plan innovations which are not widely understood or supported.

Since gender equality has no specific place in the national curriculum, the issue could be driven underground. If it is to remain an active priority in schools which have made a commitment, or to be introduced into schools which realize the need for change, it is vital that, as the schools work out how to encourage teaching and learning which is genuinely unbiased, they make governors and parents aware of how important this matter is.

The strategies needed are, of course, similar whether the issue is race, gender, improved pupil performance and behaviour, or indeed more effective reporting to parents and the wider community, but in their article 'Gender in the house of policy', Kirp *et al* suggest four principles for a sound gender policy, especially if the protection of individual liberty is also an aim. They are: the opportunity to choose; a capacity to make choices; information on which to base preferences; and a climate of tolerance in which to explore alternatives. Schools could usefully keep these conditions in mind when planning their approaches to the home.[38]

Very few parents, after all, would deliberately choose to undermine their daughters' self-esteem or ability to benefit fully from schooling if they understood the ways in which these effects were produced. Schools which are trying to eliminate sexism are therefore reinforcing the parents' natural desire that their children receive fair and equal treatment of their children. Even men with traditional expectations from marriage have been known to wake up to sexism when their own daughters are seen to be victims of it.

Some schools may have among their parents people whose cultural traditions and values may seem implicitly to make it difficult for girls to have equal treatment, especially in a coeducational setting. Negotiating change can sometimes be particularly difficult in such circumstances but some schools appear to have learned to handle the problems with considerable skill. It is, of course, important, that schools be seen to respect the values and practices of different cultures and to work out ways of collaborating with them appropriately.

But there may well be times when the drive for gender equality will cause tensions for girls, in particular, whose aspirations begin to challenge their family's expectations. In these instances the school will have to tread a delicate path in order to honour an approach to equality which it believes to be important, and therefore support girls in their aspirations, without being guilty of causing a breach in family relationships.

But many parents, whatever their backgrounds, will need considerable help if they are to understand and work with schools committed to equality, given the extent to which British family life is still profoundly sexist in its practices, if not its assumptions. Workshop sessions, talks, videos, live drama and concerts can all be presented and enticingly publicized so that parents can have a chance to learn about and discuss the issues. Open days or special events focusing on equality can be part of the school's normal calendar, or included in the traditional activities that parents share in. If the parents cannot or will not come in to the school, the school can pursue them through attractive leaflets, home visits, or even 'phone-ins on local radio. Why not use the community slots on regional television too?

Governing bodies on which parents sit, should be invited to discuss gender, during one of their regular meetings, or perhaps at special informal seminars with the staff. When new initiatives such as separate science classes for girls, careers counselling or assertiveness training workshops are being planned, the opportunity should be seized to involve parents and governors. If education for family life makes its way into the timetable the range of outside contributors who should be involved would include parents as well as social workers, health visitors, building society officers, etc.

All new approaches are fraught with difficulties and working with parents in the gender field is no exception. Fears run deep and confronting old ideas is often painful. Teachers who have undergone training for themselves can attest to the difficult and sometimes fraught exchanges that can take place as ideas are confronted and thrashed out. Skilful trainers are as crucial for work with parents and governors as they are with teachers. Efforts to include parents in moves towards sexual equality require considerable energy and commitment of time as well as courage. Without this partnership change is unlikely to take place. But if Britain in the 1990s is to be a more equal place for women and men, the effort is well worth making.

Notes

1 Rendel, M. (1985) in Arnot, M. (Ed) *Race and Gender: Equal Opportunities in Education*, Oxford, Open University/Pergamon Press.
2 *The Fact about Women is . . .* (1987). Manchester, Equal Opportunities Commission.
3 Weiner, G. and Arnot, M. (Eds) (1987) *Gender Under Scrutiny — New Inquiries in Education*. London, Hutchinson.
4 Henwood, M., Rimmer, L. and Wicks, M. (1987) *Inside the Family: Changing Roles of Men and Women*, London, Family Policy Studies Centre.
5 David, M. (1986) 'Teaching family matters', in *British Journal of Sociology of Education* Vol. 7 No. 1, pp. 35–57.
6 Nicholson, J. (1984) *Men and Women: How Different Are They?* Oxford, Oxford University Press.
7 Eisenstein, H. (1984) *Patriarchy and the Universal Oppression of Women: Feminist Debates*, reprinted in Arnot, M. and Weiner, G. (1987) *Gender and the Politics of Schooling*, London, Hutchinson.
8 Millett, K. reprint (1971) New York, Avon Books.
9 Eisenstein, H. (1984) *op. cit.*
10 *Ibid.*
11 *Ibid.*
12 David, M. (1986), *op. cit.*
13 Quoted in David, M. (1986) *op. cit.*
14 Britain 1988 (1988) London, HMSO and *The Fact about Women is . . .* (1987) *op. cit.*
15 Charles, N. (1986) 'Women and trade unions', in *Feminist Review*.
16 Henwood, M., Rimmer, L. and Wicks, M. (1987), *op. cit.*
17 Clarricoates, K. (1980) 'All in a day's work', in Spender, D. and Sarah, E. (Eds) *Learning to Lose: Sexism and Education*, London, The Women's Press.
18 Sharpe, S., (1984) *Double Identity: The Lives of Working Mothers*, Harmondsworth, Penguin.
19 Mullan, B. (1987) *Are Mothers Necessary?*, London, Boxtree.
20 Kirp, D., Yudof, M. and Franks, M. (1986) *Gender in the house of policy*, reprinted in Arnot, M. and Weiner, G. (1987), *op. cit.*
21 David, M. (1986), *op. cit.*
22 *Ibid.*

23 Wallace, C. (1986) 'From girls and boys to women and men: The social reproduction of gender', reprinted in Arnot, M. and Weiner, G. (1987), *op. cit.*
24 Nicholson, J. (1984), *op. cit.*
25 Turner, J. (1984) *Cognitive Development and Education*, London, Methuen.
26 Furlong, A. (1986) 'Schools and the structure of female occupational aspirations', in *British Journal of Sociology of Education* 7, No. 4, pp. 367–77.
27 Wallace, C. (1986), *op. cit.*
28 Whyte, J. (1983) *Beyond the Wendy House: Sex Role Stereotyping in Primary Schools*, London, Longman for the Schools Council: Millman, V. and Weiner, G. (1985), *Sex Differentation in Schooling: Is there Really a Problem?* London, Longman; Marland, M. (Ed.) (1983), *Sex Differentiation and Schooling*, London, Heinemann.
29 Kessler, S., Ashenden, D., Connell, B. and Dowsett, G. (1985) reprinted in Arnot, M. and Weiner, G. (Eds) (1987) *op. cit.*.
30 Licht, B. and Dweck, C. (1983) *Sex Differences in Achievement Orientations: Consequences for Academic Choices and Attainments* in Marland, M. (Ed) *op. cit.*
31 Lees, S. (1987) 'The structure of sexual relations in schools', in Arnot, M. and Weiner, G. (Eds), *op. cit.*
32 Equal Opportunities Commission (1982) 'Equal opportunities in craft, design and technology'. Report of a Working Party convened by the Equal Opportunities Commission, Manchester, EOC; Equal Opportunities Commission 'An equal start: Guidelines for those working with the under-fives', Manchester, EOC; Equal Opportunities Commission 'We can do it now, a report on some good practices in science, technology and crafts in schools', Manchester; EOC; Nut (1983) 'Girls and boys in primary classrooms', *in Primary Education Review*, 17, London, National Union of Teachers; NUT (1980) *Promotion and the Woman Teacher*, London, National Union of Teachers.
33 Elm Bank Teachers' Centre (1983) 'Towards equal opportunities in secondary schools — What does it means for girls?' A report from a Coventry LEA course, Coventry, Coventry LEA; Taylor, H. (1985) 'A local authority initiative on equal opportunities', in Arnot, M. (1985), *op. cit.*
34 Weiner, G. (1985) 'The Schools Council and gender: A case study in the legitimation of curriculum policy' in Arnot, M. (1985), *op. cit.*; Chisholm, L. and Holland, J. (1986) 'Girls and occupational choice: Anti-sexism in action in a curriculum development project', *British Journal of Sociology of Education*, Vol. 7 No. 4, pp. 353–65.
35 Stones, R. (1983) *Pour out the cocoa Janet: Sexism in children's books*, London, Longman for the Schools Council.
36 Whitfield, R. (1980) *Education for Family Life: Some New Policies for Child Care*, London, Hodder and Stoughton.
37 Kelly, A. (1985) 'Changing schools and changing society: Some reflections on the Girls into Science and Technology Project', in Arnot, M. (1985), *op. cit.*
38 Kirp, D., Yudof, M. and Franks, M. (1986) *op. cit.*.

4 *Equity in Diversity: The Problems Posed by Values - and their Resolution*

John Raven

Introduction: The Problems: Some Illustrations

I once attended a small invitational 'planning' meeting between the Head of a yet-to-be-established new local authority school, a few of the teachers who had been appointed, representatives of community and other interests, and a number of prospective parents.

The Head had set up an agenda with a view to getting agreement to his plans. Among the papers he had distributed was an organizational chart. One of the boxes on the chart, with some arrows going to and from it, was labelled 'guidance'. After an hour or so's inconsequential discussion, one of the parents chanced to say 'guidance, what's that?' 'Oh, that's helping pupils to think about their abilities and their problems, social education, sex education, and . . .' SEX EDUCATION. It was if a volcano had erupted. Everyone pitched in. The parents tore into each other: some were avidly in favour, some utterly opposed. In the end, the Head closed the discussion saying 'There you are, you see, you can never get agreement between parents. I will have to decide that there will be sex education and what will be covered . . . and I will set aside the next two days to listen to parents' complaints'.

I am sure that many of us have had experiences of this sort. Groups of parents on PTAs regularly decide that they want to influence the curriculum. Given an amenable Head — like the one above — a meeting between parents and staff is then convened. At that meeting it becomes clear that, although all parents want change, one group of parents wants to encourage teachers to foster qualities like initiative, creativity, and the ability to ask questions and pursue the answers. Others are utterly opposed to any such thing: they don't want their children asking questions and being adventurous: they couldn't answer their questions, they would lose control over them, and, anyway, their children might get hurt in the process. What is more, the school should not foster these qualities in other people's children either: if it did, those children would do better in life than their own (and *that* would be bad). What they want is more discipline. The pupils should learn to do as they are told. The children should have the badness beaten out of them. Society will fall apart otherwise: you can't have people deciding for themselves when they will work and what they will work at.[1] The outcome of the meeting is that the Head is left to go his own way.

This example illustrates some of the central problems in public education. It shows that the most important qualities to be fostered by the educational system are value laden. It illustrates the difficulties posed by the need to cater for people who have different priorities and the effects of the widely held belief that the public sector should treat everyone equally. It shows that the equally widely held belief that democracy means taking majority votes which will be binding on everyone, rather than coming to decisions which allow people with different priorities to go their own way, results in decisions which satisfy very few people. It illustrates the impossible situation in which innovative managers find themselves. In fact it illustrates the need to hold managers accountable, not for orchestrating democratic decisions, but for making high level and creative discretionary judgments, based on conflicting information and priorities, but which are in the best interests of as large a sector of the community as possible. Managers exist, not to implement clients' or committees' consensus decisions, but to seek out information and then come to good decisions about what to do. Yet, as can be seen from the illustration, any attempt to hold managers accountable for doing just that is itself fraught with difficulties because people have different definitions of what constitutes the public interest. (All of which is, of course, why Adam Smith and F. A. Hayek said that it was impossible anyway and that one should not even try to do it.)

In the remainder of this chapter I will address some of the issues raised in the last few paragraphs.

The Importance of Coming to Terms with Values in Education

In this section I will summarize research which shows: (i) that most parents, pupils and teachers think that the main goals of education include fostering such qualities as the ability to make one's own observations and think for oneself, the ability to take initiative, and the ability to understand and influence society; (ii) that the opinions of these parents, pupils and teachers are correct; these *are* the main qualities required to lead one's life and do one's job effectively; (iii) that most schools fail to foster these qualities; and (iv) that, while the reasons for schools' failure to foster these qualities include a lack of understanding of how they are to be fostered and assessed, they also include the dilemmas involved in harnessing and influencing values and catering for diversity.

The Main Goals of General Education

Most official documents which specify the goals of general education emphasize problem-solving ability, the ability to work with others, enterprise skills, leadership, and the ability to understand and influence what happens in society.[2] These views are echoed in surveys of the opinions of teachers, pupils, parents, employees and employers.[3] The opinions of all of these groups are supported by research into the qualities which are actually required at work and in society: the qualities which have been mentioned, and others like them, *are* required by machine operatives.[4] by navvies[5] by bus drivers,[6] by nurses,[7] by small businessmen,[8] by civil servants,[9] by doctors,[10] by scientists,[11] by engineers,[12] by managers,[13] and by politicians.[14] They are required if people are to develop their talents and contribute effectively to society.[15] They are also required if leisure is to be used in a satisfying way[16] and if economic and social development (rather than, for example, stagnation and conflict) is to occur.[17]

Most Schools Fail to Foster such Qualities

Despite the exhortations of governments, despite parents', teachers' and pupils' wishes, and despite the demonstrated importance of the qualities mentioned above, most schools do not even attempt to foster them or even such qualities as the ability to muster arguments, make good judgments, or reconcile different points of view.[18] Worse still, many schools actually stifle them and foster socially dysfunctional beliefs, understandings and values.[19] It is therefore impossible for most parents, by sending their children to state schools, to fulfil their legal obligation to provide them with efficient full-time education suited to their age, ability and aptitude.

The Nature and Development of Competence

In the light of these findings it seems essential to develop a better understanding of the nature of qualities like those which have been mentioned and how they are to be fostered. In this context, one of our most interesting findings[20] has been that, while few teachers understand how to foster them, many parents not only know *how* to do so but actually do so. It emerges that parents are their children's most important educators, not in the sense that they do the things which schools do, or even in the sense that they support schools, but in the sense that they, and they alone, foster these wider qualities. And it is these wider qualities which (unlike the knowledge conveyed to pupils at school[21]) make for the differential life success of those who do well at school.

As the parents we interviewed emphasized, if one is to foster such qualities as initiative, the ability to observe, or confidence in dealing with others, one must create situations in which young people can practise doing these things and thus learn to do them more effectively. Yet these are all difficult, time-consuming, and often frustrating activities. No one is going to make the effort required to practise them unless what they are doing is important to them — and they are also likely to be discouraged if it is not important to at least some other people as well. If people are to be brought to practise undertaking these activities, the tasks they are encouraged to undertake must therefore be tasks which relate directly to their motives, interests, priorities and talents. In short, their educational programmes must be individualized in such a way that they are tailored to their values, motives and talents.

But practice is not the only way in which qualities like initiative, adventurousness, and leadership are developed. As some of the parents we interviewed also pointed out, people learn from the example of others. It is not only other people's observable behaviour — the *results* of their thinking and planning — which it is important for children to see and to copy. The mental, emotional and striving processes which lie behind that behaviour are also important. So, if people are to develop the competencies which make for enterprise, leadership, and the willingness and the ability to understand and influence the direction in which society moves, their mentors must make these normally private concerns, values, thought processes, agonies and delights visible. In this way they can learn to be sensitive to the cues which beckon and point toward an activity which is likely to pay off, which tell them when corrective action is necessary, or which tell them that things are getting out of hand and they had better either get help or stop. They can learn how to turn a chance observation to advantage.[22]

It is because experiences gained whilst undertaking tasks which are personally significant and whilst working with other people who share one's concerns are so important that the Youth Training Scheme branch of the Manpower Services Commission is correct when it asserts — to the annoyance of many 'educators'[23] — that such qualities are best fostered and developed on the job or in the community. (It is important to emphasize that work is anything but the soul-destroying activity which many teachers take it to be. Some 83 per cent of the young people say that they have been able to identify and develop their talents at work in contrast to only 13 per cent who say they are able to do so at school,[24] and, with the exception of those who work in *large* factories and offices — which employ relatively few people — 80 per cent of young people like their work, like their employers, and find their jobs interesting.[25] They like the variety and the opportunity to use their own particular talents, work with others, and take initiative.)

Fortunately for educators, the home and the workplace are not the only settings in which such qualities can be fostered. If teachers adopt such processes as interdisciplinary, competency-oriented, enquiry-based project work grounded in the environment around the school and explicitly set out to embody important features of work experience in that activity — a *real* task to do, a variety of tasks to do during the day, an opportunity to exercise different talents from those exercised by colleagues — then educational environments *can* be made more developmental.[26] In this context it is of interest to note that more effective teachers, like more effective parents and managers, are the ones who show a greater tendency to think about, harness, build upon, and develop the talents of their pupils.[27] And they are also more likely to share their own thoughts, their own strivings, and their own feelings with them.[28]

So far, I have noted simply that, if young people are to develop a selection of important competencies, they will need to be engaged in long-term activities which they value and work with people whom they respect in the course of carrying out activities which both value.

Many people find this intrusion of values into education threatening enough. But many of the other qualities which parents, pupils and teachers believe important for the educational system to foster involve *influencing* values. Examples include fostering consideration for others or the desire to work for the long-term good of the community.

The research we have carried out into the nature of competence[29] has, however, led us to a yet more disturbing conclusion. The competencies which make for enterprise, innovativeness, leadership, the ability to work with others and other types of effective behaviour are crucially dependent on understandings of terms like 'democracy', 'participation in management', 'industrial democracy', 'management', 'money' and 'wealth'. If teachers are to foster high level competencies they will therefore have to influence pupils' understandings of these and similar terms. The thought of encouraging teachers to engage in political education of this sort — with all its attendant dangers — makes many people — including me — extremely uncomfortable. It has resulted in the government banning 'political education' from its TVEI and YTS schemes despite the fact that, as we can now see, if they are to achieve their objectives, this is the *most* important ingredient of these programmes. Nor is the discomfort generated by this conclusion entirely dissipated by the thought that teachers *already* — and (since there can be no such thing as value-free education) *inevitably* — influence these beliefs and understandings. Indeed, in an effort to avoid the problem, they give pupils the impression that politics is a dirty, unmentionable, business in which no respectable person would engage. This has had devastating consequences for our society.[30] Thus, teachers' unexamined impact in this area is often not for the better.[31] Informed and explicit action has therefore got to be the only way of handling the problem.[32]

What I hope I have now done is indicate just how crucial it is to find some way of coming to terms with values in public education. Unless we do so we will not only continue to squander some two thirds of the resources devoted to 'education' and stunt the development of many of our children, we will stunt the development of our society.

I must emphasize that I am talking about *state* education, because it is significant that private schools can inculcate political beliefs, influence values, and foster — through Cadet Corps, house activities, the prefects system and similar activities — the very competencies of which we have spoken with no qualms whatsoever. Interestingly enough, they are caught in the trap I described earlier. It is precisely *because* they are so effective in reaching these 'non-academic' goals that they are so widely opposed by people who would not send their children to them even if they could. Until we find a way of dealing with the fact that people often wish to prevent other people's children developing qualities which they do not want their own children to develop we are unlikely to make much progress in thinking through the issues associated with parent power or identify ways in which the quality of education is to be improved.

The Origins of Variance in Values and Talents

In the course of our research Sigel, McGillicuddy, Pellegrini, Tharp, Gallimore and my colleagues and I[3] have shown that parents believe that they can influence their children's values and foster important competencies by creating developmental environments in which their children can develop those competencies while undertaking tasks which interest them and which they care about. Sigel,[34] McGillicuddy,[35] Rosen and D'Andrade,[36] McClelland,[37] Bloom[38] and I[39] have also demonstrated that these beliefs are correct. Elsewhere we[40] have shown that managers can create developmental environments which release, and lead people to practise and thereby develop, such qualities as initiative, the ability to support innovative colleagues, and the ability to work with others for the long term good of the organization concerned and society in general.

In the next few paragraphs I will refine and qualify these statements in a way which will help to take us forward. Although many parents think they can influence the activities which their children value, many of them also acknowledge that their children come with sharp limits within which they, as parents, must work. Unlike most teachers, parents tend both to accept that their children are as they are and to respect their children's interests and preoccupations. Instead of trying to *change* their children's interests, parents tend to set about harnessing those interests and motives in order to get them to practise reading, observing, inventing, analyzing, planning, and working with others. They then study their children's difficulties and intervene sensitively, only when help is really required.[41]

Parents' recognition that their own children's dispositions are to a considerable extent pre-programmed is nevertheless frequently in conflict with generalizations they will make about the malleability of human nature. And they are in even greater conflict with the environmentalist stance of many teachers, psychologists and sociologists. However, some large scale research undertaken in the early 1970s[42] supports both positions. What we found was that there is almost as much variation in the values and activities of adolescents who come from similar backgrounds — indeed from the same families — as there is between children who come from different backgrounds. Some children from middle class backgrounds espouse what Kohn[43] and others have called 'working class' values: they want to develop toughness and strength, learn to do as they are told, and to have strict rules to guide their lives. Some children from working class backgrounds espouse 'middle class' values — they want to think for themselves, develop the qualities which make for creativity and originality and to assume managerial responsibilities. (Jackson and Marsden[44] have described some of the family conflicts which stem from this). What is more (as Havighurst and Taba[45] had earlier noted) the values which children espouse are at least as characteristic of the socio-economic groups they will enter as they are of those they have come from. Our own results have been confirmed by the Newsons,[46] by Sokolowska,[47] and by Lempert.[48] Kinsey[49] reported the same thing for sexual behaviour: children's sexual behaviour and attitudes anticipated those of the groups they would later enter. What is most interesting about Kinsey's results is that there is no way in which the children concerned could have acquired through discussion or observation sexual attitudes and behaviour which typify groups with whom they had as yet had little contact.

For the sake of brevity, I have summarized our conclusions by reference to 'working class' and 'middle class' values. It is, however, extremely important to note that this is a shorthand. While a much higher proportion of middle class than of working class parents endorse 'middle class values' and *vice versa*, the relationship between socio-economic status and values is far from perfect. Indeed, in absolute numbers, because there are more working class than middle class people, there are more working class than middle class parents who endorse 'middle class values'. However, because of implications which will become clear later, one of the most important facts to hang onto is that an absolute majority of parents endorses *working class* values.

Particular mention must be made of the work of Burns *et al.*[50] What they found was that Kohn's results are a product of *two* variables — *true* cultural (SES, ethnic) differences and effects of environment. This makes sense of much other work. We found that while there was a great deal of variation between parents in the qualities they wanted to encourage in their children and the activities in which they engaged in order to foster these qualities, many parents were deterred from engaging in child-rearing activities which they otherwise valued by the quality of their environments. The result is that while children from the same family usually have a predisposition to develop, and value, a wide range of very different competencies and qualities, the environments in which they are reared do have a marked effect on the concerns and competencies they develop.

Taken as a whole, these results suggest that we are dealing here with some poorly understood, but socially important and functional, process. It would seem that children are born with predispositions to develop very different concerns and talents and that, in the process of social allocation, they find their way into very different positions in society which demand different concerns and competencies. It would also seem to follow that society must need a wide range of people with very different concerns and patterns of competence.

Implications of Values Diversity and its Anticipatory Nature: the Barriers to Handling Them

The research summarized above suggests that, instead of fostering only one type of competence in schools (the ability to remember, typically for not more than a year, a smattering of out of date facts[51]), instead of creating school environments characterized by 'working class' values ('sit still, do as you are told, learn what is put in front of you, remember rather than think, be dependent rather than independent'), we may need to do as good parents do — namely to identify, respect, nurture, and find ways of capitalizing upon, the types of behaviour which young people value in order to foster a much wider range of competencies and talents. We may not only need to harness widely available, but neglected, motives (such as the desire to work with others and the wish to feel that one has really created something[52]) to fuel enthusiasm for educational activities, we may also need to find ways of accommodating the wide variety of different types of activity which young people are motivated to undertake and the diversity of the competencies they tend to display in the course of undertaking those activities.[53]

There are many barriers to respecting the variety of tasks which attract different children and fostering a number of the competencies which may be exercised in pursuit of them. These barriers include:

1. The absence of appropriate theory.
2. The absence of tools for administering individualized, competency-oriented, educational programmes.
3. The fear of exacerbating the climate of mediocrity.
4. The contempt which many teachers have for working class values.
5. The very narrow range — and general inappropriateness — of the concerns and competencies displayed by teachers for pupils to emulate.
6. The definition society has given to the term equality and widely held views about the appropriate nature of public provision.
7. The fear that treating different children in different ways will lead to a caste society.
8. The pressures which focus teachers' attention on low level goals.

I will review all of these in the paragraphs which follow. However, it may be useful first to draw attention to the fact that, if some means of respecting and catering for diversity by offering genuine variety and choice could be found, it would remove the fears of brainwashing which intrude as soon as one envisages that teachers might be encouraged to influence values, engage in political education, and treat different children in different ways. If pupils had the right to opt into and out of educational programmes depending on how congenial they found the values of the teachers concerned it would greatly facilitate the solution of some of the most important problems in education.

I will now discuss the barriers to implementing individualized, competency-oriented, education which harnesses each pupil's motives and fosters high-level, value-laden, competencies which were listed above one at a time.

1. *The absence of appropriate theory.* Although this is not the right place to pursue it, it would be inappropriate not to mention that one of the main reasons why schools do not make use of the individualized competency-oriented educational programmes which are required to foster such qualities as the ability to make one's own observations, communicate, take initiative and think for oneself is that, despite the voluminous writing on progressive education, there is no generally accepted understanding of how teachers might identify, foster, and point to the development of, these talents. As Jackson[54] has emphasized, educational theory has had particular difficulty with the *transformative* processes which occur in some homes, schools and workplaces. These transformations tend to occur when people are highly motivated and they get an opportunity to develop new self-images and competencies in the course of undertaking tasks they care about or when they are exposed to role models which they find attractive and engaging.[55]

2. *The absence of tools to administer individualized competency-oriented educational programmes.* This barrier is related to the first: if pupils are to develop a selection of important competencies whilst they are engaged on tasks which are important to them, their teachers must be able to identify the particular types of activity which engage them and monitor the development of many 'intangible' competencies. As Fraley[56] and I[57] have shown, most teachers are unable to do this even when they are in 1 : 1 relationships with children (other than their own). This is because they do not know what interests the children, cannot 'read' their body language and do not have time to reflect on its implications, and, as a result, do not know when and how to intervene. They need tools to help them to do these things.

3. *The fear of exacerbating the climate of mediocrity which the public associate with 'mixed ability teaching' and 'progressive education'.* The idea of fostering 'all of the talents of all of the children' is associated in most people's minds with 'mixed ability teaching' and 'progressive education'. These ideas are in turn associated with mediocrity. There is some justification for these associations since, although neither mixed ability teaching nor progressive education have been wholeheartedly and widely implemented,[58] the goals which were to be achieved and the educational processes which were to be used to reach them have been only intermittently articulated[59] — and often poorly at that. As Bernstein[60] noted, they have been multiple

and implicit. Individualized, competency-oriented education is, however, anything but vague and it is, in particular, quite different from the dominant, romanticist, 'leave children to do as they please' version of progressive education. It requires competent teachers as managers to orchestrate multiple and demanding programmes of personal growth.

4. *The disrespect which many teachers (and researchers) have for 'working class' values.* One observation which may be made about the research literature is that our map of middle class values is much more differentiated than our map of working class values. Researchers seem to have the greatest difficulty hearing what working class people are telling them, and they tend to dismiss it as meaningless or inappropriate if they do hear it. For example, when I have presented data which shows that the most widely endorsed child-rearing priority among working class mothers is that their children should 'really need them', I have been repeatedly challenged to say what the item means. I have never been asked a parallel question about items which middle class mothers endorse. Similarly, when some of the teachers involved in the Lothian Region Educational Home Visiting Scheme said they were concerned about imposing middle class values on working class mothers, they were met by the argument that 'We wouldn't be doing this if we did not believe in it, would we? So what's the problem?' Likewise, in the course of our surveys of pupil opinion, we have repeatedly heard pupils who asked some variant of the question 'What use will all this education be to me as a bricklayer?' being told 'You shouldn't have asked that question. You should have asked how it will help you to avoid being a bricklayer' — a reply which denigrates the pupil's interest in being a bricklayer. Yet again, we have repeatedly observed teachers ignoring pupils' interests and talents whilst 'introducing' them to 'new' interests and forcing them to practise doing things in which they were not interested, which they were not good at, and which they would probably never have to do again. (This process, particularly when it is enacted in the course of 'compensatory', 'remedial' and 'enrichment' programmes establishes a self-fulfilling cycle which *creates* a 'general factor' of 'ability'.)

One thing which should perhaps be made clear at this point is that it appears that high level competencies developed in the course of undertaking tasks which are of little social importance can be released in the course of undertaking other activities if those concerned later come to value those other activities. For this reason it is possible to respect the *competencies* which are being developed and displayed whilst young people are engaged in activities which one does not oneself value.

5. *Teachers on the whole neither present the role models to whom it would be most desirable for young people to be exposed nor, between them, offer a sufficient diversity of models.* We have seen that high-level competencies are not just developed through practice. They are also developed through exposure to people who portray the appropriate values and behaviours in the home, community and workplace. If the energies and talents of all our young people are to be released and developed, it will therefore be necessary either (a) to bring into schools, as mentors, a wide range of people who value different goals and activities and who display the competencies which are needed to translate their values into practice or (b) to develop job placements as a vital part of the educational programme of all pupils. The need for diversity is not, unfortunately, the only reason for underlining the importance of doing these things. It is unfortunately the case that teachers rarely display the competencies required to create an innovative, forward-looking, society.[61] They are rarely interested in innovation or possess the inclination or the competencies required to do new things well: they often feel unable to initiate new activities, monitor the results, and take corrective action when necessary. Instead of inventing the methods they need to do new things, they want courses in which experts will tell them how to do them. They rarely feel in control of their destinies or display the competencies which would be required to get control over those destinies: they do not think it is important to support other teachers who are trying to innovate or band with others to influence wider social forces which constrain their freedom of movement. In all these ways they are very different indeed from small businessmen.[62] They emerge as a rather down-trodden and ineffectual group. They are, therefore, not the best people to whom to expose our children. (One problem for the job placement solution is, however, that British managers and supervisors [unlike, say, Japanese managers and supervisors] rarely see it as part of their job to think about and develop the talents of their subordinates.[63])

6. *The way we, as a society, have defined equality and our understanding of appropriate public provision has tended to deflect teachers' attention away from fostering qualities like creativity and initiative.* Paradoxically, despite the fact that teachers themselves typically espouse 'middle class values', the ethos of state schools is typically 'working class'. This arises partly because, although it is only a narrow majority of

parents who actually endorse the 'working class' value for sitting still and learning what is put in front of one, many other parents end up going along with these parents because of a dilemma which confronts middle class parents. This is that there is no way in which their children can get credit in the examinations which control entry to jobs and courses of further and higher education for possessing such qualities as the ability to think, lead, or take initiative. They therefore come to recognize that schools would be jeopardizing their children's life chances if they pursued these wider goals at the expense of examination success — irrelevant though they recognize that the latter is from the point of view of developing competencies which will actually be of value in later life. Another reason why schools come to be dominated by 'working class' values is that, given current beliefs about equality and public provision, there is no way of catering differentially for the minority of parents who still want schools to foster question-asking, creativity, and initiative. Another is that those pupils who want strong, tough, teachers who discipline them (and who disrupt the work of other pupils if they don't get such teachers) drive out of classrooms the sensitive, reflective, intellectual processes which are crucial to any form of creative activity. (One cannot foster sensitivity to the fleeting feelings on the fringe of consciousness which form the germ of all creative and innovative ideas and a value for working hard at tasks set by others at the same time in the same classroom). For this reason, among others which will be mentioned shortly, it is necessary to cater for some of the diversity in values of which we have spoken by creating variety *between* classrooms and institutions and this raises the spectre of social divisiveness.

The more one moves toward project-based education, the more serious these problems become. Some pupils wish to develop the competencies needed to be successful in business; some to install sewers and electricity supplies; some to apply themselves to the beautification of their communities; and still others to devote themselves to literary creativity. It is necessary to meet the need for much of this diversity on a group basis. It might be thought that this would best be done by creating large schools rather than by having many small units, but this is not the case. Large schools preclude the very educational processes which are most important: they preclude the widespread assumption of responsibility for the effectiveness of the school as an organization and as a community; they preclude children being forced by the objective needs of circumstances (rather than the 'authoritarian' demands of teachers) into a wide range of responsible roles; they preclude the creation of an ethos which emphasizes high standards of behaviour, innovation and performance; they preclude the processes which force people to become aware of the strengths of their colleagues and the development of the capacities needed to work with others with different priorities and capitalize upon their talents.[64]

7. *The worry that treating different children in different ways in different buildings would lead to a caste society has been exacerbated by the attention which has been drawn to the imperfections in social mobility.* This is an exaggerated fear: there is a great deal of social mobility in our society. Jencks,[65] for example, found that, for the United States, the status inequality between brothers amounted to 82 per cent of status variability in general. Payne *et al*[66] found that 71 per cent of adults in Scotland had been upwardly or downwardly mobile from their fathers' socioeconomic status, and that 10 per cent of those holding class 1 jobs had come all the way from class 7 backgrounds. Hope[67] found that, by age 40, there was no difference in the rates of social mobility between Scotland and the US. What was different was that, in Scotland, pupils had been allocated to their future class status by the time they were 11 years old. The Americans floundered around for another thirty years.

8. *The pressures which focus teachers' attention on low level goals.* As I have shown in *Education, Values and Society*,[68] what happens in schools is not mainly determined by the wishes of teachers, pupils, parents, ministers of education or anyone else but by what is assessed in the certification and placement process. The tests which are available for use in both this process and in evaluation and accountability studies are only capable of assessing low level competencies. These tests therefore focus everyone's attention — including that of parents and administrators — on low level competencies.[69] This pressure is exacerbated by the absence of tools to help teachers to identify each pupil's interests and competencies, administer the individualized, competency-oriented, educational programmes which are required to foster high level goals, and monitor progress toward them. It is important to note that merely abandoning testing would not help. As Bernstein[70] has noted, people cannot work effectively toward multiple, intangible, and high level goals. What would help would be a wider range of diagnostic and prescriptive tools and formative and summative assessment instruments . . . but *that* would mean developing and operationalizing a value-based psychometric paradigm instead of pursuing our quest for value-free measures.[71]

This section may be summarized by saying that refusal to come to terms with values and, in particular, the variance in values, has driven all education which aims to foster high level competencies out of schools. Encouraging variety and respecting 'working class' values would unleash opportunities (for future middle class as well as for future working class children) to enter educational programmes which would engage their concerns and help them to develop important competencies.

Influence, Assessment and Parental Involvement

Earlier, I have shown that more variety and choice, both within and between schools, is essential if the talents of more of our young people are to be identified and developed. In this part of my chapter I will first show that the provision of choice is *in itself* neither appropriate nor effective from the point of view of improving the quality of education or enabling pupils and parents to influence what happens in schools.[72] I will then discuss the expectations, tools, and structures which are required to perform these functions.

Influence through choice

To exert effective influence through choice one must have:

(i) access to a range of distinctively different options which have been explicitly developed to meet the needs of a cross-section of pupils and about which there is good information on (a) the pupils for whom they are appropriate, (b) the distinctive features of the educational processes which are being provided, and (c) the consequences of each of the alternatives for different sorts of children, immediately, for their future lives and careers, and for the society in which they live;

(ii) *convenient* geographical access to these options;

(iii) good information on what is going on in the specific classrooms in which one's children are, or might be, enrolled (this information being distinct from information on the type of educational *programme* on offer);

(iv) access to help (guidance) which enables one to articulate one's often unverbalized needs and become familiar with the aims, processes and consequences of educational programmes

which one did not know were possible;
(v) capacity to understand, and time to review, the necessary information (one must not, for example, be preoccupied with securing a precarious hold on life).

If a 'market' system of this sort is to work, there must be some mechanism whereby the range of options which are offered to the public can be extended. In classical theory, this mechanism is provided by the entrepreneurial class whose job it is to notice a previously unmet need and to invent — and put on the market — a product which is designed to meet the need. In education, the scope for such entrepreneurial activity is very limited because the range of educational programmes which can be offered is controlled by what is assessed in public examinations and the sociological process into which those examinations feed. As far as parents are concerned, an option which may jeopardize their children's future life chances because employers will not accept the qualifications [if any] concerned is not a realistic option. To exert effective influence through choice, therefore, parents require some means of influencing the wider constraints which limit the range of options which a local authority is able to provide and which they are able to take up. This means that, if we pursue the examination example, they need some means of initiating the research and development which is required to develop means of indexing the wider outcomes of general education so that their children can get credit for possessing these qualities. And they need some means of influencing national and international manpower policies. The prospect of doing this through existing political structures is slim indeed.

One other prerequisite to the effective operation of a 'market' mechanism arises from the fact that, as has become clear even in relation to the purchase of tangible goods like cars and drugs, the information which is available on the products has become of crucial importance. If pupils and parents are to have access to the information which they will need to use a 'market' system effectively — and especially to use it to stimulate innovation — it will be necessary for them to have a mechanism whereby they can initiate research and development to generate information, the nature of which is at first only poorly articulated, but the importance of which becomes clearer as the results begin to emerge. That is, pupils and parents must have access to a mechanism which enables them to initiate social research and development and which enables them to *ensure* that it is carried through from their own perspective:

researchers tend to recast research to reflect their own perspectives and, while this is not always a bad thing — indeed social researchers have, because of their position and access to information, come to be cast in the role of guardians of the public interest and need to defend that position in the courts — there is a need for research informed by a wider range of perspectives.

Although the changes being introduced by the present government make provision for collecting and supplying partial information on school 'performance', that information does not relate to the outcomes discussed earlier, that is, it does not relate to the *most important* outcomes of education. There is no provision for ensuring that any of the other prerequisites to choice becoming influence are met. Nor are other mechanisms whereby people can influence provision and the constraints on its improvement to be established. The 'market mechanism' which the changes being introduced into education purport to offer will therefore provide neither meaningful nor useful choice nor a mechanism for school improvement. It will only offer some people a choice of supplier; it will not offer people a choice between distinctively different *types* of education.

Influence through Representation

Representation on boards of management or governors (England) or school boards (Scotland), and a requirement that Headteachers report to school boards, is, from the point of view of being able to significantly influence one's children's education or improve schools, no more satisfactory than the right to choose between schools offering educational programmes which have not been developed to differ markedly in character and which do not lead to distinctively different, but equally acceptable, qualifications.

There are two issues here: one is the nature of the information which is to be collected and disseminated on the work of individual teachers and schools. The other is the decision-taking structure into which that information is fed.

What is needed is some mechanism whereby the work of individual teachers can be assessed *in such a way that it highlights realistic possibilities for improvement*, discussed constructively with the administrators and parents concerned so as to identify realistic but challenging strategies for improvement, and monitored so as to see whether the planned changes have been introduced and had the desired effect. The whole process needs to be carried through constructively and in such a way that those concerned can learn from the things which have not turned out as had been hoped or expected. In the following paragraphs I will discuss two types of assessment which might be useful (assessment of classroom climate and teacher appraisal) and then say a little more about the kind of structure into which such information might usefully be fed.

The Assessment of Classroom Climate

For many years, we have studied the nature of the classroom processes which are associated with the development of the high level competencies mentioned earlier and those which lead teachers to be able to identify and foster very different talents in different children thus producing children who differ from each other in their *areas* of excellence and expertise instead of their 'level of ability'. In the course of this research it has become clear that the presence or absence of relevant educational processes can be indexed by asking pupils about such things as what kinds of behaviours are valued by their fellow pupils and their teachers, what kinds of activity are encouraged and rewarded, whether they themselves are encouraged to do new things and decide for themselves what they will do, whether turning in a first rate performance is applauded and a second rate performance frowned upon by their fellow pupils, and whether a wide range of pupils who have very different talents are encouraged to develop and use them and whether those contributions are recognized and built upon by others. Indices of classroom processes of this sort have, in the literature, been called measures of 'classroom climate'.[73] Both Walberg[74] and Howard[75] (like many others in the industrial sector) have shown that information collected using such measures helps groups of parents, teachers and administrators to think about what is going on and the changes which might usefully be introduced. These researchers have also shown that the same measures can be used to monitor the effectiveness of the changes in such a way that remedial action can be taken when necessary. There is therefore a clear need to initiate further development work in this area.[76]

Teacher Appraisal

Our work has shown that pupils tend to assimilate the concerns, priorities, attitudes, thoughtways and patterns of competence of their teachers.[77] It is therefore crucial to the future of this society that we have an educational system staffed by people who display high levels of innovativeness *as an educational objective in its own right.* It follows that it is necessary to create time within the school day for teachers to involve themselves in educational innovation and to create interschool networks which facilitate teacher involvement in innovative activities. It is necessary to create a staff appraisal system which enables teachers to get credit for involving themselves in the difficult, demanding and frustrating business of innovation. In the course of the requisite staff appraisals it will be necessary to find some way of giving teachers credit for doing such things as paying attention to the idiosyncratic needs of each of their pupils and inventing better ways of meeting those needs. To implement such a staff appraisal system it will be necessary to find ways of assessing teachers' ability to take initiative, invent better ways of doing things and solve problems. This is not necessarily as difficult as may appear. In one of those strokes of genius which cut through brushwood which has engulfed others, Burgess and Adams have suggested that teachers be asked to keep a record of their own achievements in a way which parallels their own and Stansbury's reporting process for pupils. Further development of the value-expectancy measurement methodology which we have ourselves pioneered offers another basis on which more appropriate staff appraisal systems might be developed.

Structures for Parental Involvement

The changes currently being introduced into the educational system are in part a response to the public's awareness that, despite all the changes which have been introduced over the past forty years, there is still something seriously wrong. They are in part a response to the public's desire to be able to exercise more choice of their own instead of being pushed about by faceless public administrators who are not noted for taking their priorities seriously. They are in part a response to the public's desire to be able to influence what happens in schools. However, the Conservative government, while being much more sensitive to these and similar feelings than any of the other political parties, has characteristically not thought the issues through. The structures being introduced will not provide any form of choice worth the name because the research needed to identify and develop the options which are needed is not being put in hand. They will not yield parent power because it is not possible for the diverse views of parents to be represented in any form of small 'representative' committee. And they will not lead to the improvement of education because that requires the creation of an innovative educational system supported by the fundamental research and development activity which is required to develop the necessary understandings, tools and procedures. Edward Heath was therefore correct to describe the government's Bill as a 'con trick'. There is no connection between the problems which are correctly diagnosed and the remedies which are prescribed.

The reasons *why* the government has not thought the issues through themselves merit serious attention. To do anything about the problems the government has correctly identified it would be necessary for the public to accept and encourage diversity *in public provision*. It would be necessary to introduce new forms of democracy through which people could monitor public provision and exercise choice and influence. It would be necessary to accept that supervising and managing public provision is a genuinely wealth-creating activity which merits financial reward. It would be necessary to establish policy research and development units to develop the concepts and tools which are required to run the public sector effectively and generate the information which is required to monitor its effectiveness.

The school boards and boards of governors currently being introduced are inadequate to the task of stimulating the radical changes which are needed in education. As we have seen, one of the most urgent needs is for a comprehensive range of distinctively different sorts of provision suited to the cross-section of the population who live in each geographical area. No single school board could take the overall perspective which is essential if this is to be done. Likewise, most of the barriers to educational innovation are beyond the control of individual schools: they stem from the absence of clear, research-based, thinking about the type of programme which is required to cater for different types of children, and they stem from the constraints which the centrally-prescribed testing and examination system places on what happens in schools. No single school is in a position to challenge and revise those requirements.[78]

But even if one ignores these wider problems, representative bodies do not provide a mechanism which can ensure that a cross-section of parents who have different priorities are elected and then insist that the school find some way of meeting all of their diverse needs. Compulsory annual reports by Headteachers to school boards are unlikely to be very effective. Experience shows that officials who are required to report to elected boards (including local authority committees) are typically able to manipulate the information they report in such a way as to conceal real problems and options, to stifle debate, and to gain endorsement for the proposed policies.

Traditional representative structures are not suited to this purpose. Instead we need: (i) some kind of participative, or network, structure which makes it much easier for groups of interested parents and other citizens to find out about, comment on, press effectively for change in, and monitor subsequent developments in, the work of individual teachers, schools and groups of schools; and (ii) new concepts of the role of public servants. We need to expect our public servants to solicit, and take steps to generate, the necessary information, invent — or initiate the invention of — ways of catering for a cross-section of pupils and parents, to take steps to monitor the quality of that provision, and to come to good discretionary judgments about what is in the long term best interests of the public. We need to expect them to study parents' and pupils' needs and wishes and to invent ways of accommodating *all* of them. We need to expect them to initiate studies to investigate problems which are not yet clear, the methodology for studying which is not yet formulated, and to develop forms of provision and tools to administer and evaluate diversity for which there is as yet no demand. In other words we need to expect them to be entrepreneurs and innovators. And we need to hold them accountable in these terms. That is, we need some tools and structures to help us to find out whether they are doing these things and structures which will enable us to ensure that remedial action is taken if they are not.

Toward a More Satisfactory Model

We have seen that we need to find some way of holding individual teachers (public servants) accountable for studying each of their pupils' talents and inventing ways of helping them to develop them. We have seen that, in order to find out whether teachers are doing this, we need new, research-based, classroom appraisal instruments. We have also seen that, if teachers are to monitor their performance and take the initiative needed to find better ways of meeting their pupils' needs, they must devote a great deal of time and energy to risky, frustrating and innovative activity. Their job descriptions need to change so that they are *expected* to take initiative and be adventurers and inventors. They therefore need to work in a structure which encourages contact with teachers in other classrooms and schools and which supports them when their attempts at innovation go wrong, as they surely will. It is important to note that teachers need to be encouraged to do more than improve classroom processes. They need to be encouraged to spend more time outside their own classrooms. They need to spend more time working with parents and bringing effective pressure to bear on politicians and examination boards. This is because what they *can* do in their classrooms is mainly determined by forces from outside.

If the tools, the information they produce, and the structures for innovation mentioned in the last paragraph are to be *used*, it will be necessary to have some public supervisory structure which does not depend on a long chain of authority to a distant elected representative who is necessarily ignorant of the work of a particular teacher and the issues in his or her school — and who, in any case, has many other things to do. Teachers therefore need to be accountable to some local group. Since what it is appropriate for one teacher to do must necessarily depend on what other teachers, locally and nationally, are doing and on what is emerging from national and international research, any one teacher, and his or her supervisory group, must be part of some network of monitoring groups. Some of these would focus on the work of individual teachers, some on schools, some on groups of schools, and some on research, but they would be linked to each other by their overlapping memberships. All should have links with local and national media.

In this description I have focused only on classroom teachers. The work of administrators also needs to be brought within its remit. The administrative structure which has grown up around schools over the past forty years was, indeed, supposed to perform some of the functions which I am now proposing to hand over to this new monitoring structure. The problem with our existing structures has been that they have not functioned very effectively. This is partly because the information which has been collected has often been regarded as if it was for internal use only and not for public consumption or debate. Its use has been constrained by a concept of democracy which limits it to 'that which happens in city hall'. Furthermore, the job of the administrator (manager) has generally not been understood as involving the creation of an innovative climate in the educational system and society. It has not been understood as involving responsibility for ensuring that there is a balance of different types of provision in a particular geographical area. It has not been defined as involving drawing the attention of politicians and the public to the linkages between educational policy and other aspects of policy (such as employment policy or equitable payment). In other words it has been defined as doing politicians' bidding rather than drawing previously unnoticed problems and tasks to the attention of the public. Clearly, therefore, it will be necessary to establish an exactly parallel set of tools and monitoring groups to oversee the work of public servants as is required to oversee the work of teachers. We are now in a position to draw two other points out of this discussion.

First, if the kind of innovation in the social process which has been envisaged above is to come about, there is a need for an unprecedented public debate, not just about education and educational goals, but about the goals of society, the state of our society and how it is to be run. This debate could occur through the network of monitoring and discussion groups which have already been mentioned, but it could not take place without the assistance of the media, and those who take part in that debate need some mechanism through which they can make their views known. As Toffler[79] has pointed out, modern information technology (such as Prestel) makes it easy for people to do this from the comfort of their living rooms. But the value of the information collected through such referenda is not only dependent on the dissemination of information about the range of possible activities and their consequences, it is also dependent on the development of survey questions which yield more meaningful information than that generated from opinion polls. Furthermore, if useful conclusions are to be drawn from the data which are collected, it will also be necessary for those concerned to develop an understanding of democracy which does not assume that majority decisions are sovereign, but which instead demands that some means must be found to enable people with different priorities to get equitable treatment, geared to their priorities, from the public service.

Second, the time required for many members of the population to engage in the kind of participative — as distinct from representative — democratic process which is required to oversee the public-sector activities which dominate our society will be considerable. Wider recognition that such civic activity contributes to the efficiency of our society and the quality of life of all, and should therefore correctly be viewed as a *wealth creating* activity, is therefore essential. Such activity merits financial reward. (It is not inappropriate at this point to emphasize that the costs of operating the economic marketplace [which provides for quality control and innovation through the choice mechanism instead of through a managerial and democratic structure] are enormous: two thirds of the cost of the average article goes on distribution and marketing and more goes on the enforcement of safety, health, and other standards. Yet this work — unlike the chore of supervising the public sector — tends to be viewed as contributing to wealth creation, and is certainly thought to merit financial reward.)

To give the ideas I have put forward here greater credibility, it may be useful to mention that one of the most striking features of Japanese society is the network of discussion groups — supported by policy research and development units — which have been set up over the years to examine various aspects of public policy and to bring into being desirable futures. This was how they moved out of shipbuilding and took up Information Technology (IT). It is also relevant to note, with Toffler, that the orchestration of such debates represents one of the most important, but as yet neglected, uses of IT. The evolution of new structures of participation and influence is one of the key issues of our time. What is more, it is an evolution to which research can contribute: what we need to do is to experiment more freely and to compare and contrast the operation and effects of alternatives.

The question of how all this is to be paid for will lead many to dismiss what I have said as unrealistic. However, just as we urgently need new concepts of democracy, so we urgently need new concepts of money, wealth, and wealth-creation. I have discussed these elsewhere[80] and there is room for only a few assertions here. The main point is that one does not have to have money *before* one initiates wealth-creating activity. Nor is wealth something which one must have before embarking on a programme of economic activity. Rather it is a product of wealth creating activity. Nor is wealth to be equated with money. Money is a tool to be used to orchestrate wealth creation, and, like other tools, more can be manufactured (printed) if it would be useful. However, money as the main tool for use in managing wealth-creation and accounting has outlived its usefulness and needs to be replaced by multiple-bottom line, information-based, accounting procedures which take account of replacement and other externalized costs. Finally, the quality of our lives — our wealth — is now primarily determined by what our public servants do: they are the main producers of wealth.

Education must Remain in the Public Domain

Currently fashionable beliefs about appropriate ways of running society will undoubtedly lead many to think that the need for choice and variety, the need to find ways of combating the deadening hand of the bureaucratic process and its press toward uniformity, and the need to combat the prescription of content by central examination boards point, separately and collectively, to a need to privatize education. It is suggested that there will then be more choice and that market mechanisms will then generate the necessary variety. There are two fundamental objections to this view.

The first is that privatization is in fact no solution even to the problems which have led to its introduction into industry and commerce. It simply does not engage with the nature of modern society. Whether we like it or not, we now, for the best of reasons, live in economies which are managed by public servants. It is public servants who, more than anyone else, determine trade, prices, and profitability. It is they who, more than anyone else, control the quality of our lives: our wealth is now overwhelmingly defined by the quality of public provision. We need public servants to develop and enforce international policies relating to pollution, the exploitation of non-renewable resources, and the replenishment of renewable resources. The word 'customer' as used in free-enterprise propaganda conjures up an outdated image: nowadays most customers are no longer people voting with their pennies to influence the direction of development but corporate giants purchasing on behalf of pension companies, health services, airlines, countries and consortia of countries. Even the increased efficiency apparently gained by the privatization of manufacturing and service industries is illusory, being typically achieved by forcing the weakest members of society to accept casualized working conditions and to forego benefits which must be provided by law for full time employees.

The second is that the measures being introduced by the present government in the educational sphere have focused entirely on only one prong of the supposed benefits of choice in the marketplace — i.e. the efficiency of the supplier. They have not only entirely ignored the stimulus to the development of new products which Smith, Hayek and others have argued that the marketplace could provide, but actually stifled such developments by prescribing a common curriculum for all schools.

Given what we have seen about the need for variety, choice and innovation in education, it would therefore behove us to be much clearer about why education should remain in the public sector and be funded by the general public rather than by those who are engaged in education.

It is inappropriate to expect people to pay for the education of only their own children or for these children to pay through repayable loans because:

(a) all citizens of well-educated societies — and not just those who have children — reap the benefits of an educated workforce and citizenry;
(b) those who are best able to perform the crucially important task of leading and managing our society in the public interest do not come exclusively from well-off families. Yet they *are* in short supply. We would therefore deprive society of the benefits of crucially important talents if those who were born into poor families were unable to obtain a suitable education;
(c) different people confer quite different benefits on society. It is therefore in society's interests to develop the talents of all of them. This will not happen if some people are unable to pay for their children's education;
(d) as Robertson[81] has shown for the United Kingdom, and as Winter and McClelland[82] have shown for the United States, as things stand, the people who contribute most to society rarely get what is generally considered to be equitable financial reward for their efforts. There is therefore little reason to believe that, in general, those who are going to contribute most to society will be best able to repay any debts they may have incurred in the course of their education;
(e) socio-psychological processes work their wonders in mysterious (ie psychological rather than logical) ways. For example, early Calvinists worked hard, contributed disproportionately to society, needed to know they were doing 'well' in income

terms in order to assure themselves that they were among 'the elect', but then dared not spend that money other than on further investments, still less enjoy the comfortable life it could have purchased. Others who did not have this need to adopt an austere and hard-working life style enjoyed the benefits the Calvinists produced. Both benefited from this symbiotic relationship. (Since his standards were norm-referenced, the Calvinist could not do 'well' if someone else was not indolent). This process is still at work today among 'achievement-oriented' individuals. A similar 'illogicality' is that the innovators on whom we are so dependent are typically comfortably situated and do not have to worry about their financial futures.[83] Security, not insecurity, breeds creativity. Conversely creativity and innovation breeds social instability and financial insecurity (not necessarily so much for the innovator as for others). Those who are responsible for crucial ideas rarely benefit from them financially.[84] Although these people contribute disproportionately to society, they do not get commensurate benefits. Furthermore, creativity and innovation are typically dependent on the possession of unique combinations of up-to-date specialist knowledge. We would choke our life blood if we deprived these people of access to the knowledge they require. Once again, then, the links between earnings and contribution to society are so weak that we cannot afford to rely on them as a mechanism to fund education;

(e) we need in each and every community a balance of institutions offering quite different forms of provision. This is best illustrated by an example. Outstanding entrepreneurs require for their success access to outstanding academics. To produce prototypes of their inventions they may need to employ outstanding machinists who are able to take good discretionary judgments about what should be done and invent ways of doing things. To market their product they may need outstanding managers and sales personnel — they have to sell the idea that there is a need for such a product as well as the idea that buying their product will best satisfy that need. They need customers who are well enough off to purchase their innovations. Yet in a market driven system only the education of those who are going to obtain to the highest-paying jobs would be adequately funded;

(f) a market mechanism would not lead to improvement in the

quality of education in the current economic circumstances because people would buy — are buying — passports to entry to good jobs rather than education itself. The marketplace would offer better ways of beating the system rather than better educational programmes. This is why improvement in educational practice must come from the intervention of public servants (an argument which is also true across most of the developments which are needed to improve the quality of our lives and to conserve resources).

The final three comments relate to the funding of university education:

(g) if our society is to develop, we need an educational system which is very different from the legitimizing-of-rationing-of-privilege system that we have at the moment. We need an open system which admits adults at any time in their lives to the seminar atmosphere characteristic of research-style universities so that they can develop the concepts and tools they need. To flourish, this atmosphere requires continuing funding. (The remarks made in this paragraph of course imply radical change in the universities[85] and the application of new criteria of accountability, not the restoration of the atmosphere of the 1970s);

(h) we cannot expect those who are most conscious of personal benefits and costs to be willing to pay the fees needed to maintain the risky research which society so badly needs;

(i) contract research is not an appropriate way of creating the research climate needed in the universities. All the evidence is that those who have made worthwhile contributions to research have devoted their lives to their chosen topics. (Contract research has proved to be highly inefficient in cost-benefit terms, having high costs and yielding few benefits.)[86]

In conclusion

In the course of this chapter we have seen that the key development needed to improve the quality of education is an increase in the range of distinctively different options on offer. Unfortunately, the notion that public provision should cater for different people in different ways is a heresy which, even if it entertained, is regarded as dangerous. If I am right in arguing that it is important for education to remain in the public domain, it follows that the effective administration of the educational system demands new concepts of the role of public servants and new concepts of democracy. It demands new concepts of management and new supervisory structures. It demands new concepts of citizenship, wealth, and wealth-creating activity.

There are three striking things about this collection of unexpected, and often unwelcome, conclusions. The first is that they all involve new understandings and new concepts in political-economy. Those who have administered the Manpower Services Commission's (MSC) enterprise programmes have made the same discovery. However the MSC has reacted to the dangers inherent in encouraging old-style political education by banning it. The second is that exactly parallel conclusions emerge from the study of other sectors of the economy: if we are to handle pollution, the balance of payments, conservation of renewable and non-renewable resources, agricultural policy, or international security more effectively, we need public servants who initiate the collection of information about issues which have not yet become clear and we need to get them to link that information together and come to good discretionary judgments which are in the public interest. We need to be able to monitor and influence their work and their decisions. The third is that the evolution and introduction of these new shared understandings is an unmistakably educational task. But it is an educational task which embodies two key features of the educational process envisaged in the first part of this chapter: the educational process requires evolutionary, research-based activities and involves the initiation of further research. The evolution of this new understanding will not depend mainly on the communication of received wisdom. Educators should therefore focus on fostering among students the competence to evolve new civic understandings. If they did so, many of the fears of political brainwashing which represent such serious barriers to the introduction of effective education would disappear.

Acknowledgements

I am very deeply indebted indeed to Bryan Dockrell and Stanley Nisbet for their invaluable help and encouragement in preparing this chapter.

Notes

1 Durkheim (1925) has argued their viewpoint more coherently.
2 HMI (1978), DES (1977), CBI, Scottish Education Department (1965), HMI (1980), 'Munn' Report (1977), MSC (1984–85), DES (1985), Educaton for Capability Manifesto (see Burgess [1986]), Boyer (1983), National Task Force for Economic Growth (1983), National Commission on Excellence in Education (1984), Passow *et al* (1976), Little (1983), Marimuthu (1983).
3 Bill *et al* (1974), Raven, Handy *et al* (1975), Raven (1977), Morton-Williams *et al* (1968), Macbeath *et al* (1981), CES (1977), Flanagan and Russ-Eft (1975), Johnston and Bachman (1976), DeLandsheere (1977).
4 Flanagan and Burns (1955), ITRU (1979).
5 Sykes (1969).
6 Van Beinum (1965).
7 Fivars and Gosnell (1966).
8 See McClelland (1961), Burgess and Pratt (1970), Schwartz (1987).
9 Raven (1984). What is most notable about Schwartz's (1987) study is that, although Schwartz was nominally studying businessmen's responsiveness to changes in their environment, their ultimate success in reaching the objectives the country (ie civil servants) had set for them was dependent on the quality of civil servants' judgments both in establishing the objectives and in correctly understanding how to manipulate prices, grants and the 'business environment' in order to get 'independent entrepreneurs' to achieve these objectives. Their job is, it seems, to manage both businessmen and the economy.
10 Price, Taylor *et al* (1971).
11 Taylor and Barron (1963).
12 Burgess and Pratt (1970), Fores and Pratt (1980).
13 Klemp, Munger and Spencer (1977).
14 Raven (1984).
15 Raven (1984), Flanagan (1978, 1983).
16 Raven (1984), Flanagan and Russ-Eft (1975).
17 Benedict (1976), Raven (1977, 1984), McClelland (1961), Graham and Raven (1987).
18 Raven (1977), HMI (1980), Raven, Johnstone and Varley (1985), MacBeath *et al* (1981), Johnston (1973), Bachman *et al* (1971), Flanagan (1978), Goodlad (1983).
19 Raven (1977), Raven, Johnstone and Varley (1985), Goodman (1962).
20 See Raven (1980), Sigel (1985).
21 Bachman *et al* (1971), Jencks (1973, 1979), Hope (1985).
22 Raven (1977, 1980, 1984), Raven, Johnstone and Varley (1985), Winter, McClelland and Stewart (1981), Klemp, Munger and Spencer (1977), Jackson (1986), McClelland (1965).
23 Benn and Fairley (1986).
24 Johnston and Bachman (1976).
25 Morton-Williams *et al* (1968).
26 Smith (1964, 1966, 1969), James (1968, 1969), Mason (1970), Raven (1977), Raven *et al* (1985).

27 Raven *et al* (1985), Winter *et al* (1981), Schneider, Klemp and Kastendiek (1981), Klemp *et al* (1980), Huff *et al* (1982).
28 Raven *et al* (1985), Jackson (1986).
29 Raven (1984).
30 Raven (1984), McClelland (1975), Winter (1973).
31 Raven and Litton (1976), Litton and Raven (1977/82).
32 See McClelland (1965), Raven (1977), and Raven (1988) for a fuller discussion of this issue.
33 Pellegrini *et al* (1985), Sigel and McGillicuddy-Delisi (1984), McGillicuddy *et al* (1982), Tharp *et al* (1984), Gallimore (1988), Raven (1980).
34 Sigel (1985, 1986).
35 McGillicuddy (1985), McGillicuddy *et al* (1987).
36 Rosen and D'Andrade (1959).
37 McClelland (1961, 1982).
38 Bloom (1985).
39 Raven (1980).
40 Raven and Dolphin (1978), Raven (1984).
41 Raven (1980), Sigel and Kelley (1986), McGillicuddy (1985), Tough (1973), Gallimore *et al* (1974), Tharp *et al* (1984), Tizard and Hughes (1984), Tizard, Schofield and Hewison (1982), Heath (1983), Hewison and Tizard (1980), Bloom (1985).
42 Raven (1977).
43 Kohn (1959; 1969; 1977), Kohn *et al* (1986).
44 Jackson and Marsden (1962).
45 Havighurst and Taba (1949).
46 Elisabeth Newson, personal communication.
47 Sokolowska *et al* (1978).
48 Lempert (1986).
49 Kinsey (1948).
50 Burns *et al* (1984).
51 Numerous studies (for example, Goodlad [1982], ORACLE, HMI [1980], Raven [1977], Raven, Johnstone and Varley [1985]) have demonstrated that school days are typically filled with activities concerned with the repetitious coverage of out of date, low level, factual material. Other evidence, summarized in Raven (1977) and Goodlad (1982), shows that half of what is learned is typically forgotten within one year and 75 per cent within two years. There is little exercise of judgment, creativity, thinking or even writing of continuous prose — let alone the revision of that material to communicate a message which is important to the writer to a recipient who needs to get it.
52 See Raven (1977) for a review of these.
53 Hatch and Gardner (1986), like Calvin Taylor (1971; 1973; 1976) and ourselves, have been delighted by the range, diversity and importance of children's interests and talents which come to light if one bothers to look for them.
54 Jackson (1986).

55 Bachman *et al* (1978), Jackson (1986), Flanagan (1978), Raven, Johnstone and Varley (1985).
56 Fraley (1981).
57 Raven (1980).
58 ORACLE, HMI (1980), Bennett (1976), Powell (1985), Goodlad (1983), Raven, Johnstone and Varley (1985).
59 The goals of mixed ability teaching have, to the best of my knowledge, nowhere been satisfactorily articulated. However, in 1977, (Raven, 1977) I set out the alternative goals of this process insofar as they could be discerned from interviews with teachers. The chaotic activities perpetrated in the name of progressive education are well illustrated in the work of Barth (1972), Aiken (1942), Rathbone (1971), Rugg (1926), Rugg and Schumaker (1928), Wright (1950, 1958), ORACLE, Leith (1981) and Bennett (1976). Cremin (1961), Fraley (1981) and Ravitch (1974) have provided useful summaries of the progressive education movement in America. What is notable is that none of these authors identify even a section of the progressive education movement as wishing to *replace* conventional educational goals by a distinctively different set. None of the teachers Bennett asked to define progressive education did so by reference to distinctive goals. It was seen as a different method of achieving the same goals. By and large, 'progressive education' has involved little more than a reaction *against* a single-valued concept of human quality and excellence — ie one based on performance at school tasks which could be seen to have few correlates outside the classroom but which, as part of a sociological system for allocating position and status nevertheless led, on the one hand, to the wrong (ie purely self-interested) people being placed in influential positions in society and, on the other, to many people who did contribute in very worthwhile ways to society not getting the respect and financial rewards they deserved. The problem was that this reaction against a dysfunctional system did not lead to a better system — but only to teachers addressing themselves mainly to pupils of 'average' ability and even, in some cases, to pouring scorn on those who sought to do 'well' in those terms — and thus to the cult of uniformity and mediocrity. Few sought to implement a 'talents unlimited' (Taylor, 1974; 1985) form of educational programme. Several writers sought to add goals without seeking to basically change teachers' focus. Thus Dewey (1899; 1910; 1916) seems to have been preoccupied with, on the one hand, fostering the skills of the research scientist (the ability to conceptualize, analyze and experiment), and, on the other, with creating 'democratic' classrooms. His writing does not encourage teachers to make use of multiple-talent concepts of ability (for example by encouraging them to think about a wide range of alternative talents which schools might foster), still less encourage them to foster different competencies in different children. Kilpatrick (1918) indicates that, in translating a plan into reality, pupils should practise purposing, planning, executing and judging. These are high level competencies, but Kilpatrick does not analyze them and present them in a way which would encourage teachers to reflect on what it means to, for example,

plan and execute, or on the prerequisites to getting pupils to practise (and thereby develop) the activities which are necessary. Counts (1932) and Rugg (1926) seem to have set out to introduce *particular* understandings of socio-politico-economic processes. Perhaps the largest group of progressive educators — the 'child-centred' teachers who have suggested that the child should be left to do his or her own thing and thereby learn 'instinctively' what is important to him or her to learn — have been opposed to the very idea of stating objectives, believing that these should emerge from an evolving situation. However, they have nowhere discussed how teachers are to facilitate the development of these multiple talents. The 'bible' of the progressive education movement (the 1926 Handbook of the NSSE) nowhere identifies the competencies which are to be fostered, how they are to be fostered, or how they are to be assessed for either formative or summative purposes. French (1957), Stratemeyer *et al* (1947), Caswell and Campbell (1935), Tyler (1936), and the Educational Policies Commission (1938) do attempt to identify goals, but have muddled together goals at a wide variety of levels, the frameworks are not multiple-talent frameworks, and the goals are only weakly linked to curriculum processes. Most accounts of classroom processes focus on encouraging students to take 'democratic' decisions within the compulsory attendance framework of schools (a framework which deprives pupils of citizenship rights and in which most of the sources of power and influence [for example, the option to withdraw and the opportunity to influence decisions and gain treatment suited to their own priorities through the marketplace] which are open to people in capitalist 'democracies' are unavailable) and in which teachers could not allow students to implement many decisions which would command majority support from pupils, on 'discovering' information which the teacher already knows (mostly in classrooms, but sometimes in field trips), or on 'discussions' which involve guessing what the teacher has in mind. Among the few exceptions to the rather damning picture of progressive education presented in this footnote are the writings of Barnes (1932) and her colleagues at the Lincoln school. Unfortunately few students of education are likely to come into contact with this work since it is not referred to in more recent writings on progressive education, such as those of Barth (1972), Ravitch (1974) or the thirteen-volume *International Encyclopaedia of Education*.

60 Bernstein (1975).

61 Raven (1977).

62 Raven (1977).

63 Raven (1984).

64 Raven (1977), Barker and Gump (1948), Raven, Johnstone and Varley (1985).

65 Jencks (1973).

66 Payne *et al* (1979).

67 Hope (1985).

68 Raven (1977).

69 Raven, Johnstone and Varley (1985), Raven (1988).

70 Bernstein (1985).
71 Raven (1984; 1988).
72 Elmore (1986) has also shown from an extensive review of the available evidence that 'there is little evidence that greater choice will, . . . by itself, dramatically change the performance of schools'.
73 To avoid confusion it is important to distinguish measures of process which are theoretically related to aspects of competence from attempts, like those of Pace and Stern (1958), to index the *overall* climate of the classroom.
74 Walberg (1979; 1985), Walberg and Haertel (1980).
75 Howard (1980–82).
76 Preliminary forms of such measures for use in taking stock of organisational climate are available in *The Edinburgh Questionnaires*, Raven (1982).
77 Raven and Varley (1984), Raven (1977).
78 One would, of course, like to see schools banding together to insist on change and to experiment with alternatives. This is something we are only likely to get if we concentrate on introducing an innovatory educational system instead of — as the government is doing — trying to *prescribe* precisely what pupils should be studying.
79 Toffler (1981).
80 Raven (1983).
81 Robertson (1985).
82 Winter, McClelland and Stewart (1981).
83 Raven (1984).
84 McClelland (1961), Freeman (1974).
85 Raven, (1984).
86 Raven (1984, 1985).

References

AIKIN, W.M. (1942) *The Story of the Eight Year Study: Adventure in American Education, Vol. I*, New York, Harper Bros.

BACHMAN, J.G., GREEN, S. and WIRTANEN, I.D. (1971) *Youth in Transition III: Dropping Out — Problem or Symptom?* Ann Arbor, Michigan, The Institute for Social Research.

BACHMAN, J.G., O'MALLEY, P.M. AND JOHNSTON, J. (1978) *Adolescence to Adulthood: Change and Stability in the Lives of Young Men*, Ann Arbor, Michigan, The Institute for Social Research.

BARKER, R.G. and GUMP, P.V. (1948) *Big School Small School*, California, Stanford University Press.

BARNES and YOUNG (1932) *Units of Work: Children and Architecture*, Lincoln School, New York, Bureau of Publications, Teachers' College, Columbia University.

BENEDICT, SISTER M. (1976). 'An analysis of the philosophy of Paulo Freire' MEd thesis, Maynooth, Eire, Department of Education, St Patrick's College.

BENN, C. and FAIRLY, J. (1986) *Challenging the MSC: An Enquiry into a National Disaster*, London, Pluto Press.
BENNETT, N. (1976) *Teaching Styles and Pupil Progress*, London, Open Books.
BERNSTEIN, B. (1975) 'Class and pedagogies: Visible and invisible', in DOCKRELL, W.B. and HAMILTON, D. (Eds) *Rethinking Educational Research*, London, Hodder and Stoughton.
BILL, J.M., TREW, C.J. and WILSON, J.A. (1974) *Early Leaving in Northern Ireland*, Belfast, Northern Ireland Council for Educational Research.
BLOOM, B.S. (Ed) (1985) *Developing Talent in Young People*, New York, Ballantine Books.
BOYER, E.L. (1983) *High School: A Report on Secondary Education in America*, The Carnegie Foundation for the Advancement of Teaching, New York, Harper and Row.
BURGESS, T. (Ed.) (1986) *Education for Capability*, Windsor, Berks, NFER/Nelson.
BURGESS, T. and PRATT, J. (1970) *Polytechnics in Pakistan*, London, North East London Polytechnic.
BURNS, A., HOMEL, R. and GOODNOW, J. (1984) 'Conditions of life and parental values', *Australian Journal of Psychology*, **36**, pp. 219–37.
CASWELL, H.L. and CAMPBELL, D.S. (1935) *Curriculum Development*, New York, American Book Co.
CENTRE FOR EDUCATIONAL SOCIOLOGY, UNIVERSITY OF EDINBURGH (1977) *Collaborative Research Dictionary*.
COUNTS, G.S. (1932/69) *Dare the Schools Build a New Social Order?* New York, John Day, (1969: Arno).
CREMIN, L.A. (1961) *The Transformation of the School*, New York, Knopf.
DE LANDSHEERE, V. (1977) 'On defining educational objectives', *Evaluation in Education, 1, No. 2*, pp. 73–190. Oxford, Pergamon Press.
DEPARTMENT OF EDUCATION AND SCIENCE (1977) *Education in Schools: A Consultative Document*, Cmnd 6869, London, HMSO.
DEPARTMENT OF EDUCATION AND SCIENCE (1985) *The Development of Higher Education into the 1990s*, Cmnd 6869. London, HMSO.
DEWEY, J. (1899) *The School and Society*, Chicago, University of Chicago Press.
DEWEY, J. (1910) *How We Think*, New York, D.C. Heath.
DEWEY, J. (1916) *Democracy and Education*, New York, Macmillan.
DURKHEIM, E. (1925, 1961) *Moral Education*, New York, Free Press.
EDUCATION POLICIES COMMISSION (1938) *The Purposes of Education in American Democracy*, Washington, D.C., National Education Association.
ELMORE, R.F. (1986) *Choice in Public Education*, New Brunswick, Rutgers University, Center for Policy Research in Education.
FLANAGAN, J.C. (1976) *Planning Life and Career Goals: A Cluster of Materials and Manuals*, Monterey, CA, CTB/McGraw-Hill.
FLANAGAN, J.C. (1978) *Perspectives on Improving Education from a Study of 10,000 30-year-olds*, New York, Praeger Publishers.
FLANAGAN, J.C. (1983) 'The contribution of educational institutions to the

quality of life of Americans', *International Review of Applied Psychology*, **32**.

FLANAGAN, J.C. and BURNS, R.K. (1955) 'The Employee Performance Record', *Harvard Business Review*, **33**, pp. 95–102.

FLANAGAN, J.C. and RUSS-EFT, D. (1975) *An Empirical Study to Aid in Formulating Educational Goals*, American Institutes for Research, Palo-Alto, California.

FORES, M. and PRATT, J. (1980) 'Engineering; Our last chance', *Higher Education Review*, **12**, pp. 5–26.

FRALEY, A. (1981) *Schooling and Innovation: The Rhetoric and the Reality*, New York, Tyler Gibson.

FREEMAN, C. (1974) *The Economics of Industrial Innovation*, London, Penguin.

FRENCH, W. *et al* (1957) *Behavioural Goals of General Education in High School*, New York, Russell Sage Foundation.

GALLIMORE, R. (1985) *The Accommodation of Instruction to Cultural Differences*, Los Angeles, University of California, Department of Psychiatry.

GALLIMORE, R., BOGGS, J.W. and JORDAN, C. (1974) *Culture, Behavior and Education*, Beverly Hills, CA, Sage.

GALTON, M. and SIMON, B. (1980) *Progress and Performance in the Primary Classroom*, London, Routledge and Kegan Paul.

GALTON, M., SIMON, B. and CROLL, P. (1980) *Inside the Primary Classroom*, London, Routledge and Kegan Paul.

GOODLAD, J. (1983) *A Place Called School*, New York, McGraw-Hill.

GOODMAN, P. (1962) *Compulsory Mis-Education*, London, Penguin Books.

GRAHAM, M.A., RAVEN, J. and SMITH, P.C. (1987) 'Identification of high level competence: Cross-cultural analysis between British, American, Asian and Polynesian labourers', to be published in *Organisation Forum*.

GRAHAM, M.A. and RAVEN, J. (1987) 'International Shifts in the Workplace — Are We Becoming an 'Old West' in the Next Century?', Provo, BYU Dept. Organisational Behaviour.

HATCH, T.C. and GARDNER, H. (1986) 'From testing intelligence to assessing competencies; a pluralistic view of the intellect', *Roeper Review*, 8, pp. 147–50.

HAVIGHURST, R.J. and TABA, H. (1949/63), *Adolescent Character and Personality*, New York, Wiley.

HEWISON, J. and TIZARD, J. (1980) 'Parental involvement and reading attainment', *British Journal of Educational Psychology*, 50, pp. 209–15.

HMI (1978) *Primary Education in England: A Survey by HM Inspectors of Schools*, London, Department of Education and Science, HMSO.

HMI (SCOTLAND) (1980) *Learning and Teaching in Primary 4 and Primary 7*, Edinburgh, HMSO.

HOPE, K. (1985) *As Others See Us: Schooling and Social Mobility in Scotland and the United States*, New York, Cambridge University Press.

HOWARD, E. (1980) *Some Ideas on Improving School Climate*, Colorado, Department of Education.

HOWARD, E. (1982) *Instrument to Assess the Educational Quality of Your School*, Denver, Colorado Department of Education.

HOWARD, E. (1982) *Successful Practices for Making the Curriculum More Flexible*, Denver, Colorado Department of Education.

HUFF, S., LAKE, D. and SCHAALMAN, M.L. (1982) *Principal Differences: Excellence in School Leadership and Management*, Boston, McBer and Co.

INDUSTRIAL TRAINING RESEARCH UNIT (1979) *The A–Z Study: Differences between Improvers and non-Improvers among Young Unskilled Workers*, Cambridge, The Industrial Training Research Unit.

JACKSON, B. and MARSDEN, D. (1962) *Education and the Working Class*, London, Routledge and Kegan Paul.

JACKSON, P.W. (1986) *The Practice of Teaching*, New York, Teachers' College Press.

JAMES, C. (1968) *Young Lives at Stake*, London, Collins.

JAMES, C. (1969) 'Being enquiring, enquiry and enquiries', *Ideas*, II, pp. 2–3.

JENCKS, C. *et al.* (1979) *Who Gets Ahead*, New York, Basic Books.

JOHNSTON, L. (1973) *The American High School: Its Social System and Effects*, Ann Arbor, Michigan, Institute for Social Research.

JOHNSTON, L.D. and BACHMAN, J.G. (1976) 'Educational institutions', in ADAMS, J.F. (Ed.) *Understanding Adolescence*, Third Edition, pp. 290–315. Boston, Allyn and Bacon.

KILPATRICK, W.H. (1918) 'The project method', *Teachers' College Record,* **19**, pp. 319–35.

KINSEY, A.C. (1948) *Sexual Behaviour in the Human Male*, New York, Saunders.

KLEMP, G.O., MUNGER, M.T. and SPENCER, L.M. (1977) *An Analysis of Leadership and Management Competencies of Commissioned and Non-Commissioned Naval Officers in the Pacific and Atlantic Fleets*, Boston, McBer.

KOHN, M.L. (1969) *Class and Conformity: A Study in Values*, Illinois, Dorsey Press.

KOHN, M.L. (1977) *Class and Conformity: A Study in Values, Second Edition*, Chicago, Ill, Chicago University Press.

KOHN, M.L., SLOMCZYNSKI, K.M. and SCHOENBACH, C. (1986) 'Social stratification and the transmission of values in the family: A cross-national assessment', *Sociological Forum*, **1**.

LEITH, S. (1981) 'Project work: An enigma', in SIMON, B. and WILLCOCKS, J. *Research and Practice in the Primary Classroom*, London, Routledge and Kegan Paul.

LEMPERT, W. (1986) 'Sozialisation und Persönlichkeitsbildung in beruflichen Schulen, dargestellt am Beispiel der Entwicklung moralischer Orientierung', *Die berufsbildende Schule,* **38**, pp. 148–60.

LITTLE, A. (1983) 'Employers and qualitifications: Learning from developing countries', *International Review of Applied Psychology,* **32**, pp. 327–46.

LITTON, F. (1977/82) *Aspects of Civics Education in Ireland: Final Report,* Dublin, Institute of Public Administration. Also available in *Collected Original Resources in Education* (1982), 6 (2), F4E7.

MACBEATH, J., MEARNS, D., THOMSON, B. and HOW, S. (1981) *Social Education.*

MCCLELLAND, D.C. (1961) *The Achieving Society,* New York, Van Nostrand.

McClelland, D.C. (1965) 'Toward a Theory of Motive Acquisition', *American Psychologist,* **20**, 321–33.
McClelland, D.C. (1975) *Power: The Inner Experience*, New York, Irvington.
McClelland, D.C. (1982) *Education for Values*, New York, Irvington.
McClelland, D.C. (1982) What behavioural scientists have learned about how children acquire values', in McClelland, D.C. (Ed), *The Development of Social Maturity*, New York, Irvington Press.
McGillicuddy-DeLisi, A.V. (1982) 'The relationship between parents' beliefs about development and family constellation, socio-economic status, and parents' teaching strategies', in Laosa, L.M. and Sigel, I.E. (Eds) *Families as Learning Environments for Children*, New York, Plenum, pp. 261–99.
McGillicuddy-DeLisi, A.V. (1985) 'The relationship between parental beliefs and children's cognitive level', in Sigel, I.E. (Ed) *Parental Belief Systems: The Psychological Consequences for Children*, Hillside, NJ, Erlbaum.
McGillicuddy-DeLisi, A.V., DeLisi, R., Flaugher, J. and Sigel, I.E. (1987) 'Family influences on planning', in Friedman, S.L., Scholnick, E.K. and Cocking, R.R. (Eds) *Blueprints for Thinking: The Role of Planning in Cognitive Development*, New York, Cambridge University Press.
Marimutha, T. (1983) 'Education and occupation in Peninsular Malaysia', *International Review of Applied Psychology* **32**, pp. 347–60.
Mason, E. (1970) *Collaborative Learning*, Edinburgh, Ward Lock.
Morton-Williams, R., Finch, S., Poll, C., Raven, J. and Ritchie, J. (1968) *Young School Leavers* London, HMSO.
Manpower Services Commission (1984) *TVEI Review*, London, MSC.
Manpower Services Commission/DES (1985) *Review of Vocational Qualifications in England and Wales: Interim Report*, Sheffield, MSC.
Manpower Services Commission (1985) *Developing the Youth Training Scheme as Part of an Integrated Vocational Training Provision*, Statement of Intent, Sheffield, MSC.
Manpower Services Commission (1985) *Two-Year YTS: Guide to Scheme Content and Quality*, Sheffield, MSC.
Munn Report (1977) *The Structure of the Curriculum*, Edinburgh, HMSO.
National Commission on Excellence in Education (1984) *A Nation At Risk*, Washington, D.C., US Government Printing Office.
National Society for the Study of Education (1926) *Twenty Sixth Year Book: The Foundation and Techniques of Curriculum Making*, Bloomfield, Ill., Public School Publishing Co.
National Task Force for Economic Growth (1983) *Action for Excellence*, Denver, Education Commission of the States.
ORACLE *See* Galton and Simon (1980) Galton, Simon and Croll (1980), Simon and Willcocks (1981).
Pace, R.C. and Stern, G. (1958) 'An approach to the measurement of psychological characteristics of college environments', *Journal of Educational Psychology*, **49**.
Passow, A.H., Noah, H.J., Eckstein, M.A. and Mallea, J.R. (1976)

An Empirical Study of Twenty-One Educational Systems, Stockholm, Almqvist and Wiksell.

PAYNE, G., FORD, G. and ULAS, M. (1979) *Education and Social Mobility: Some Social and Theoretical Developments*, Organization of Sociologists in Polytechnics, Paper No. 8.

PELLEGRINI, A.D., BRODY, G.H. and SIGEL, I.E. (1985) 'Parents book-reading habits with their children', *Journal of Educational Psychology*, **77**, 332–40.

POWELL, J.C. (1985) *The Teachers' Craft*, Edinburgh, The Scottish Council for Research in Education.

PRICE, P.B., TAYLOR, C.W., NELSON, D.E. *et al.* (1971) *Measurement and Predictors of Physician Performance: Two Decades of Intermittently Sustained Research*, Salt Lake City, University of Utah, Department of Psychology.

RATHBONE, C.H. (Ed) (1971) *Open Education: the Informal Classroom*, New York, Citation Press.

RAVITCH, D. (1974) *The Great Schools Wars*, New York, Basic Books.

RAVEN, J. (1977) *Education, Values and Society: The Objectives of Education and the Nature and Development of Competence*, London, H.K. Lewis; New York: The Psychological Corporation.

RAVEN, J. (1980) 'The most important problem in education is to come to terms with values', *Oxford Review of Education*, **7**, pp. 253–72.

RAVEN, J. (1980) *Parents, Teachers and Children*, Edinburgh, The Scottish Council for Research in Education.

RAVEN, J. (1982) *The Edinburgh Questionnaires: A Cluster of Questionnaires for use in Organizational Development and in Staff Guidance, Placement and Development*, London, H.K. Lewis.

RAVEN, J. (1983) 'Towards new concepts and institutions in modern society', *Universities Quarterly*, **37**, pp. 100–18.

RAVEN, J. (1984) *Competence in Modern Society: Its Identification, Development and Release*, London, H.K. Lewis; North America, Toronto: Guidance Centre — OISE press.

RAVEN, J. (1984) 'Quality of life, the development of competence, and higher education', *Higher Education*, **13**, pp. 393–404.

RAVEN, J. (1984) 'The role of the psychologist in formulating, administering and evaluating policies associated with economic and social development in western society', *J. Econ. Psychol.*, **5**, pp. 1–16.

RAVEN, J. (1985) 'The institutional framework required for, and process of, educational evaluation: Some lessons from three case studies', in SEARLE, B. (Ed) *Evaluation in World Bank Education Projects: Lessons from Three Case Studies*, Washington, DC, The World Bank, Education and Training Department Report EDT5 pp. 141–70.

RAVEN, J. (1986) 'A nation really at risk: a review of Goodlad's "A Place Called School", *Higher Education Review*, **18**, pp. 65–79.

RAVEN, J. (1987) *Learning to Teach in Primary Schools: Some Reflections. Collected Original Resources in Education*, **11**, F3, DO7.

RAVEN, J. (1988) 'The assessment of competencies', in BLACK, H.D. and DOCKRELL, W.B. (Eds), *New Developments in Educational Assessment:*

British Journal of Educational Psychology, Monograph Series No. 3, pp. 98–126.

RAVEN, J. (1988) 'A model of competence, motivation and its assessment', in BERLAK, H. (Ed.) *Assessing Academic Achievement: Issues and Problems*, Madison.

RAVEN, J. (1988) 'Developing the talents and competencies of all our children', *Gifted International*, **5**, pp. 8–40.

RAVEN, J. and DOLPHIN, T. (1978) *The Consequences of Behaving: The Ability of Irish Organizations to Tap Know-How, Initiative, Leadership and Goodwill*, Edinburgh, The Competency Motivation Project.

RAVEN, J., HANNON, B., HANDY, R., BENSON, C. and HENRY, E.A. (1975) *A Survey of Attitudes of Post Primary Teachers and Pupils, Volume 2: Pupils' Perceptions of Educational Objectives and their Reactions to School and School Subjects*, Dublin, Irish Association for Curriculum Development.

RAVEN, J., HANNON, B., HANDY, R., BENSON, C. and HENRY, E.A. (1975) *A Survey of Attitudes of Post Primary Teachers and Pupils, Volume 1: Teachers' Perceptions of Educational Objectives and Examinations*, Dublin, Irish Association for Curriculum Development.

RAVEN, J., JOHNSTONE, J. and VARLEY, T. (1985) *Opening the Primary Classroom*, Edinburgh, The Scottish Council for Research in Education.

RAVEN, J. and LITTON, F. (1976) 'Irish pupils' civic attitudes in an international context', *Oideas*, Spring, pp. 16–30.

ROBERTSON, J. (1985) *Future Work: Jobs, Self-Employment and Leisure after the Industrial Age*, Aldershot, Gower/Maurice Temple Smith.

ROSEN, B.C. and D'ANDRADE, R.G. (1959) 'The psychological origins of achievement motivation', *Sociometry*, **22**, pp. 185–218.

RUGG, H. (1926) in NSSE Yearbook.

RUGG, H. and SHUMAKER, A. (1928) *The Child-Centered School*, Yonkers, George Harrap.

SCHNEIDER, C., KLEMP, G.O. and KASTENDIEK, S. (1981) *The Balancing Act: Competencies of Effective Teachers and Mentors in Degree Programs for Adults*, Boston, McBer and Co.

SCHWARTZ, H.H. (1987) 'Perceptions, judgment and motivation in manufacturing entrepreneurs', *J. Econ. Behavior and Organisation*, **8** pp. 543–66.

SCOTTISH EDUCATION DEPARTMENT (SED) (1965) *Primary Education in Scotland*, Edinburgh, HMSO.

SIGEL, I.E. (Ed) (1985) *Parent Belief Systems: The Psychological Consequences for Children*, Hillside, NJ, Erlbaum.

SIGEL, I.E. (1986) 'Reflections on the belief-behavior connection: Lessons learned from a research program on parental belief systems and teaching strategies', in ASHMORE, R.D. and BRODZINSKY, D.M. (Eds) *Thinking about the Family: Views of Parents and Children*, Hillsdale, NJ, Erlbaum.

SIGEL, I.E., and KELLEY, T.D. (1988) 'A cognitive developmental approach to questioning', in Dillon, J. (Ed) *Classroom Questioning and Discussion: A Multidisciplinary Study*, Norwood, NJ, Ablex.

SIGEL, I.E. and MCGILLICUDDY-DELISI, A.V. (1984) 'Parents as teachers of their children: A distancing behaviour model', in PELLEGRINI, A.D. and YAWKEY, T.D. (Eds) *The Development of Oral and Written Language in Social Contexts*, Norwood, NJ, Ablex.

SIMON, B. and WILLCOCKS, J. (Eds) (1981) *Research and Practice in the Primary Classroom*, London, Routledge and Kegan Paul.

SMITH, L.A. (1964) 'Starting IDE', *Ideas*, **I**, pp. 2–5.

SMITH, L.A. (1966) *The Raising of the School Leaving Age: Pilot Course Report*, London, Goldsmiths' College.

SMITH, L.A. (1969) 'Starters', *Ideas*, **II**, p. 1 and pp. 27–30.

SMITH, L.A. (1969) 'Starting and supporting a project', *Ideas*, **II**, pp. 4–7.

SOKOLOWSKA, M., FIRKOWSKA-MANKIEWICZ, A., OSTROWSKA, A. and CZARKOWSKI, M.P. (1978) *Intellectual Performance of Children in the Light of Socio-Cultural Factors*, Warsaw, Polish Academy of Sciences: Institute of Philosophy and Sociology, Department of the Social Problems of Health.

STRATEMEYER, F.B., FORKNER, H.L. and MCKIM, M.C. (1947) *Developing a Curriculum for Modern Living*, New York, Teachers' College, Columbia University Press.

SYKES, A.J.M. (1969) 'Navvies: Their work attitudes', *Sociology*, **3**, 21f and 157f.

TAYLOR, C.W. (1971) 'Multi-talent potential', in *Igniting Creative Potential*, Utah, Jordan School District.

TAYLOR, C.W. (1973) 'Developing effectively functioning people', *Education, Vol. 94, Nov/Dec,* **No. 2**, pp. 99–110.

TAYLOR, C.W. (1976) *Talent Ignition Guide*, Salt Lake City, University of Utah and Bellvista Public School.

TAYLOR, C.W. and BARRON, F. (Eds) (1963) *Scientific Creativity*, New York, Wiley.

THARP, R.G., JORDAN, C., SPEIDEL, G.E., AU, K.H.P., KLEIN, T.W., CALKINS, R.P., SLOAT, K.C.M. and GALLIMORE, R. (1984) 'Product and process in applied developmental research: Education and the children of a minority', in LAMB, M.E., BROWN, A.L. and ROGOFF, B. (Eds) *Advances in Developmental Psychology*, Vol. III, Hillsdale, NJ, Lawrence Erlbaum.

TIZARD, B. and HUGHES, M. (1984) *Young Children Learning*, London, Fontana.

TIZARD, J., SCHOFIELD, W.N. and HEWISON, J. (1982) 'Collaboration between teachers and parents in assisting children's reading', *British Journal of Educational Psychology*, **52**, pp. 1–15.

TOFFLER, A. (1980) *The Third Wave*, New York, Bantam Books.

TOUGH, J. (1973) *Focus on Meaning: Talking with Some Purpose to Young Children*, London, Allen and Unwin.

TYLER, R.W. (1936) 'Defining and measuring the objectives of progressive education', *Educational Research Bulletin*, **XV**, p. 67f.

VAN BEINUM, H. (1965) *The Morale of the Dublin Busman*, London, Tavistock Institute of Human Relations.

WALBERG, H.J. (Ed.) (1979) *Educational Environments and their Effects*, Berkeley, CA, McCutchan.

WALBERG, H.J. (1985) 'Classroom psychological environment', in HUSEN,

T. and POSTLETHWAITE, N., *International Encyclopaedia of Education*, London, Pergamon.

WALBERG, H.J. and HAERTEL, D. (1980) 'Validity and use of educational environmental assessments', *Studies in Educational Evaluation*, **6**, pp. 225–38.

WINTER, D.G. (1973) *The Power Motive*, New York, Free Press.

WINTER, D.G., MCCLELLAND, D.C. and STEWART, A.J. (1981) *A New Case for the Liberal Arts*, San Francisco, Jossey Bass.

WRIGHT, G.C. (1950) *Core Curriculum in Public High Schools: An Enquiry into Practices, 1949*, Office of Education Bulletin No. 5. Washington, DC, Federal Security Agency.

WRIGHT, G.S. (1958) *Block-Time Classes and the Core Program in the Junior High School*, Bulletin 1958, No. 6, US Dept. Health, Education and Welfare, Washington, DC, US Government Printing Office.

Part 2: Accountability to Parents and the Community

5 *Toward an Independent Education for All*

Antony Flew

'Let me call your attention to the curious incident of the dog in the night-time.'
'The dog did nothing at all in the night-time.'
'That was the curious incident', said Sherlock Holmes.

What is to be done?

When the editor of the present volume first approached possible contributors the subject proposed for discussion was, in general, 'Families and Schools: Issues in Equalizing Opportunity and Increasing Accountability'. One socialist introduced as such and one right wing thinker were asked to address themselves more particularly to the relevant 'changes of political thinking — over the last thirty years or so'. Since this has been the period of the comprehensive revolution it is appropriate to examine such issues in that context. Since this revolution, like the similarly radical and similarly non-violent Glorious Revolution of 1688–9, was effected through Parliament the most authoritative source for its officially expressed aims is the operative resolution of the House of Commons. The then Labour Minister, Anthony Crosland, forthwith implemented the resolution by issuing DES Circular 10/65,[1] instructing all LEAs to prepare their plans to go comprehensive:

> That this House, conscious of the need to raise educational standards at all levels, and regretting that the realization of this objective is impeded by the separation of children into different types of secondary schools, notes with approval the efforts of the local authorities to reorganize secondary education along comprehensive lines, which will preserve all that is valuable in grammar school education for those children who now receive it and make it available to more

> children; . . . and believes that the time is now ripe for a declaration of national policy.

This resolution makes it plain that the stated, official aims of the revolution were: both to raise the educational standards actually achieved by all our children — the House was 'conscious of the need to raise educational standards at all levels'; and to increase the proportion actually benefiting from 'all that is valuable in grammar school education'.

The adverb 'actually' has to go in because there is a world of difference between the setting and the meeting of standards. Much more to the present point, the qualifications 'official' and 'stated' have not only to be entered but also to be emphasized. For, from the beginning, many of the militants of the comprehensive revolution certainly cherished quite other and even incompatible purposes. With the passage of time most of these militants, as well as many less fiery supporters — as is entirely understandable if rather less easily forgivable — have become committed to defending the policy for its own sake; and almost if not altogether regardless of any actual educational or other effects of its implementation.

As we now know from the memoir written by his widow, the Minister responsible for putting that decisive resolution before the House of Commons expressed himself in private in a coarser and less constructive way: 'If it's the last thing I do, I'm going to destroy every fucking grammar school in England and Wales. And Northern Ireland.'[2] Presumably Crosland saw his revolution of destruction as what moral philosophers of an earlier generation would have called an intrinsic good; something to be pursued for its own sake rather than to be judged by its actual consequences. Certainly there are many others who have by deed or word or both made it clear that for them universal compulsory comprehension is just such a non-instrumental, intrinsic good. White, for instance, a Lecturer in Philosophy at the University of London Institute of Education, proclaimed his own commitment in positive terms, and with none of Crosland's vulgarity: 'Comprehensive schooling is an integral part of the socialist vision'.[3]

It is important to recognize this variety of motivation, past and present. For, unless we do, we shall be unable to understand why so many defenders of the comprehensive revolution have been, and still are, not merely indifferent but hostile to any first-order and truth-concerned discussion of evidence or argument suggesting that that revolution has not in fact yielded the excellent, strictly educational results promised in the parliamentary resolution of 1965.

Here and hereafter the phrase 'strictly educational' is so employed that, in strictly educational terms, a programme has to be accounted a success if and insofar as, and only if and insofar as, it results in the educational achievements of all our children approaching more closely to the limits of their abilities. The reason for inserting the further qualification 'first-order and truth-concerned' is to exclude the diversionary contributions of those eager to change an embarrassingly revealing subject by making suggestions about the motives of anyone daring to dissent.[4]

The reason why we here, however reluctantly, do have to inquire into the motives of some of the defenders of the new status quo is in order to understand their otherwise incomprehensible lack of interest in, or of anxiety about, the strictly educational results of the comprehensive revolution. The explanation is that, although they are perhaps themselves not overmuch concerned about the strictly educational progress of at any rate other people's children, such persons cannot but know that there are some, and in particular the parents of those children whose education may be suffering, who do care. Suppose that investigation were to show that those 1965 promises have not been fulfilled, then the caring of the parents whose children have been and are being victimized might well lead these parents furiously to challenge a policy to which, as we have been suggesting, some of its defenders either always were, or have since become, totally devoted for reasons by no means strictly educational.

Take, for instance, Halsey,[5] who has been a leading figure, both in researching into supposed social and educational inequalities and in campaigning for universal and compulsory comprehension. The very first sentence of his article on '*Education and Equality*', published in *New Society* for June 17 in the year of the parliamentary resolution, is altogether frank and explicit: 'Some people, and I am one, want to use education as an instrument in pursuit of an egalitarian society.' Other people, however, and here I am one, do not want to sacrifice either the education of their own or of other people's children, or indeed anything else whatever, to the realization of Halsey's Procrustean ideal.[6]

What it is to increase accountability and equalize opportunity

The next necessity is to get a little clearer about both what is and what ought to be understood by the key phrases 'increasing accountability' and 'equalizing opportunity'. Let us take each in turn, for there is much to be made of the frequent, indeed well nigh universal, failure to press either of these two elementary and fundamental questions.

Accountability

For an individual, or for a set of individuals, or for an institution, to be effectively accountable to another individual, or another set of individuals, or to another institution, two things are required. (By Cantor's Axiom for Sets[7] the sole essential feature of a set is that its members have at least one common characteristic, any kind of characteristic.)

First, whoever or whatever calls persons or institutions to account for their performance or non-performance has to be able and willing to monitor that performance or non-performance. Second, whoever or whatever is effectively to call persons or institutions to account has to be able and willing to offer incentives to satisfactory and disincentives against unsatisfactory performance.

If once we recognize these glimpses of the obvious to be the truisms which they are, and proceed to fix them firmly in our minds, then we can scarcely fail to notice that the arrangements for public education in Britain fulfil neither of the two necessary conditions of accountability — and of accountability to individual parents least of all. First, and it should be notoriously, we have no fully comprehensive, independently assessed, criteria-related, national system of examinations.

GCE A-level (and the recently assassinated O-level) is (or were) intended only for the top 20 per cent of the ability range. And furthermore — under an ukase issued in the early sixties by the Secondary Schools Examinations Council — both were to be norm-related; thus formally invalidating all direct year on year comparisons of standards achieved. (*Cui bono?*) The new GCSE, supposedly directed at at least that top 60 per cent which previously attempted GCE or CSE, and providing for a large or even a predominant element of continuous assessment and Mode III, looks like becoming by far the most catastrophic consequence of all Sir Keith Joseph's ministerial capitulations.[8] But his expressed concern for the bottom 40 per cent, along with some other enlightened initiatives, seems to have sunk without trace. So we still have no compulsory exit examinations for those resolved to leave school at the minimum age of 16.

One regrettable result of this negligence is that, whenever official committees are set up to report on the problems of illiteracy or innumeracy, they have, in order to estimate the extent of the problem, to start by scratching around for indirect evidence. Another, and more immediately distressing matter, is that nearly half of the sixteen-year-olds leaving school during the summer of 1987 cast themselves or were cast upon the labour market with no credible certification to show what, if anything, which might perhaps help them to earn their own livings, they had contrived to learn in all those long years of compulsory, state-supplied schooling. It is impossible to emphasize facts of this kind either too much or too often: both because such insistence might eventually stay the torrent of books by doctrinally infatuated Marxists, contending that the public educational systems in all 'late capitalist' societies must be always and magically responsive to 'the needs of capital'; and because these facts contribute so crucially to the case for fearing that only a really radical and correctly directed reform of our own state system can reverse Britain's century-long relative decline.[9]

There is another sort of evidence of what educational value we are getting for our ever-increasing expenditure of taxpayers' money — another sort of evidence of the educational output accruing from an ever-increasing input of real resources.[10] It is provided by the national and local inspectorates. Such evidence is far and away less satisfactory than that which would be provided by a comprehensive system of independently assessed criteria-related examinations: both because inspectors can at best sample only a tiny proportion of all classroom hours; and because their investigations during those scanty hours are able to yield only the most sketchy and conjectural estimates of what and how much has actually been learnt by even the very few pupils involved in such inspections. Parents, whose offspring are present during every classroom hour, are in a far better position to monitor what goes on — even, or especially, what goes on when official inspectors are neither present nor expected.

As late as the early 1980s the HMIs appeared to believe that, in general, there was nothing seriously wrong which still more cash would not cure: they were inclined rather to rebuke LEAs spending less per pupil than the national average than to commend those — often the same ones — achieving above average results.[11] Recently, however, even they have begun to be alarmed. In May 1986, commenting on their own 1985 findings, they opined:

> Few involved in providing or providing for education can take much, if any, pride in a national service within which three tenths of all lessons seen were unsatisfactory . . . (*ibid.*, p. 49).

Later, reporting on their attendance at 200 science lessons given during the summer term of 1985 under the most richly resourced of all LEAs, they described their devastating assessments, with a characteristic restraint, as 'a matter for concern'. For, out of that 200, 110 were 'substandard': 15 per cent 'good'; 30 per cent 'satisfactory but not good'; 40 per cent 'less than satisfactory'; and 15 per cent 'unrelievedly bad'. They proceeded to detail instances of the grossest idleness and incompetence (*ibid.*, p. 136).

Inadequate as these present monitoring arrangements are, even an ideal alternative would only go part of the way towards making schools and teachers accountable for their performance. For, as we insisted earlier, 'whoever or whatever calls persons or institutions to account has to be able and willing to offer incentives to satisfactory and disincentives against unsatisfactory performance.' That this second necessary condition of accountability has by no means been always and sufficiently satisfied is most aptly indicated by quoting a letter to *The Times*,[12] published during the period of writing: 'Two years later, in the summer term of 1987, the ILEA's own inspectors went into schools in Greenwich to check, one assumes, on the government's inspectors. This latest inspection found a situation that had become even worse. Only 10 per cent of science classes could be called good, with a figure up to 59 per cent for poor or worse.'

Equal opportunity

The expression 'equalizing opportunity' can be, and has been, construed in two different ways. In the first, traditional understanding of equality of opportunity would be better described as fair and open competition for scarce opportunities. The equality here lies in the sameness of the treatment of all the competitors, and the only opportunity which is equal precisely is the opportunity to compete on these fair terms. Certainly in the great French Revolution of 1789, when the cry was raised '*La carrière ouverte aux talents!*', the drive was to open all (and only) public appointments to competition from members of formerly excluded groups. Thus in that year, in the *Declaration of the Rights of Man and of the Citizen*,[13] we read:

> The law is the expression of the will of the community . . . it should be the same to all . . . and, all being equal in its sight, are equally eligible to all honours, places and employments, according to their different abilities, without any other distinction than that created by their virtue and talents (Article VI).

The practice of dividing grammar school pupils from secondary modern pupils by means of the old 11+ examination was established and maintained as an instrument for realizing this first ideal of equality of opportunity. Yet the actual realization, like all things human, was less than perfect: both because there were those who both could and would have benefited from grammar schooling who nevertheless failed that often too early test; and because the proportions of grammar school places varied in no properly relevant way from one LEA to another. No doubt it was with these deficiencies in mind that many were originally persuaded that, if reorganization 'along comprehensive lines' did in the event 'preserve all that is valuable in grammar school education' for those previously subjected to it, then it would also make an education of that sort 'available to more children'. Certainly this first ideal of equality of opportunity is nowadays shared almost universally.

'Equalizing opportunity' and similar expressions are, however, also taken to refer to the very different ideal of providing everyone with actually equal opportunities. Applied in the context of 1789, equalizing opportunity in this second sense would presumably have required not just that appointments to the command of armies should be open to all the talents, regardless of social class background; but rather that everyone, or everyone so desiring, should each have their necessarily brief day of command.

Applied in the present context this second ideal clearly requires that all our children without exception be compelled to attend comprehensive schools; comprehensive schools which in their provision and in their recruitment are as near as may be identical, and in which all classes and any examinations are completely mixed ability. It has often been argued that all this and more follows from the inner logic of the comprehensive revolution. If and insofar as this is true, then it becomes, surely, unnecessary to spell out the arguments for concluding that the consummation of that revolution must be in practice, if not also in theory, incompatible with the realization of either of its officially stated aims?

Most discussion here is confused by failures to distinguish these two different and indeed ultimately incompatible conceptions of equalizing opportunity. The confusion is further confounded by failures to distinguish these in their turn from other conceptions and from other ideas of equality. Two constantly collapsed distinctions must be of especial interest to us: first, that between equality of opportunity, in the first sense, and equality of achievement or of outcome; and second, that between an equal chance — a fair chance — in a properly run competition and an equal chance — an equal likelihood — of succeeding in that competition. Someone has said that invalid inference from unequal achievement to unequal opportunity is the occupational disease of the sociologists of education[14]: '. . . and in a way one might agree with that. But for a sneaking suspicion that it's their occupation'.[15]

So far little has been seriously attempted

The motto at the head of the present chapter is one of 170 specimens of Sherlockisms collected by the fictitious German scholar Ratzegger.[16] It is appropriate because so extraordinarily little has so far been nothing more nor less than actually done in order either to increase accountability or to discover whether the comprehensive revolution has in fact produced the results publicly promised by its promoters.

Consider a remarkable yet also altogether typical boast by Crosland,[17] a member of the 1964–70 Labour administration: '. . . expenditure on education rose from 4.8 per cent of Gross National Product (GNP) in 1964 to 6.1 per cent. As a result, all classes of the community enjoyed significantly more education than before'. The second of these two propositions was presumably being drawn as an immediate inference from the first. For the only further reason offered for believing that conclusion was that 'The huge expansion in the supply of teachers produced a steady reduction in the pupil/teacher ratio.'

What is so astonishing is that this manifestly unsound inference from input to output was presented as a compulsive argument by an extremely able man; a man who had, before entering professional politics, earned his living as the Economics Fellow of an Oxford college. He of all people should have known: first, that it is only in conditions of ideally perfect competition that all consumers can reasonably hope to get equally good value from freely chosen suppliers; but, second, that in Britain today primary and secondary educational services are normally supplied to captive customers by local education monopolies. (Is there any anti-monopoly legislation anywhere which would not be activated long before a single supplier had gained 94 per cent of the market, even if the monopolists there were not — unlike ours — engaged in predatory, priceless pricing?)

When such an intellectual tiger as Crosland is capable of committing himself to baseless complacencies in premeditated print there is no call to be surprised by the impromptu bleatings of the sheep. Consider, as a more recent instance, a typical House of Commons debate under the rubric 'Education'. In 1981 the Opposition motion, introduced by Neil Kinnock,[18] took it similarly for granted that the relations between input and output are here direct, constant and uniform: 'That this House', it began, 'recognizing the direct relationship between the maintenance and enhancement of educational standards and an appropriate investment of resources . . .'; and so it went on, and on and on.

The Ministerial amendment moved by Mark Carlisle did at least mention value for money. It expressed 'confidence in the ability of the education service . . . to secure maximum educational value from the extensive resources which continue to be available to it.' Yet in the rest of his speech the Minister made no attempt to justify such confidence. Like so many of his predecessors in similar debates he could think only of offering formidable figures of ever increasing expenditure. From these, and from these alone, he felt entitled to conclude: 'There has been a gradual improvement in standards.'

Thus, sheeplike, he followed in the self-interested steps of the National Union of Teachers (NUT) and of other elements in what — with acknowledgments to President Eisenhower — we could call the bureaucratic-educational complex; he followed these supply-side spokespersons in stubbornly refusing to distinguish standards of resource input from standards of achieved output.[19] If the assumption presupposed by this equation were correct, then it would presumably mean, what is manifestly not the case, either that effective accountability had already been achieved or that it is totally unnecessary. It is, as the most formidable of British political thinkers, Hobbes, once remarked, 'easy to see the benefit of such darkness, and to whom it accrueth'.[20]

From the beginning militants of the comprehensive revolution have manifested what in Ernest Bramah's Kai Lung stories[21] is delicately described as 'well-sustained no-enthusiasm' for the discovery of any evidence or the examination of any argument suggesting that it might be prudent at least to pause a while and reflect, and then perhaps, on reflection, to change course in some way.

So note well, what I have argued more fully elsewhere[22] that all those sincerely pursuing any purpose of any kind whatever must be concerned to monitor their progress towards that objective, and must be eager to examine with open-minded anxiety evidence suggesting that it is not in fact being attained. We have therefore to suspect — to put it no stronger — that those who have been uninterested in or even positively hostile to honest investigations of the actual results of that revolution either never did cherish, or else have long since ceased to cherish, the two aims specified in the original operative resolution.

Since the name of such persons is legion, we lack the sorts and amounts of evidence which we might like to have. Having elsewhere recently reviewed what is available, and at much greater length than would be possible here, I will confine myself now to brief remarks about each of those two stated aims. We were promised, and this we should never forget, as results of the comprehensive revolution: both that more children, and in particular more children from the Registrar General's social classes IV and V, would enjoy the benefits of 'all that is valuable in grammar school education'; and that the levels of educational achievement of all our children would rise. There seems to be precious little excuse for believing that either of these promises has in fact been fulfilled.

In the bright confident morning of 1968 the DES published a paper estimating that the next ten or fifteen years would compass a great leap forward.[23] In England and Wales there were by 1976 going to be 124,600 secondary school age children getting two or three A-level passes. By 1981 it was to be 171,900. Yet somehow something went wrong. For 1976 saw a shortfall of 34,300 — over a quarter. By 1981 this had become 68,000 — more than a third. It seemed that a percentage plateau in A-level achievement had been reached in 1971. Further analysis, significantly neither made for nor commissioned by the (official) DES but the (unofficial) National Council for Educational Standards (NCES), revealed that between 1969 and 1978 the percentage of boys in state schools getting one and two A-level passes actually fell, with that of those getting three not rising but staying steady.[24] The picture would have looked still more disappointing but for the noteworthy but not strenuously publicized DES practice of mixing up the performance figures of the maintained with those of the independent schools. For there the minority had in fact achieved the kind of improvement which had been expected for all (*ibid*).

As for the more particular hope for the offspring of social classes IV and V, it looks as if it is rather the reasoned fears of those doubleplus ungood crimethinkers the *Black Paper*[25] writers which are in fact being realized. Consider the percentages of those from such working class homes admitted to our universities. Throughout what the revolutionaries tell us were the black days of the twenties and thirties, the annual figures hovered around 26 per cent — far and away higher than any reported from any of the supposedly so much less class-ridden countries of Western Europe. They reached a peak at 31 per cent in 1968. By 1973 they were down to 28 per cent, while by 1978 it looked as if they were bottoming out onto a new and lower plateau. The latest figures are: 1978 — 23 per cent; 1979 — 22 per cent; 1980 — 19.4 per cent; 1981 — 17.5 per cent; 1982 — 18 per cent; 1983 — 19.5 per cent; 1984 — 19.7 per cent; and 1985 — 20.5 per cent.[26]

The fact that militants of the comprehensive revolution are reluctant to attend to these figures, and even to attempt any alternative interpretation thereof, is bound to suggest that these people do not sincerely share that concern for the opportunities of able boys and girls from disadvantaged homes which was a golden thread running through all the *Black Papers*.

As for the claim that, thanks to the comprehensive revolution, 'the levels of educational achievement of all our children would rise', we are, in the absence of any system of independently assessed, criteria-related examinations — much less of a fully comprehensive system embracing that neglected bottom 40 per cent — forced to resort to the rather less direct and less satisfactory evidence of *Standards in English Schools* (by Cox and her colleagues).[27] As all readers of the present book will surely know, when this study of examination results was first published both the authors and their work were subjected to an all-out campaign of vilification. Most was made of an internal and hence supposedly confidential document in which DES statisticians were said to have 'rubbished' this 'seriously flawed' and 'grossly incompetent' work.

What many readers will not know — not, that is, if they

depend for their misinformation upon comprehensively committed politicians, journalists and union officials — is that, once the authors were at last permitted to see a copy of that DES critique, they were able to demonstrate, in face to face discussion with the statisticians, arranged and chaired by the Minister at the DES, that the supposed flaw was not in fact a fault in their own work, but the result of a simple misreading on the part of their critics. These honourable public servants at once apologized, withdrawing their original reservations but not their several commendations of a path-breaking and exhaustive enterprise. These commendations had, of course, never been quoted by any of those making so much of the leaked critique. The DES statisticians also agreed to release more information about the social class composition of school intakes, information which will make possible a still more adequate allowance for such differences. All this was clearly recorded in a statement issued by the DES on the results of this confrontation between the three authors and those who had supposedly 'rubbished' their work.[28]

It is what happened next, and perhaps still more what did not happen, which is so relevant to the argument of the present chapter. For most of those who had made so much of the alleged 'rubbishing' by the DES statisticians never withdrew or apologized for their false assertions, but instead continued to treat both the authors and their findings as if both had, as their accusers had so long and so savagely maintained, been utterly discredited. Thus the *Times Educational Supplement*,[29] having throughout presented the debate in an overwhelmingly hostile way, never even reported the DES apology. Similarly true to form *The Teacher*,[30] house organ of the NUT, first followed that example, and then compounded this fault by flatly refusing to print any corrective protest from the authors. That DES statement of apology was issued on 28 November 1983. In what was clearly a later letter to *The Times* on 3 December, 1983 Giles Radice,[31] the then Labour Party Parliamentary spokesperson on Education, simply ignored all withdrawals, reiterating every previous charge in even fiercer indignation, and a very similar letter,[32] signed by various teachers' unions' officials, appeared three days later still.[33]

The moral which we have to draw is that the last thing which these militants of the comprehensive revolution desire is to discover and to be called to account for its actual, strictly educational results. For the authors of *Standards in English Schools* printed their summary conclusion in block capitals:

> Substantially higher O-level, CSE and A-level examination results are to be expected for pupils in a fully selective system of schools compared with pupils in a fully comprehensive system of schools. This finding applies to all the indices of examination success which we studied and, according to our data, is as robust as the generally accepted finding that examination results are highly correlated with social class (p. 61).

This finding was later confirmed by little publicized work done within the DES.[34] It had already been indicated by comparisons of the disappointing A-level results for England and Wales, mentioned earlier, with those for Northern Ireland, which Crosland and his comrades had reluctantly left as an uncomprehensivized control group. There the figures — which being for maintained schools only, are not bumped up by the strikingly superior performance of any independents — are now, for leavers with one or more A-levels, 50 per cent higher and, for those with five or more O-levels, 40 per cent higher than for England.[34]

The belated Conservative awakening

The first indication that anxiety about the performance of the state education system in Britain had reached cabinet level in either party of government was Prime Minister Callaghan's 1976 Ruskin Speech.[35] The account of the background to this intervention in Donoughue's *Prime Minister* published in 1987[36] is invaluable; most especially since Donoughue's expressions of home truths both about the NUT's lack of interest in educational achievement and the indoctrinated obstructiveness of the DES would, coming from an enemy of socialism, be dismissed by *bien-pensants* as 'ultra right-wing' and therefore inconsiderable.

Unfortunately that speech contained an inhibiting hint which Shirley Williams — then the responsible Minister at the DES — was only too eager to take. Callaghan, who had presumably never himself read any of the *Black Papers*, and relying solely upon information supplied, put down all their contents as worthless '. . . prejudices. We all know those who claim to defend standards but in reality are simply seeking to defend old privileges and inequalities.' The resulting Great Debate[37] therefore resembled those sometimes staged by Marxist–Leninist regimes. For it was so structured as to ensure that no really radical criticisms were openmindedly entertained, or even heard. Above all there was to be no reversal of, or even check to, the comprehensive revolution.

In 1979 the Conservative manifesto promised to encourage an experiment with education vouchers; a notion which properly left-thinking readers of *The Guardian* might be inclined to discredit to Milton Friedman. In fact it was first introduced by Tom Paine[38] and later revived by J.S. Mill.[39] But, in the event, the 1980 Education Act did only two relevant things: it removed the compulsion to comprehensivize; and it required that all maintained schools publish their examination results. The importance and the value of this second innovation can be deduced from the fact that the NUT declared its 'total opposition'.

Although Sir Keith Joseph in entering the DES proclaimed his 'philosophical sympathy' for the voucher idea he was quickly brought to heel by classic *Yes, Minister* manoeuvres.[40] In his Education Act the main relevant innovation was the introduction of a substantial set of elected parents into the governing bodies of maintained schools. But this measure of decentralizing accountability was offset by his authoritarian insistence that no school, maintained or even nominally independent, was to be allowed to prepare pupils for O-level or CSE examinations. Under Joseph's Law — like Gresham's — bad currency must replace good.

However, towards the end of what historians may eventually come to call the second Thatcher Parliament, there were several signs that some of the ideas which had for many years been brewing in the Institute of Economic Affairs, in the Centre for Policy Studies, and in the Adam Smith Institute, might soon, at least in some partial and qualified form, become Conservative Party policy. For instance: in 1986 a group of fifteen Conservative MPs, several believed to have ministerial prospects, published, from the Conservative Political Centre, *No Turning Back*;[41] while early in 1987 members of the Hillgate Group were seen entering or leaving Number 10 Downing Street. In due course the winning 1987 manifesto promised what the brewers of such ideas hoped would eventually be seen to have been the first short, hesitant and even contradictory stage in the realization of their ideal — 'Neither a grammar school, nor a comprehensive, but an independent education for all!'[42]

These people, of whom the present writer is of course one insist: both that LEAs are, in effect, LEMs — local education monopolies; and that this monopoly provision of educational services in fact suffers from all the familiar faults of monopoly provision in other areas. The proposal is to turn all schools into separate educational 'firms', subject like the present independent schools to the incentives and disciplines of the market. Whether paid from private purses or the public pocket, school fees must be paid directly to whichever separate educational 'firm' provides the children of particular parents with the educational services they wish their children to have. This finance should be available to each individual school to spend (more or less) as it sees fit.

The proposal here most emphatically is NOT to have all schools run by elected parent governors: that would be as silly, as inefficient and as burdensome as having all grocers' shops or all garages operated by customers' committees. The power which the proposed arrangement would give to parents, and the effective accountability which it would impose upon individual schools, is exactly that power which paying clients hold over the independent professionals who undertake to serve them, while the effective accountability is exactly that which such independent professionals have to the clients who employ them. It says a lot, and all nasty, about the true aims of the (non-professional) unions of (public sector) teachers, as well as of that union creature the Labour Party, that, despite much talk of the need for professional pay and status for teachers, any suggestion of real power for individual parents, or of effective accountability to them, is wholly abhorrent.

These proposals are relevant also to questions about equal opportunity. For there are two ways in which a monopoly system of neighbourhood comprehensive schools is bound to produce inequalities of provision; especially if these schools have fixed 'standard numbers' of 'places', to be filled up as requisite by LEA dictation. In the first place, without a politically and perhaps even physically impossible programme of compulsory bussing, without the intolerable imposition of direction of labour upon teachers of scarcity subjects, and with a monopoly system of neighbourhood comprehensive schools in often vastly different neighbourhoods, there are bound to be large differences both in the quality and variety of teaching and in the stimulus to learning offered by different schools.

Consider, for example, one of the first cases to come to light. In 1978, when, in the name of the party of open government, Shirley Williams was still permitting and indeed encouraging authorities to conceal the examination results from their individual schools, Dr Rhodes Boyson got his hands on the separate examination results for that year of every school under the City of

Manchester LEA — all-comprehensive since 1967. His analysis of and commentary upon these findings ended with a still unanswered question: 'What equality is there in opportunity between children going to Parrs Wood with 1562 pupils and 210 A-level passes this year, and those attending Spurley Hey with 1119 pupils and only eight . . .?'[43]

It appears that Parrs Wood must indeed have been preserving much if not 'all that is valuable in grammar school education'. But it must also have been offering this to many less able pupils from more prosperous families while at the same time many other more able pupils from less prosperous families were directed into their strikingly inferior neighbourhood comprehensives. This was, of course, one of the immediate consequences of the comprehensive revolution both foreseen and deplored by those whom its militants have been and still are ever ready to misrepresent and abuse as defenders of 'old privileges and inequalities'.

In the second place, as should be well known from Rutter's study,[44] under such a system it is possible for two neighbouring schools, equally well-resourced, and with very similar pupil intakes, to produce vastly different educational results; and for this disparity to continue indefinitely. But what is not possible, where consumers have a choice, is for an unsubsidized firm to stay in business when a nearby competitor is offering two or three times better value for money. Perhaps it was some belated and surely almost invincibly reluctant recognition of the equalizing and improving tendencies of supplier competition and of consumer choice which led that lifelong socialist Halsey, to give at least some brief hospitality to the voucher idea. All that is certain, however, is that his vision occurred on the road not to Damascus but Carlisle.[45]

Notes

1 Department of Education and Science (1965). Circular 10/65 *The Organization of Secondary Education*, London, HMSO.
2 Crosland, S. (1982) *Tony Crosland*, London, Cape, p. 149.
3 Shaw, B. (1983) *Comprehensive Schooling: The Impossible Dream*, Oxford, Blackwell.
4 Wragg, E. (1983) 'Personal', in *The Times Educational Supplement*, 15 July.
5 Halsey, A.H. (1965) 'Education and equality', *New Society*, 17 June, pp. 13–15.
6 Flew, A.G.N. (1981) *The Politics of Procrustes*, London, Temple Smith.
7 Cantor, G. (1915) *Contributions Towards the Founding of the Theory of*

Transfinite Numbers, New York, Dover (Translated by Philip E.B. Jourdians)
8 NORTH, J. (Ed) (1987) *GCSE: An Examination*, London, Claridge.
9 See, for an account of this decline BARNETT, C. (1986) *The Audit of War*, London, Macmillan.
10 FLEW, A.G.N. (1987) *Power to the Parents: Reversing Educational Decline*, London, Sherwood.
11 *Ibid* p. 48.
12 OLLERENSHAW, E. (1987) ILEA member for Kensington in a letter to *The Times*, 9 December, p. 17.
13 [1793] *Declaration des Droits de l'Homme et du Citoyen*, Paris, F. Dufort.
14 FLEW, A.G.N. (1981) *op. cit.*
15 AUSTIN, J.L. (1961) *Philosophical Papers*, Oxford, Clarendon.
16 KNOX, R.A. (1928) *Essays in Satire*, London, Sheed and Ward.
17 CROSLAND, C.A.R. (1974) *Socialism Now, and Other Essays*, London, Cape, p. 20.
18 KINNOCK, N. Opposition Motion 13 January 1981 *Hansard* Vol. 996 Column 1236.
19 FLEW, A.G.N. (1987) *op. cit.*, p. 46.
20 HOBBES, T. (1951) *Leviathan*, London, Chapter, XLVII.
21 BRAMAH, E. (1900) *Kai Lung Unrolls his Mat* and *Kai Lung's Golden Hours* Re-published by Penguin 1937 and 1938 respectively.
22 FLEW, A.G.N. (1987) *op. cit.*, Chapter 2.
23 DEPARTMENT OF EDUCATION AND SCIENCE (1968) Circular 10/67 *A Great Leap Forward*, London, HMSO.
24 BALDWIN, R.W. (1981) *Secondary Schools 1965–79*, London, National Council for Educational Standards.
25 COX, C.B. and DYSON, A.E. (Eds) (1969) 'Fight for education: A Black Paper', *Critical Quarterly*, London.
COX, C.B. and DYSON, A.E. (Eds) (1970) 'Black Paper Two', *Critical Quarterly*, London.
COX, C.B. and BOYSON, R. (1975) *Black Paper*, London, Dent.
COX, C.B. and BOYSON, R. (1977) *Black Paper*, London, Dent.
26 FLEW, A.G.N. (1987) *op. cit.*
27 COX, C., MARKS, J. and POMIAN-SRZEDNICKI, M. (1983) *Standards in English Schools*, London, National Council for Educational Standards.
28 DEPARTMENT OF EDUCATION AND SCIENCE (1983) *The School Curriculum* Circular 8/83, 6 December, London, HMSO.
29 GRAY, J. and JONES, B. (1983) 'Disappearing data' *Times Educational Supplement* 15 July 1983 and subsequent reports and letters.
30 NASH, I. (1983) 'Discredited research "Used against Teachers"' *The Teacher* 7 October, p. 1 and subsequent reports and letters.
31 RADICE, G. (1983) letter to *The Times*, 3 December.
32 JARVIS, F. *et al* (1983) letter to *The Times*, 6 December.
33 FLEW, A.G.N. (1987) *op. cit.*
34 For the full story of this unscrupulous campaign to discredit *Standards in English* see, for example NAYLOR, F. and MARKS, J. (1987) *Comprehensives Fail the Test*, London, Centre for Policy Studies; and COX, C. and MARKS, J. (1988) *The Insolence of Office*, London, Claridge.
35 CALLAGHAN, J. (1976) 'Towards a national debate', *Education* **14**,

pp. 332–3 (Text of a speech given at Ruskin College, Oxford, October 1976).

36 DONOUGHUE, B. (1987) *Prime Minister*, London, Cape.

37 This was the semi-official description of a debate that was organized by Shirley Williams, MP subsequent to Jim Callaghan's Ruskin College speech in October 1976.

38 PAINE, T. [1791] (1984) *The Rights of Man*, Harmondsworth, Penguin.

39 MILL, J.S. [1859] (1962) *On Liberty*, London, Collins/Fontana.

40 SELDON, A. (Ed.) (1985) *The Riddle of the Voucher*, London, Institute of Economic Affairs.

41 BROWN, M. *et al* (1986) *No Turning Back*, London, Conservative Political Centre.

42 FLEW, A.G.N. (1987) *op. cit.*

43 BOYSON, R. (1978) 'Verdict on comprehensives', in *The Free Nation*, 29 September to 13 October.

44 RUTTER, M. *et al* (1979) *Fifteen Thousand Hours: Secondary Schools and their Effects on Children*, London, Open Books.

45 FLEW, A.G.N. (1987) *op. cit.*

6 *Parent Power*

Ted Wragg

Introduction

The general push for greater and more public accountability in education has been a feature of the 1970s and 1980s. It has sometimes been pressed more vigorously by politicans speaking, as they would say, on behalf of the electorate than by ordinary folk themselves, but it has been a regularly recurring theme nonetheless.

Demands for an account to be given should not cause surprise. Education costs billions of pounds each year, it employs well over half a million teachers at all levels, and for local authorities it is the most expensive service they run, requiring, often, half their total budget. For many parents education embodies their hope for a successful adult life for their children, especially at a time of high unemployment. In what is often called our 'credential society', where those who acquire a range of formal qualifications are more likely to find employment than those who do not, parents will want the best for their children, even if they are not always sure what this actually entails or how to set about securing it.

Three Decades of Change

During the last thirty years the role of parents in the education power structure has changed. In political terms they have, as a group, been placed in a more central position, having the right to be full members of school governing bodies, for example. Indeed this particular right is now becoming so taken for granted it is difficult to remember that books in the 1960s, like Patrick McGeeney's *Parents are Welcome*,[1] deplored the presence, in some schools, of a line in the playground which marked the point beyond which parents were not allowed to proceed.

In some respects, if one takes an even longer perspective, power has both ebbed to and flowed from parents. They do not have some rights they may have had in the early nineteenth century, for legislation has forbidden them to send young children out to work, beat them savagely or keep them away from school. The requirement to send children to school of itself brought with it a further loss of rights. In Britain, more than in many other countries, it has been schools rather than parents, which decided what children should wear during the day and even the length and style of their hair. Furthermore critical decisions about choice of subjects, or which public examinations were taken, could be made with little or no reference to parents.

The late 1960s was a watershed in the development of home-school relationships. The Plowden Report[2] on primary education published in 1967 marked the time when power began to flow back to parents. A number of factors came together to cause this movement. A significant one was that research for the Plowden Report highlighted the importance of such matters as parents' attitudes on children's achievement. It had long been believed that social class was influential, but research in the 1960s attempted to break down the global notion of class into discrete components such as parental attitudes.

The assertion in the Plowden Report that these were positively related to achievement led to the assumptions (a) that the relationship was a causal one and that raising parents' interest and concern would of itself improve children's learning and (b) that parents should be given more responsibility within the power structure of education. The Plowden Report was unusual for having a whole chapter devoted to parents, and the first outcome of the Report and the development projects it spawned, like Patrick McGeeney's book *Parents are Welcome*[3] and the film he produced with the same title, was the spread of more parent–teacher associations.

Parent–teacher associations actually produced relatively little direct power for parents. They had no standing in law and were principally bodies which raised extra funds, held social events or were at best consulted over decisions the head and staff intended to implement. In some cases they had higher status, but this depended very much on the willingness of the head to put policy matters to them or discuss details of classroom process. Many were cosmetic, valuable enough for all that as a meeting forum or to head off potential aggravation, but not any more significant than a staff social club would be in a commercial business.

Nevertheless the rapid development of the PTA movement during the 1970s did lay the foundations for some of the legislation which was eventually introduced a decade later. One reason was the identification of the heirs of the Heads who had a line in the playground in the 1950s. These were the Heads who refused to have a PTA, not for the perfectly valid reason that they wished to consult all parents and a PTA might easily become dominated by a small committee of professional middle class members, but because they did not wish to hear the views of parents at all. This excessively territorial stance by a few led to demands for parents to be given real powers by law, and the wish was expressed by people of all social and political backgrounds, driven especially by those who felt frustrated at their inability to penetrate what they saw as professional mystique.

The Education Acts of 1980, 1981, 1986 and 1988, have given parents more rights. These include the requirement that schools issue a prospectus containing a number of key pieces of information; the right of parents whose child has special educational needs to see the written statement about his or her educational future; the establishment of an annual report to parents by governors and an annual meeting at which parents, if they wish, may pass a motion on some aspect of school governance; membership, as equal partners with teachers, politicians and members of the community, of the school governing body; wider choice of school, supported by an appeals system.

What Power?

Not all these rights, however, amount to any real power. The right to be given a prospectus is not the power to say what should be in it, and the right of parents as a group to provide between two and five parent governors is not the same as power to all parents to determine the conduct and curriculum of a school. Rights must not be confused with power. A right represents nothing more than an entitlement. Power, on the other hand, is the ability to influence action. The two may be related, but they equally may not. Furthermore power usually carries with it responsibility and this in turn can inhibit as easily as it can facilitate. Representative parents on governing bodies, for example, may feel more inhibited about pressing the case of their own child, for fear of being seen as abusing their privileged position, than would have been the case had they not been a governor.

This raises the question about parents' actual as opposed to hypothetical powers. It is one thing for them to be given what seem to be increased powers, but quite another to translate these into actuality. A related matter is the issue of what powers parents ought to have in our society. It is to these two questions that the remainder of this chapter is devoted.

An interesting first concern is the whole question of admissions to schools. By granting parents the right to appeal to a formally constituted panel if their choice of school was not met, the 1980 Education Act certainly did strengthen what had previously been a weak position. Before 1980 parents had to accept what were sometimes arbitrary decisions by the LEA and only had the right to appeal to the Secretary of State, which few did, although many of those who actually pressed their case were successful.

The consideration of parental power over admissions raises several related issues. One of these is the extent to which free parental choice is achievable or whether it is merely a Utopian dream. Giving the power of choice to one parent may take it away from another. The matter of single sex education illustrates this very effectively. In one city in the South of England there were mainly mixed secondary schools but also two single sex schools, one for boys another for girls. The girls' secondary school sought an annual intake of at least ninety but usually had only about forty to fifty actual requests. As a result some forty to fifty girls who wished to attend a mixed school had to be coerced into joining a girls' school.

Eventually the LEA decided to abandon this unpopular role and merge the two single sex schools into a further mixed school, thus annoying and frustrating the forty to fifty parents each year who wanted their daughters to be educated separately from boys. Inevitably this produced an accusation that the LEA was failing to pay due regard to the wishes of parents, yet no easy solution to the dilemma was available, because an intake based solely on those who wished for single sex education would not have been viable at a time when secondary pupil numbers were in any case falling rapidly.

The market philosophy implicit in some of the proposals in the 1988 Education Act holds that free competition resolves the question of parental choice more effectively than direction by the LEA. The notion of open enrolment is a variation of the voucher scheme which was considered but rejected by the Conservative party prior to the 1987 General Election. Under the voucher scheme parents would have direct financial power, in that they would be able to use their entitlement voucher, with or without topping up, to purchase a place at a school of their choice. Open enrolment under the 1988 Act is aimed at preventing LEAs from putting artificial limits on their quotas for schools.

The enhancing of parental choice of school does appear to give more direct power to parents as a group, but not necessarily to all individuals. In the situation described above, where meeting every single parent's need is Utopian, but society must strive to maximize choice, there will always be some parents whose individual or collective power is stronger than others. Those with greatest influence on admissions will probably be (a) the more articulate, willing to write letters or go to appeals panels, (b) the better off, able to pay fees or higher travel costs to attend a school further afield, (c) those belonging to a pressure, interest or religious group, who can argue that their children must be educated alongside those of like-minded parents and (d) parents with a special case, like an elder child already in attendance or some specific social need. The least potent will be working class parents who do not understand how the education system works, or indeed how power is exercised in society. Though the legislation of the 1980s has undoubtedly strengthened the position of 90 per cent of parents on admissions, it has by no means ensured that all will be granted their wish, nor could it.

Another matter of considerable interest is parents' power over decisions on curriculum in the school. Prior to the 1980s although governors had, in theory, some say over both the conduct and curriculum of a school, not all had this in practice. Some local authorities omitted the words 'and curriculum' in their articles of government and, at that time, relatively few had established parent governors as of right. Michael Golby elsewhere in this volume cites evidence which suggests that many parents feel relatively impotent on governing bodies, so actual control over the curriculum may be more imagined than real.

A good illustration of this is the situation in many secondary schools at the third year 'options' stage, when children make choices of new areas of study or discard existing subjects. In a country like Sweden such critical decisions are taken much more as a three-way partnership, with parents and pupils more centrally involved. In Britain not only do parents have little say over the content of the curriculum but they have little status, compared with their counterparts in other countries, at crucial decision points.

Tension and its Resolution

There is some tension within government policy over this same matter. On the one hand the 1988 Education Act appears to strengthen the position of parents in terms of their influence at local level. On the other hand the introduction of a National Curriculum has removed to central government a considerable chunk of influence over what is taught. Since teacher supply is also under the direct control of the Secretary of State it is even more difficult for parents to gain a purchase on what is taught in schools. Were there a demand from parents for more Spanish classes, for example, the implications of this would have to ripple right through to the Secretary of State when he determines the quotas of trainee teachers for each three year period so that a higher quota could be established. In practice it is factors other than parental demand which influence the setting of quotas. Until the more widespread development of supported self study and distance learning in schools this position will not change very much.

Compared with areas of the United States where certain organized political or religious groups can exercise influence over curriculum, British parents are in a much weaker position. In some states, particularly in the south and mid-west of the United States, groups of parents who are members of the John Birch Society, the Moral Majority or religious fundamentalist groups, have sometimes been influential on, for example, the choice of school textbooks, set literary works or on syllabus content. There have been occasional attempts by British parents to influence what is taught, but it has usually been confined to isolated objections to particular lessons, textbooks or activities, rather than an organized attempt to be proactive.

The most striking examples of parental power have come at two levels. The first is at national level through parents' organizations such as the National Confederation of Parent–Teacher Associations (NCPTA) and bodies like the Campaign for the Advancement of State Education (CASE) which have many parent members. Both the NCPTA and CASE have undertaken their own surveys of parental opinion, and have shown themselves to be very sophisticated in their understanding of the workings of the mass communications media. CASE in particular has also fostered enquiry and action at local level. For example the report by the East Devon branch of CASE on the state of resources in local schools was widely cited and probably had a direct influence on the County Council which then endeavoured to improve matters. Although some of the more active 'parents' in such groups are sometimes also teachers or people working professionally in education, others are not. James Hammond, who has often spoken on behalf of the NCPTA, is not involved professionally in education, but he is one of a number of spokespeople for organized parental pressure groups who have been comfortable on national radio or television whether answering questions about the NCPTA report, or debating with politicians or even the Secretary of State.

At local level parents have also shown an increasing awareness of how to influence the power structure independently of national parents' organizations, though sometimes aided and advised by these. A feature of the 1980s has been the proliferation of pamphlets for parents produced by bodies like the Advisory Centre for Education (ACE) on such matters as school closure, books for parents advising them how to exert influence, like *A Parent's Guide to Education*[4] and *Education: an Action Guide for Parents*[5] or for parent and other governors, such as *A Handbook for School Governors*,[6], or radio programmes, like *The Education Roadshow* on BBC Radio 4, which travelled the country with a panel of experts giving advice to parents who attended or phoned in.

On one occasion a local authority tried to remove hundreds of teaching posts, mainly from small village schools.[7] Over a thousand parents marched to County Hall on the day when the decision was to be confirmed by the County Council. Faced by the massed ranks of their own electors councillors reversed the decision.

The successful campaign waged by the parents of Plymtree when their small two teacher village primary school was threatened with closure, illustrates well the new found sophistication of many parents. First of all they interviewed every family with children under five in the region and found that the LEA had underestimated future numbers. Next they invited key members of the Education Committee to the school to see the children and their work, on the grounds that it is psychologically more difficult to close a school you have actually seen than one which is merely a name on a list. They also wrote individual letters to councillors and their MP. Finally they attended the actual meeting of the Education Committee at which the future of their school was to be decided.

Not only was this shrewd campaign successful but it whetted the appetite of Plymtree parents for more battles with the local authority. When numbers began to increase, as they had predicted, they needed a third classroom. The LEA protested that no money was available, so the parents identified a school with a surplus portable classroom and struck a deal with the authority that they themselves would erect it if the LEA paid for the transport.

This remarkable story is one of the more striking examples of parent power in action, but it does illustrate several important basic principles. The first is that organized parents may have to do their own research, especially if they are to counteract official estimates or projections. Parents may lack the tools of information gathering or the accumulated data banks of professional bureaucrats, but they do have the advantage of local knowledge. Secondly many have now discovered the power of personal persuasion, especially of elected politicians. Personal letters written to councillors or MPs are more effective than petitions or sponsored write-ins of identical messages. One letter read out by a councillor during the debate on the reduction of a school's teaching staff, began 'I am the mother of three children at our local school and I have interrupted my washday to write you this letter, so please do me the courtesy of reading it carefully'. It had clearly made an impact on an elected member alarmed at the possibility of electors about to switch allegiance.

Most significantly Plymtree parents had realized the importance of personalizing the issue. They not only invited councillors to the school but also exercised their right under the Public Bodies (Admissions to Meetings) Act of 1960 to attend the very meetings at which decisions were going to be made. In the past parents might well have been ignorant of their local authority's decision making structure, but many of the well-organized and informed today realize that it will be the Schools Sub-committee which makes the first important decision, that the Education Committee itself will discuss the matter subsequently, and that the full County Council will have to give the final approval. Not only have they become aware of the cycle of committees and the power structure, but they may also lobby skilfully and then attend meetings with their children. The unspoken visual message, that callous councillors are about to deprive children of something, is a highly potent one, especially when the press are in attendance, as they usually are.

What Role for Parents?

This degree of sophistication shown by some parents is not universal, however. Many remain ignorant of both their actual and potential collective power. Just as social security benefits may go unclaimed and charitable trusts find that no-one applies for their funds, so too parents may be oblivious of their rights. The distribution of awareness of these matters is enormous, varying from parents who may be extremely knowledgeable, may even be lawyers or politicians, to those who, despite considerable publicity, press coverage, letters from schools, handbooks and prospectuses, have little idea what to do in cases of adversity, or indeed how to influence events. At the one extreme parents neither claim nor seek any power, at the other they press at the very frontier which divides professional and lay responsibility for education.

This demarcation line is not a clear one. It is much more diffuse than would be the case in law or medicine where, rightly or wrongly, massive expertise is assumed to be necessary. The nearest to challenging these powerful professions may come only from clients or patients who feel sufficiently well-informed, after reading magazine articles perhaps, to challenge the need for an episiotomy during childbirth or query the slowness of house conveyancing. In education matters seem more related to personal experience and everyday commonsense, and teachers themselves have sometimes been reluctant to claim special expertise and have lost confidence after sustained public attacks from politicians and some newspapers.

Questions have arisen, therefore, about what role parents who are lay people can properly play. Already parent governors may find themselves members of a staff selection committee or of a group discussing a pupil suspension, or be expected to take part in a discussion on aspects of the curriculum. Under the 1986 Act they also have direct responsibility for such matters as the contents of the school's programme on sex education.

The introduction of teacher appraisal has led to a consideration of who should legitimately be involved,[8] because the act of appraising 400,000 teachers in England and Wales will be complex and time-consuming. Thus teacher appraisal presents a test case. If parent governors already take part in appointments, in larger schools have responsibility for finances, perhaps even take the lead in persuading fellow parents to opt out of local authority control under the provisions of the 1988 Education Act, might they not also participate in the appraisal of staff, since their position is closer to that of employer than it might have been in previous times?

Writing as someone who has spent a great deal of time supporting greater power for parents both individually and collectively my own view is that there is little or no role for parents either as governors or individuals to play in the appraisal of teachers. It is, quite simply, a professional matter. Feedback from parents, whether favourable or otherwise, should certainly figure in the appraisal process provided it is reliable and not based purely on hearsay or the views of the malevolent, prejudiced or ill-informed. But properly done the evaluation of teaching should be based substantially on a sustained appraisal over a period of time with appropriate observation of lessons and discussion of objectives and progress. That is what makes it essentially a professional responsibility.

With an average of over eight million children in schools over the past decades, reviewing the actual, as opposed to putative, power of their successive generations of parents, is not a simple or straightforward matter. Social pressures and legislation have certainly increased the influence that parents may have if they are well informed, articulate, persistent and listened to, but the distribution of these necessary circumstances and characteristics is by no means even. The most powerful have shown they can not only exert direct influence but occasionally cause discomfort to teachers, administrators and politicians. It remains the case, nonetheless, that the majority of parents are still relatively impotent and that many have no ambition for the situation to be any different, until such time as there is a clear identifiable source of aggravation.

Notes

1 McGeeney, P.J. (1969) *Parents Are Welcome*, London, Longman.
2 Central Advisory Council for Education (1967) *Children and their Primary Schools* (Plowden Report), London, HMSO.
3 McGeeney, P.J. (1969) *op. cit.*
4 O'Connor, M. (1986) *A Parent's Guide to Education*, London, Fontana.
5 Wragg, E.C. (1986) *Education: An Action Guide for Parents*, London, BBC.
6 Wragg, E.C. and Partington, J.A. (1989) *A Handbook for School Governors*, London, Routledge.
7 Wragg, E.C. (1986) *op. cit.*
8 Wragg, E.C. (1987) *Teacher Appraisal*, London, Macmillan.

7 *Parent Governorship in the New Order*

Michael Golby

Introduction

Parental involvement, we all know, is an enormously good thing. But how much of a good thing we will only know when its limits have been tested. That is something which has so far not happened, except in some isolated and inconclusive cases. In widely publicized affairs parents in Dewsbury and Brent, for example, have asserted their views about multicultural education and their demands over matters such as the appointment of teachers and the allocation of pupils to schools. Matters such as these have hitherto been regarded as the LEAs' sphere and in fact that, legally speaking, is what they are. The LEAs own the maintained ('state') schools and employ the teachers; they are responsible for running the education service efficiently. These responsibilities do lie squarely with the LEAs and, in regard to the example of the choice of school for their children, parents have the legal right only to 'express a preference' which the LEA must take into account. The consumerist atmosphere of the eighties has led to much practical confusion within the general relationship between parents and professionals and the big issues have been fudged.

In Brent, for example, the Secretary of State used a reserve power to overrule the LEA in the case of a Headteacher suspended by the LEA but popular with at least some parents. The disagreement there was largely an ideological one between an LEA with a distinct anti-racist policy and central government with equally decided and opposing views. Parents were implicated in that case as part of the rhetoric of politics but the point is that this was an exception which is not, yet at any rate, the rule. If it became so we would have direct rule from Elizabeth House, Downing Street or the Gray's

Inn Road (exactly where in central government such powers might come to rest is part of the problem). The destabilizing of LEAs, possibly their dismantling, has been sought in part by the appeal to parent power under a social darwinist belief that competition produces quality. But it is arguable how far an efficient and just service can be provided within a market for education devolved to the parents. Would not the free play of parental choice be both inefficient and unfair as well as chaotic in implementation?

There is a lack of clarity of principle in such cases which is mirrored in the less spectacular but equally important daily practice of thousands of teachers making decisions about the extent of parental involvement they can encourage. For involvement can take many different forms ranging from supportively mild interest to membership of a governing body having executive powers.

It is the contention in this chapter that only when the parents' interests are worked out in relation to those of other parties to the work of schools can a satisfactory settlement be accomplished. Socially satisfactory solutions are necessary and these extend beyond satisfying the demands of the parents.

The Present Position

At present parents still exercise a mainly supportive or 'advise and consent' relationship to the predominant values underlying the work of schools. This is so whether in classrooms, fund raising through PTAs or even in the post-1980 governing bodies. It is an open question how far and in what ways it will be legitimate to involve parents in the many different functions of schools. 'Involvement' is very much an umbrella term for a multitude of relationships to a great diversity of practices. The charting of the whole field has simply not been done. For example, we might very well encourage all parents to work with their own children in school where we might have reservations about some (or all) parents working with other parents' children. Parents themselves might very well have views on this in particular cases. But on what principles can we conscientiously make up our minds?

As a contribution to the development of ideas about legitimacy I will consider the particular form of parental involvement found in school governing bodies. This may cast some light on the general issues as well as being of some passing interest as the greatly increased number of parents acting as school governors (provided for by the 1986 Education Act) move into the era after the 1988 Education Act with its provision for greater powers for school governors over financial and curricular aspects of school life.

Ideological Background

First, the deeper political background needs to be considered. Why the emphasis on parents at this time? Is this just a welcome and overdue recognition of natural rights, a system at last come to its senses, a change of heart and mind on a large scale? Or is there more to be said? In any case we have at least to ask why, if all is to the good, it should come about at precisely this juncture of our educational and political history. Much could be brought into such a discussion including the rise of consumerism generally with a metaphor of 'the market' being applied widely to what have since the beginning of the welfare state been considered as social services. Health, for example, is now to be 'delivered', like the curriculum to 'customers'. This pervasive image extends to water supply but not, interestingly, to the police or armed services. There are also factors such as falling rolls in the school system, economic stringency and unemployment at above the ten per cent level. These and other factors need to be related together in an effort to understand the grip of current ideological forces. Only the passage of time and historical analysis will allow of this yet it is an urgent task if we are to make policy decisions in areas such as parental involvement in schools. For the present we may usefully consider the roots of the 1988 Education Act which may well set the climate for as long as its predecessor of 1944.

Political measures are seldom the unadulterated product of pure ideology. Even governments with large majorities have to put together packages of legislation that catch the prevailing mood. A *Zeitgeist* more than a coherent overall theory explains political initiative and response. The mature Thatcher government of 1988 brought in an Education Act with four main components so far as schools were concerned. It was to be possible for schools to opt out of the control of local education authorities into 'grant maintained' status, that is to say into central control; enrolments were to be 'open' up to certain maxima based on past, historically high, rolls; governing bodies were to exercise stronger powers, especially over the financial and curricular aspects of school policy making; and there was to be a national curriculum backed up by national tests of pupils at seven, eleven, fourteen and sixteen.

Parents figure centrally in the first three of these measures but little in the fourth. To opt out a majority of parents was to be required. Thus parents of one generation would commit their successors to a school administered from the centre. The educational character of schools opting out was to be unchanged so this looks like a simple change of proprietorship based on dissatisfaction with the LEA regime but in ignorance of the full implications of the alternative. Open enrolments were to buttress parental choice, a principle established in the 1980 Act, which had legislated for the expression of a preference but not for it necessarily to be granted in every case. Stronger powers for school governors in the 1988 Act came at a time when the provisions of the 1986 (No 2) Act were coming into force, increasing parental representation on school governing bodies above that of the teachers and equal with that of the LEA appointees.

Only in the matter of the national curriculum were parents not centrally part of the machinery brought in by the 1988 Act. There was, on the contrary, evidence that parents objected to some aspects of this part of the legislation, especially the proposals to test children against national 'benchmarks'. This points to a contradiction within the 1988 legislation between the 'free market' concept and the idea of a compulsory national curriculum in maintained schools. Any colour you like so long as it is black. Whereas parents were to have the power to choose and to be involved in the government of schools at the local level, what was to be taught was for the central authority to determine. There is thus a conflict between the central direction of the curriculum and local freedom at the periphery. This needs puzzling out even granted that the idea of a national curriculum had bipartisan political and popular support.

It is social darwinism that lies behind the parental cause, the belief that quality in education, as in species, is ensured through competition in an environment of scarce resources. Enough had been done to ensure the scarcity of financial resources, through central stringency and then through rate-capping throughout the years since the first international oil crisis and under successive governments. Then the birth rate had ensured that the most precious lifeblood of all to schools, their pupils, was also in short supply. But scarcity is not enough; competition is made effective only where there is choice and where that choice is well founded in information. In the marketing metaphor the publication of HMI reports and of school and LEA policies play the role of advertising.

The measures of 1988 went as far as was possible to approximate the provision of schooling to the selling of a product on the open market. Teachers were the 'deliverers' of the curriculum and parents its 'consumers'.No consideration was given to the idea that other individuals and interest groups could equally claim to be consumers. The professions, the universities and polytechnics, and the churches did not enter into the equation. School governors were required to seek representation of business interests and to consult in appropriate circumstances the local Chief Police Officer.

Uneasy companions, these, for many parents seeking only a healthy grassroots relationship with schools for the benefit of their own children. Some indeed began to voice disquiets at being used as stalking horses in a political crusade against local authorities. More far-sighted critics pointed out that if competition was a good thing it had to be fair competition. This educational competition was confined to the public sector and designed to discipline schools there to the wishes of parents locally and within the straitjacket of the National Curriculum: the expansion of the Assisted Places Scheme and the establishing of city technology colleges were both providing publicly subsidized escape routes for children with ambitious parents. The net result, whether by intention or not, would be the erosion of the maintained sector into at best a basic safety net for those not privately educated.[1] The National Curriculum would be the educational equivalent of the emergency sickness service left when the NHS had been run down in favour of private medicine.

The political rhetoric of parents' freedom to choose was very much of a piece with a general libertarianism underlying a range of privatizing and anti-monopolistic measures. The opticians and the solicitors had lost their right to provide socially important services on their own terms and nationalized industries had been sold off on the stock market. But this general politics of freedom had not been the subject of a principled debate. The editor of *Philosophy Today* commented:

> Despite repeated philosphical warnings against viewing freedom as an absolute value, the term 'freedom' has continued to be used as a blanket justification for all kinds of controversial positions . . . The most systematic abuse of the concept of freedom is to be found, however, among neo-conservative theorists and politicians. In the name of 'freedom of choice', public housing is to be reduced, the

> extra resources needed to meet the increasing demand on public health facilities are not to be made available, better provisions for state education are not given, and a lot less is to be spent on the public sector generally because more money could then be channelled back to people in the form of tax cuts to enable them to spend it as they freely choose. But this completely ignores the rationale of establishing a wide range of public services in terms of meeting the basic needs of people *regardless of their spending power*. Instead of maximizing the freedom of choice of those who can most afford to choose between all the options, a government should aim to address the question of when and to what extent the freedom of choice of some should be limited for the sake of meeting the needs of others.[2]

In education the natural desires of parents to become involved in their children's schooling were being harnessed to a political agenda whose deepest implications were not up for inspection. In an interview with John Clare in *The Times*, the Education Secretary, Kenneth Baker, revealed his educational values and their connection with the individualistic, competitive and meritocratic society they entail. Demanding greater rigour in teaching, he said

> But that's not the way they have been taught. Instead, they're all roped together on the side of the hill to ensure that no one falls down and no one gets to to the top. It's the convoy philosophy: keep them together instead of allowing them to go at their own speed and achieve things in their own way.[3]

Such a metaphor is not particularly well chosen even for Baker's purpose since most social achievements are the product of team work, not the happy product of uncoordinated individual competition. Think of any engineering project, any exploration or research, any warfare; all such endeavours involve a vision of an overall social aim beyond the self-interest of individuals within it. A narrowly individualistic view of society is not true to the historical facts of human achievement though it may for a while discipline a workforce by causing internal strife and competition. Certainly, the price of such an ideology is the divide between those who succeed and those who fail in the social darwinist struggle:

> There is now, I believe, a great gulf in our nation that is dividing us: on the one side are those who have made it, those for whom the Thatcherite vision has brought success,

> money and the good things of life; on the other side are those who have been used, exploited so that the few might succeed. They are the poor, the sick, the women, the handicapped, the blacks, the lesbians and the gay men,

said Jeremy Younger, a gay vicar leaving the Church because of its failure to respond to the homophobia sweeping the nation in 1988.[4]

It is unclear where the teachers stand. Perhaps they bestraddle the divide. If that is so, parents could hardly be expected to formulate a collective view. Their honest intentions to do well by their own children were part of a larger scene. The above considerations were a long way from the thoughts of most parents doing their best for their own children and schools in 1988. Raising funds, getting elected to the governors, visiting classrooms, accompanying out of school activities, fighting for resources for their school in competition with neighbouring schools; all of these are activities with a more than local meaning. Only systematic research can help us to clarify what is going on and little enough of that has been done. Can it be an accident that policy-oriented research is now so hard to get funded while research on technicalities such as assessment and testing is relatively easy to set up?

Some Research Evidence

Fortunately, some evidence about the parental frame of mind comes to hand from the Leverhulme Parents as Governors Project at Exeter University School of Education. A team of teacher-researchers interviewed eighty parent-governors of Devon secondary schools and then conducted intensive case studies of individual governors at work.[5]

Devon had introduced parent- and teacher-governors following the 1980 Education Act. Unlike some other authorities which had exercised their discretionary power to introduce teacher-, parent- and in some cases pupil-governors, Devon was late in the field. The research group was interested in the perceptions, firstly of teacher governors and subsequently of parent governors in this new situation. How did teachers and parents think of their role and especially their relationship to those who elected them? Were they in danger of 'co-option' into a ruling elite or were they bringing a grassroots democratic interest to bear? Were they effective in their own terms? Did they perceive any great impediments to their effectiveness? What educational values did the parents in particular hold? What were their training requirements? These were the central questions of the research.

No adequate account of the complete findings can be given here but perhaps the most relevant general finding for the purposes of the present discussion is that parents were not all of a like mind. There was no single 'common sense' viewpoint on educational issues which would, for example, press towards opting out of the LEA system into a quasi-independent status. There was considerable goodwill towards the maintained schools and there was an enormous amount of energy given up to make school governorship productive for all parties. Parent governors were definitely not motivated by purely personal and selfish interests and they generally greatly respected the endeavours of professionals. They had no strong desire to control the schools though they conscientiously hoped to be involved and consulted thoroughly. There was no commando force of parents ready to leap into ideological battle with the school system.

Instead it was possible to identify three broad categories of parents subscribing to rather different educational values. There was a substantial number of parents who adhere to what may be called grammar school ideology. There was another set who saw schooling as a service industry, principally to employment. A smaller third group of egalitarians promoted comprehensive school ideals. Respectively, these groups stressed the values of the traditional grammar school curriculum and all the associated forms of behaviour, dress etc; the skills required by the world of work, especially all the modern guises of computer technology, together with associated attitudes towards earning a living, industriousness etc; and the broad curriculum and cooperative ethos of the supposed good comprehensive. Thus parents, far from siding with a single view, themselves exhibited a wide range of educational ideas and the deeper political and social assumptions current in the broader political debates.

There was no mandate from parental opinion as discerned in Devon in 1987 and 1988 for policies which would have the ultimate effect of withering the maintained sector. That is the broad view. But within the parents' experience can also be discerned a network of tensions between the various interests at stake in education generally. School governing bodies in 1988 were showing in microcosm the evolving strains in the system brought about by the ideological offensive against education that had been going on for at least ten years. Though parents were mainly unwitting combatants in this struggle their reports clearly demonstrate some of the strains.

Though there was little rancour and few flashpoints, parents report a general suspicion of political involvement in the deliberations of governing bodies. An alliance of those closest to the grassroots, the parents and the teachers, went together with a dislike of local politicians who on occasion used a governing body as an arena for the further pursuit of their own political interests. One parent recently elected as Chair of the governors, found his authority publicly challenged at an open governors' meeting and could only attribute this to local politics and goings on at County Hall where a hung council was in crisis, having to elect a Chair separately for each of its committee meetings since no inter-party agreement could be found. Though a member of a political party, this parent found himself coping with the ramifications of local politics with deep historical roots. As a relative newcomer to the district, he experienced the effects of conflicts within and between the local political parties which he could not hope to fully understand. His professional and his well-researched knowledge of the educational system were no match for the intricacies of the local political situation. This is by no means to say that he was ineffective. It is only an illustration of the interaction between parents, however well informed, and those who have traditionally come forward as governors of schools. It is to be hoped that the new governing bodies with their stronger representation of parents and their wider powers will help democratize society generally, a process which could be extended to hospitals, the police and other social services. In this way, it could be that education will be in advance of other agencies.

The Crisis in Local Government and Parental Power

Meanwhile, though, there is a crisis in our system of local government. The local authorities have been under assault throughout recent years. They have presented in the main a soft target, for their public image has been one of bureaucratic wastefulness and inefficiency. Their democratic function has been lost in the noise of accusation and derision. Yet the local authorities still own the schools and employ the teachers and the elected councillors hold legal responsibilities and powers of great importance. At school level the fact that LEA nominees are not necessarily elected councillors at all, nor even members of the political party that nominates them, may add to their lack of authenticity in the eyes of some parents.

The relationship to LEA nominees was central to parents' accounts of their work given to the researchers. In this way parents recognized the legitimacy of the local authority but they did tend to regard the local authority as a distant bureaucracy rather than a supportive presence. This ought not to blind us to the fact that there is indeed a wider authority to be represented in the work of schools beyond that of their immediate clientele. Parents are indeed the 'parents of the day' and there will be a new set of parents with each new intake to school. Parents as such have a temporary interest in the work of their child's school but their children are certainly of permanent interest, so to speak, to all of us. Nationally, we will want to know that there will be enough doctors and teachers for the future; locally, we will be interested in the kind of citizenship our younger generation will be exercising. These things matter continuously for they reflect and affect the quality of life of all of us and our successors. Parents as governors should therefore not be accorded the status of ultimate 'consumers' of education. The training agenda for parents should stress more their social responsibility than their self-interest. And, to be fair, this is very much the thinking of most of the parents interviewed in the research. Few considered themselves as delegates and most as representatives exercising their own judgment within their governing bodies. Here again the vision of a purely competitive society is inadequate to ordinary views of the social world. It is not then that local democracy has failed, more that it has not been seriously tried elsewhere than in a few urban and traditionally left-wing authorities.

School governing bodies present perhaps a last opportunity for a rebirth of citizen participation in the work of public institutions. With local councils hedged in financially and ideologically (with prohibitions about the use of such monies as they are allowed to retain), could it be that the schools will see new local democratic growth in their midst?

The omens for this are not entirely unpropitious. School governors have traditionally had mainly ceremonial and rubber-stamping functions. There were sure signs from the research that this was very rapidly changing. Governors, including parents, are now regularly and routinely involved in such important activities as selecting new staff and formulating curricular policies. These achievements have been built on a secure base of home-school relationships developed over a good number of years. With local management of schools, including financial aspects, there is a reasonable prospect of this democratic representation going from strength to strength. This itself would of course be dependent upon sufficient parents coming forward for the new governorships and it is important to the success of school governorship in an increasingly centralized state that candidates be found. If they can be found the schools will have the change of participating in the vital task of keeping democracy alive at the grassroots.

There are further requirements if this optimism is to be justified. Democracy requires not simply involvement but representation. Parents in Devon reported considerable worries about their relationship to the parental constituency as a whole. Elections were not heavily contested, in numerous cases not contested at all. Once elected parent governors had problems in reporting back. The LEA regulations do not allow parents to use the school post for newsletters etc. This is an echo of the idea that all governors are one flesh and all communications must be from the governors as a whole and through the Chair. This trusteeship concept seems to be waning and parents are clearly seeing themselves as a separate constituency with a need for its own lines of communication. So PTAs are rapidly moving to fill the gap between parent governors and the parent body. In some cases there is even reciprocal membership between governors and PTAs, with governors invited to PTA committees and PTAs providing ready-made candidates for governorships. Thus parents are indeed getting their act together in many places, perhaps particularly in the urban secondary schools.

The idea of governing bodies as representative forums is strengthened by the inclusion of representatives from business and the community by co-option. Thus, there are LEA, teacher, parent, business and community interests to be negotiated within the governing bodies. This is, of course, a recipe for potential conflict between those interests. But it is not clear along what lines such conflict might break out. Is it possible that the stereotypes will break down (the industrialist as philistine, the teacher as unworldly, the parent as self-seeking, the LEA as obstructive) in a new local political settlement? Disparities of view will hardly go away and the world would be the poorer without them. But can we envisage a responsible democratic process centred on the schools with a knock-on effect well beyond them? We have already seen in this discussion that educational views do entail societal assumptions. In debating a curricular programme or financial priorities for the coming year, will not a governing body also and at once be deliberating its desired society?

Training Governors

There are strong implications for the training of school governors in all this. Devon respondents were unanimously of the view that training was inadequate. Yet what sort of training could be adequate for a set of tasks so far reaching and complex? Beginners need basic information on the rights and duties of governorship. All governors need committee skills and knowledge of procedures (an area where parent novices felt particularly inferior to their practised political colleagues). The work of schools is fast changing and a mystery to most outsiders. Beyond all this, a full enough agenda for training, there lie the deeper levels of political and moral consciousness without which any form of government is mere rule following. How can we hope to stimulate such deeper thought while also responding to the demands of the moment? Training must be multi-faced, rather as INSET ought to be for teachers. It should offer learning for people at all stages of their governorship careers, for example by encouraging and assisting parent governors into other categories of governorship where their experience will be so valuable. Training should be specialized and not merely a blanket coverage for all. Chairmanship makes special demands; the clerk needs to understand the full needs of all constituencies; Headteachers need to move away from proprietorship to genuine consultation but without losing their professional responsibility. The rise of the parent governor should not blind us to the needs of their colleagues. Governor training then will be a priority for a future where schools will be host to a rebirth of democracy. It must put issues of principle high on the agenda alongside items of technique and information.

Supported in this way, parent power, which has come into political play for one set of reasons, may well serve broader, more liberal and democratic causes in the longer run.

Notes

1 SIMON, B. (1988) *Bending the Rules: The Baker Reform of Education*. London, Lawrence and Wishart.
2 Editorial, *Philosophy Today*, Spring 1988.

3 BAKER, K., (1988) *The Times*, 26 February.
4 YOUNGER, J. (1988) in *New Statesman*, 26 February.
5 GOLBY, M. and BRIGLEY, S. (1987) *Interim Report*, Leverhulme Research Project, Parents as School Governors, School of Education, University of Exeter and final report, *Parents and School Governors* (1989) Fair Way Publications, Tiverton, Devon.

8 *The Politics of Parental Involvement*

Ian Morgan

In the Conservative Manifesto 1987 *The Next Moves Forward* the Conservative Party promised 'four major reforms':

(i) 'we will establish a National Core Curriculum'
(ii) 'within five years governing bodies and head teachers of all secondary schools and many primary schools will be given control of their own budgets'
(iii) 'we will increase parental choice'
(iv) 'we will allow state schools to opt out of LEA control'

Here is a subtle mix of hub-and-rim political dynamic, giving the impression of rolling back the boundaries of the state while at the same time serving to consolidate the power of the state at the centre: the miller observes the stir of the wind active at the edge of his sails, but he it is who engages and governs the stones.

An influential adviser to the New Right in contemporary Conservatism, Roger Scruton, has written: 'the conservative attitude seeks above all for government, and regards no citizen as possessed of a natural right that transcends his obligation to be ruled',[1] not even, that would say, the right, incorporated in the Education Act 1944 that 'so far as is compatible with the provision of efficient instruction and training and the avoidance of unreasonable public expenditure pupils are to be educated in accordance with the wishes of their parents.'[2]

Respect for parental choice is inbuilt into the Education Act 1944, that great landmark of national consensus. It places on the parents of every child of compulsory school age the 'duty to cause him to receive efficient full-time education suitable to his age, ability and aptitude either by regular attendance at school or otherwise.'[3] Although the onus of proof rests on the parent to show that the other-than-school arrangement is 'appropriate', the conditions of acceptability for the alternate provision are not so impossible as to make redundant the services of a national agency like Education Otherwise. The take-up of this parental option is so minimal, however, that its use may reasonably be termed eccentric.

The following advertisement is sufficient to show further scope for the exercise of parental choice under the 1944 Act:

> Education. The right to choose. As parents, we know you are concerned that your child receives the best education possible and the classified section of the Lancashire Evening Post can help you make the right decision. On Friday, August 28, we will be publishing our highly successful feature Independent Schools. If you run an independent school, private tuition service, assisted fees scheme etc, you need to promote your organization through this feature in order to ensure the message is read by, and acted upon by the right people at the right time.[4]

The book *Which School? A Parental Guide to All British Independent Schools*, 1988, published by the Truman and Knightley Trust, was the 64th Edition.

The vast majority of British parents, whether by choice or circumstance, send their children to the non-fee-paying schools maintained, controlled or aided by the local education authorities and jointly funded by central government. In this system also parents who can afford to do so are able to exercise choice, as any estate agent will avow, offering as he or she will do not only houses for sale but a valuation of which schools in which area are 'good'. In any case, legislation does not tolerate the concept of the enforceable catchment or the neighbourhood school, and subject to the ability to pay the extra costs incurred in travel, say, parents can choose a school even in a different local authority area. The right of parents in exercising such choice is protected by access to local councillors and officials, statutory appeals machinery, reference direct to the Secretary of State for Education and Science, and the services of the Ombudsman.

The success of some Scottish parents in resorting to the protection afforded by the European Court of Human Rights in the matter of the use of the tawse led eventually, albeit by a majority of one in the House, to the abolition of corporal punishment from 15 August 1987 in all maintained schools in England and Wales, and parents whose choice it is to send their child(ren) to a school where corporal punishment *in loco parentis* is allowed are now restricted in that choice to paying full fees, without state assistance, at an independent school. In this case the limitation on parental choice was achieved by other parents exercising theirs.

The opportunity given to parents to vote that 'their' school secede from the control of the local education authority does not appear to give them any extra choice: it does introduce into the system a school managed in a distinctive form but it is intended that the nature of the school shall remain. The establishment of 'chosen' schools will lead to the closure of other schools in the area (for the supply of children is finite) and it is hard to see how the closures of schools increase parental choice. Perhaps it is unfair, it is certainly illogical, to look for improved democratic participation within the concept of 'parental choice'. The National Union of Teachers (NUT) shares the ambition of the Campaign for the Advancement of State Education (CASE) in looking towards a day when every local school will be so well-resourced and well-regarded that parents will have no reason to choose other than to send their children to the local school, valued at the heart of their community.

In his essay 'Education in Crisis' Stuart Hall has written:

> For a brief period in the 1960s and 1970s the involvement of parents with the school was the left's most democratic trump card. The dismantling of this into 'parental choice' and its expropriation by the right is one of their most significant victories. They stole an idea designed to increase popular power in education and transformed it into an idea of an educational supermarket.'[5]

The balance of argument would seem to indicate that educational provision is not something to be crudely assigned to the action of market-forces. The commodity of education is dealt *with* not dealt in or out: it can even be said that in education the commodity *is* the consumer. The counterview, that education is no less marketable than soap or beefburgers, fails to identify the consumer: identification hovers between the local employer, some vague holder of the perception of national needs, the funding agency (which as well as wanting value for money also wants its money back), and the parent.

If there is a consumer, it is most properly the child. *The Omega File on Education,*[6] providing a rationale for the New Right's policies, acknowledges the difficulty, without resolving it, in the following note:

> It is worth emphasizing that parental choice effectively means family choice. The family, including the children, normally discuss and decide on educational matters though the parents, as legal guardians, make the actual decision.

In the text supporting the promise of four major reforms the writers of the Conservative Manifesto 1987, already referred to, presented their view of the enlightened consumerism of parents:

> The most consistent pressure for high standards in schools comes from parents . . . But parents still need better opportunities to send their children to the school of their choice. That would be the best guarantee of higher standards . . . Popular schools, which have earned parental support by offering good education will then be able to expand beyond present pupil numbers. These steps will compel schools to respond to the views of parents.[7]

There is much here that deserves analysis, discussion and commentary, not least with regard to the accuracy of what is said. I will linger upon the last of these sentences, 'These steps will compel schools to respond to the views of parents'.

The word 'compel' here has about it a complexion that ranges from annoyance to fury. Some emotion has gone into the use of the word. Behind this resort to authoritative coercion there lies an obvious history of frustration at the way in which, despite the opportunities given to parents in the 1980 Education Act and the Education (No 2) Act, 1986, to receive more information about schools and to be represented on boards of governors, sparks were not flying fast enough. Perhaps the latter phases of this frustration were caused more by anticipation than in retrospect; for the legislation in the Education (No 2) Act, 1986, making the annual meeting of parents statutory did not come into effect until 1 April 1987 and very few meetings had been held in the few weeks of late May when the Manifesto was compiled. The evidence to hand at the time was that these meetings were being poorly attended, even in some cases ignored by parents, and that the schools must be run with more severity.

'These steps will compel *schools* (my emphasis) . . .' The use of 'schools' in this sentence can only mean the collective group of people in schools other than parents (who are separated in the equation). Those accused of not responding to the views of parents are therefore either the governing bodies, or the Headteachers, or the teachers, or the non-teaching staff, or the children themselves.

We are not in a position to know what evidence there is for non-response and do not have access to such evidence. If it means that at a governing body meeting parents, either individually or collectively, have pronounced a view, or views, that the majority of their fellow-governors has not accepted, that is one thing; if, on the other hand, it is thought that because parents have pronounced a view it has to become a decision, whether or not the majority disagree, that is another. Until we know the context in which the views were put and, perhaps, what the views were, the judgment must be reserved on whether 'schools' have set out to disregard 'the views of parents', as is implied in this assertion. Whatever the truth of the charge, I do not accept that the separation of 'parents' from 'schools' is as real as the writers of the Manifesto feel it is.

Much has happened in the field of 'parental involvement' since, in 1969, in their study *Society and the Teacher's Role*, Musgrove and Taylor were able to write: 'The freedom of teachers is the profession's glory; it is the people's shame.'[8] Such freedom is grossly exaggerated, and anyone reading the Plowden Report of 1967 should have known that it is. That Report did much to promote the concept of 'positive discrimination' in its efforts to come to grips with the enormous inequalities parents and children endure in their circumstances and expectations. 'The higher the socio-economic group, the more parents attended Open Days, concerts and parent–teacher association meetings, and the more often they talked with Heads and class-teachers . . . Manual workers and their wives were more likely to feel, when they had visited the schools, that they had learnt nothing fresh about their children, or that teachers should have asked them more . . . Almost half the manual workers, as compared with less than a quarter of non-manual workers, had not been to their child's present school at all.[9] The Report exhorted: 'They (i.e. teachers and parents) should be partners in more than name; their responsibility become joint instead of several.'

The involvement of parents means much more than visits to schools and consultations. In many schools, particularly primary or first schools, parental support is practical, within the school and involves helping other people's children learn. When Her Majesty's Inspectorate began their survey of primary schools in England in the Autumn of 1975 they were able to find:

> parents helped teachers in nearly a third of the 7-year-old classes and in just under a fifth of 9- and 11-year-old classes. The proportion of classes receiving parental help was lower

> in the inner city areas than in 'other urban' or rural areas. Typically, where parental help was given, an average of two parents a week visited the class. In over three-quarters of the classes where help was given parents assisted teachers in matters concerning the children's welfare and in the supervision of children on visits outside the school. Teachers reported that parents were involved with children's learning in over two-thirds of the classes where help was given. This type of involvement most commonly took the form of assisting with practical subjects or hearing children read.[10]

Even so, at a national primary conference held at Scarborough in 1987 Joan Sallis, Chairperson of the Campaign for the Advancement of State Education and a doughty campaigner for parental rights, exhorted:

> Teachers must show parents what they are doing in the classroom. If they had done that in the past when there was plenty of money around, then they would not be facing the difficulties that they are facing today. If you don't let parents in, they won't see. If they don't see they won't understand, and if they don't understand then they won't fight. If the public don't know anything about what is going on then how can they be anything but taken in by the doorstep salesmen?[11]

At the same Conference the Case Studies included a presentation by Gustav Macleod, Headteacher of Hotspur Primary School, Newcastle-upon-Tyne: 'Our school has taken the concept of parental involvement on such a scale that although we have 280 junior school children on roll, we have something like 4000 people passing through the school each week.'[12]

The position of the National Union of Teachers on parental involvement (as distinct from parent power) is clearly set out in the booklet, *Pupils, Teachers and Parents.* While accepting in the foreword that 'In the past, the relationship between parent and teacher may well have remained well-intentioned, but distant' the Union's support for parental involvement in education is unequivocal

> The Union has always supported the involvement of parents in the education of their children, acknowledging that there should be 'a partnership between school and home which secures the greatest possible benefit for the child individually,

for the school collectively, and for the parent, whose natural interest is in the welfare of his or her child'.[13]

If the child is to derive the greatest possible advantage from the part of the day spent working with teachers, the support and cooperation of the adults who guide him or her for the remainder of the time are vital.[14] The statement continues: 'The Union recognizes that this relationship demands extensive managerial skills on the part of the teacher. These skills enhance the teacher's own professional status . . .'[15] Whether it is true or not that the teacher has a professional status rather than that of a bureaucratic employee is a matter for debate, but the self-perception of a majority of teachers is plain: they would like to be professionals. However, there is a gap between the declaration of the assurance of support for parental involvement and its delivery. A reason for this may well be the teacher's uncertainty about professional status and what that involves.

It is the opinion of Hargreaves, the former Chief Inspector of Schools for the Inner London Education Authority, that 'anarchism' (the term he chooses to use to describe the exercising of the power by the deprofessionalized, non-bureaucratic, voluntary collective in the interests of community action) 'is committed to principles which command much support in contemporary Britain: first, a massive decentralization programme; and secondly, a belief in fraternity or the capacity of people to cooperate for the common good through voluntary associations.'[16] Whether a move to anarchism is what the Conservative Party has in mind and whether Hargreaves is correct in thinking that contemporary Britain is eager for it I doubt. In the same essay, writing as one 'committed to the community', he says:

> Teachers are forced to speak with a forked tongue: they know that parental involvement is desirable, but they also know that this implies a shift in the balance of power between parents and teachers: so many teachers find excuses for taking no immediate action, while uttering the appropriate rhetoric.[17]

What is this power that teachers are supposed to have? In what does it subsist? Teachers differ from other skilled workers only in the nature of the knowledge they require and the specificity of their training, which, in the case of teachers, is to diagnose the state of learning readiness of children and to foster their development. It is not teachers who spread abroad the gossip that they have the power of sorcerers, rainmakers or hypnotists to make people anxious about their hold on life; teachers do not live in sacred groves; they pay the same price for bread and circuses. They, too, are parents.

It is not sufficient to assert that before parental involvement in schools can be fully achieved the mystique of teacher professionalism must be dispelled. Midwinter, for instance, believes: 'If there is to be popular oversight then it must be based on informed choice. The demythology of the professions, including teaching, is the prerequisite for this.'[18]

In the USA, where there is a lively and long history of public (as distinct from parental) involvement in the local school, similar concern, particularly from the radical left, is frequently a theme. Calling for the same demystification of teaching, Densmore, in her essay *Professionalism, Proletarianization and Teacher Work* says:

> The issue of democratizing control over schools challenges its (*sic*) bureaucratic dimension; provides opportunities for debate about, and public involvement in, defining educational purposes; and helps to counteract the isolating and individualistic features of teacher professionalism (for example, hostility or suspicion towards parents and community involvement).[19]

She is confident that when such protectionism is by some means removed from schools, teachers would find that the environment so opened up to a free and confident involvement of parents would create a more sympathetic understanding of the teacher's tasks, would lead to the mobilization of improved resourcing for schools, and would enlist parents in the great cause of extending and improving educational opportunity for all. A similar view, from a different perspective, is held by Sarason:

> the single most significant mistake made by educational personnel was to accept responsibility for schools; i.e. willingly, (even eagerly) to permit parents and others to give them responsibility . . . there has *never* been a time when educators had the resources to deal with problems as they and the community defined these problems.[20]

In the USSR the word for 'professional' is not used of any worker and every school has its parents' committee. It is salutary to note the conditions under which these parents' committees are formed and what they are intended to do.

> All schools have a Parents' Committee, made up of one elected representative per class, which is very active in aiding, abetting and reinforcing the work and purposes of the school.
>
> The Parents' Committees are in no sense vehicles for the receipt of parental opinion about teaching or schooling but are instead used to reinforce and explain the work of teachers, guaranteeing its effective impact and also increasing parents' esteem for teachers.[21]

This is not what the British government had in mind when it made mandatory from 1 April 1987 the holding at every school of an Annual Meeting of Parents. In the USSR, of course, the teacher is a form of hero (or, more typically, heroine), for the teacher serves as the promoter and advocate of the national curriculum and is an open and honoured agent of the body politic.

The provision of power for parents through direct and significant representation on the governing board of schools will test out the capacities of parents to act in a representative rather than a personal capacity. The interest taken in a particular school by a particular parent is often a restricted one, especially when active participation in the committees at that school begins with the educational progress and well-being of his or her own child or children. That this is so is indicated by the fact that attendance by parents at meetings convened to discuss the progress and well-being of children are invariably better attended than meetings called for more general purposes.

Once a parent has cultivated a broader sense of commitment to the progress and well-being of *all* the children at the school, to lobby for improving the resourcing and reputation of the school, to a campaign for celebrating and championing the achievements of the children at the school, to protesting at any proposal to close the school, to leadership in fusing the culture of the community with that of the school, then that parent has become fully a governor.

It will be important to monitor how far the offer of power given to parents in the Education (No 2) Act 1986, in terms of influence in a school, is properly taken up. Much will depend on how real that power will be: for the limitations on decision-making imposed on a governing body when the curriculum is dictated and the revenue and capital budgets directed and constrained will make the scope for executive action at school level little more than marginal.

There will still be scope, of course, for the fund-raising operations, so successfully carried out by parent teacher associations in recent years, to such an extent that currently about 30 per cent of the money spent on books, materials and equipment in primary schools in England and Wales, schools that are not fee-paying, has been raised through voluntary activities.

If the invitation to take power is effective and that power is real, it can be expected that schools will see parents being organized into political caucuses and being lobbied by interest groups and the locus of potential opposition to the policies of central government at present apparent in the local government authorities will be shifted, and in what is already an unequal contest central government, by dismantling the local apparatus for protest and dispersing the pieces, will be consolidated. 'Power at community level may be no more than a token if power to make the important decisions lies elsewhere, either with higher levels of government or private corporations . . .'[22] 'Community action within the confines of state-sponsored schemes of neighbourhood decentralization assists in the reproduction of the system of domination represented in the state itself. Neighbourhood decentralization may become a form of repressive tolerance'.[23]

The response of the National Union of Teachers to the increasing involvement of parents in the operations of schools will therefore plainly depend upon what parents, and others, do with their power. The Union exists to encourage the promotion of education and its members are committed to securing the fullest educational development of every child; it also exists to defend the interests of its members, which includes protecting their qualifications, the integrity of their professional judgments, their conditions of work, their livelihood, job-prospects and tenure, their reputations, and their just treatment as employees within the law. It may be a surprise to learn that neither the Union nor any of the teacher and Headteacher associations has formal representation on the governing body of a school. It may become necessary for the Union to develop more sharply its organization in the work-place, especially in larger schools and in schools which secede from the control of LEA employers if its influence is to be effective.

An illustration of what I have called 'the gap between the declaration of the assurance of support for parental involvement and its delivery' and its consequence on relationships between the Union and organized groups of parents warrants study. As indicated earlier, a Regulation arising from legislation in the Education (No 2)

Act 1986 made the holding of an annual parents' meeting statutory; the first of these meetings was to be held in the Summer Term, 1987. The following Union Circular (No 181/87) of 11 May 1987 is self-explanatory in showing that the Union was not given assurances about the conduct of these meetings with regard to the protection of the reputations and employment rights of members. The Assistant Masters and Mistresses Association (AMMA) made a similar declaration.

> *Circular No 181/87*
> *Re: Education (No 2) Act 1986*
>
> As mentioned in the *Summary and Comment No 1 Circular 170/87* on the *Education (No 2) Act 1986*, the Union was concerned about the guidance given in the DES Circular 8/86 on Annual Parents' Meeting. It seemed that the government was envisaging that the annual parents' meeting could give rise to criticisms of named individuals, such as members of staff. The Union made representations to the Secretary of State on this question. He indicated that the government believed that parents should be able to voice their concern about any aspect of the school and that many aspects must touch in some way on the conduct of pupils and staff. The Secretary of State stated, 'We readily accept that criticism of individuals is a sensitive issue and it would clearly be undesirable and unproductive if a meeting turned into a recital of complaints against pupils and staff.' He went on to say, 'The guidance given in Circular 8/86 is thus not intended to replace LEA's established procedures for the handling of complaints against individuals; it would not, in any case, appear to be inconsistent with these arrangements'
> The Secretary of State's reply was before the Law and Tenure Committee at its meeting on Friday, 8 May. The Committee took the view that the reply was unsatisfactory and resolved:
>
> 1 Having regard to the reply by the Secretary of State to the Union's representations relating to the guidance given in the DES Circular on the annual parents' meeting and the possibility of criticism of individual members of staff *the Executive advises members of the Union not to accept an invitation by the governors to attend their annual parents' meeting*

> 2 Teacher governors, however, and Headteachers are advised to attend these meetings
> 3 Approaches be made to the other Teachers' Associations with a view to agreeing a common policy on the position of staff at the annual meeting
> 4 The resolution of the Committee be communicated to local associations and divisions as a matter of urgency.
>
> The Union urges Divisions if they have not already done so, to make representations to their local education authorities, and diocesan authorities in the case of the Aided Schools, to ensure that appropriate guidance is given to Chairpersons of governing bodies so that criticisms of individual members of staff are not debated at the annual parents' meetings.

Leaders of parents' interest groups were naturally aggrieved by the advice the Union and AMMA issued to their members. They regard the newly-introduced meeting as a breakthrough in parental involvement and considered the decision of the Union and AMMA as a grave error of judgment: teachers had everything to gain from being present at these meetings; they had opportunity to convince parents of their commitment to the school and to enlist the support of parents: the opportunity had been spurned.

The advice to teachers not to attend these meetings in case of consequences leading to litigation or general hazard to employment rights was not the reason for what is generally regarded as a most disappointing response by parents to the opportunity. Very few meetings were quorate. In one area a school with 1700 pupils on roll hired a Civic Hall to be sure of housing the meeting; it was attended by thirty, including some teachers; only ten pupils were represented by a parent or parents. In an article reviewing the first run of meetings and looking forward to the next, Sheila Naybour, Press Officer for the National Confederation of Parent–Teacher Associations (NCPTA) in England and Wales, wrote:

> The NCPTA welcomes them (i.e. the annual parents' meetings), for they have provided many parents with their first opportunity to have a closer knowledge and understanding of the way their child's school functions . . . AMMA and NUT need to reconsider their decision to boycott such meetings. I've heard of very, very few 'teacher bashing' meetings, but, undoubtedly the teaching profession is demoralized and feels unloved. Has there ever been a

more urgent need for parents and teachers to understand each other?

The advice of 11 May 1987 was reconsidered in due course, as the following extract from *Circular No 244/88(E)* dated 22 June 1988 indicates:

> *Annual Parents' Meetings*
>
> The Executive has reconsidered the advice given last year with regard to meetings held under the Education (No. 2) Act 1986. At that time, in the light of the guidance contained in DES Circular 8/86 and in the absence of sufficiently detailed advice to governing bodies from LEAs, the Executive advised members not to attend annual parents' meetings other than in their capacity as Headteachers or teacher governors. This was done to protect members' interests, particularly against the raising of matters which were not properly the concern of those meetings.
>
> Experience of the meetings which have taken place since then suggests that the Union's action successfully highlighted the urgent need for governing bodies to obtain advice, primarily from their local education authorities, on the conduct of such meetings. The Executive believes the time has now come to advise members to attend annual parents' meetings in their capacity as teachers where invited and looks to governing bodies to make that possible.
>
> The powers and responsibilities already carried by governors under the 1986 Act lend greater weight to the significance of an understanding between the school and the community it serves. Those powers and responsibilities will be increased as a result of the legislation currently under discussion. The Executive believes members will wish to participate in the opportunity which may be afforded to them by the annual meeting to ensure that the school's best interests are served.

Sheila Naybour of the NCPTA went on to voice several complaints about parents' meetings: that in a primary school parents had small chairs to sit on, while the governors sat in normal ones; that the chairman of one meeting unsuccessfully attempted to ban discussion on the annual report because he had received no written questions; that notices of some meetings were so formal that they read like a legal summons; that some Headteachers were now precluding from the agenda of PTA ordinary meetings educational matters that they considered should now be raised at the annual parents' meeting; that some Headteachers were attempting to curb all activities other than fundraising; that governing bodies were not taking their responsibilities seriously enough; and that the LEAs should provide support and training for governors.

The relationship between the Union and the NCPTA is a cordial one. Strains were obvious during the two years or so of the dispute with the government in 1984–87, during which some 150,000 NUT members took part in strike-action at some time or other and there was a general withdrawal from voluntary activities; but the NCPTA, along with other parents' groups, gave strong support to teachers during the Parliamentary passage of the Teachers' Pay and Conditions Bill, and have conducted forceful campaigns for the improved resourcing of schools. In fact, so high was the profile in the Spring of 1987 that officers of the NCPTA became conscious that in the eyes of the Department of Education and Science they were being too closely identified with the cause of the teachers. Understandably, they kept their heads down in the run-up to the General Election of June 1987.

The issue of possible complaints against individual employees raised in the NUT Circular 181/87, previously quoted, is one over which the Union and other teacher organizations have negotiated, from time to time, procedures and agreements. These negotiations have been with local education authorities and diocesan authorities. There is a 'Burgundy Book' of agreements and guidelines for practice in the areas of Conditions of Work and Conditions of Service, which, although non-statutory, are incorporated in local contracts of employment. Some of these are in process of amendment as a result of the Teachers' Pay and Conditions Act 1987, but there will remain a substantial corpus of arrangements which underpin the understandings made by employers with their work force. There is no reason why the increase of parental power as such should diminish the effect of these agreements, but parents should be under no illusion that the varying of terms and conditions of employment calls for consensus if it is to be meaningful. Additionally, teachers are by no means the only group of employees to be taken account of in the running of a school: nursery nurses and clerical staff, generally members of the National Association of Local Government Officers (NALGO), catering staff, cleaning staff, and caretakers generally of the National Union of Public Employees (NUPE), the General Municipal Boilermakers Allied Trades Union (GMBATU) or Transport and General Workers Union (TGWU); in some schools technicians may belong to Manufacturing, Science,

Finance (MSF).

Another area of Union protest and action would arise if parental involvement in a school were to be mobilized in such a way as to lead to the engagement on a regular basis of voluntary unqualified or even qualified persons in any activity that is described as teaching. If the governing body of a school considers that such voluntary participation, on a regular basis, is desirable, it has the means to employ properly paid and trained personnel. The Union is not in the business of being passive to practices which keep qualified teachers on unemployment registers when in some schools work may be being done on an unpaid and voluntary basis.

In *Pupils, Teachers and Parents* (Para 55) the Union spells out its alertness to the danger of parental support being exploited to provide a non-cost provision: 'It must be emphasized that such parental support should not be used to dilute the local authority's responsibility to provide adequate ancillary help.'[25]

When parental support is made available to a school, or when the use of school premises is extended, special demands are placed on teachers and others. Most of these can mainly be met if teachers are given time within their working day to meet with parents and to organize their work so that it is compatible with the progress of the children. Time is also needed to give clear guidance to helpers so that they operate fully within the prevailing ethos of the school, of which working cordially with parents will be part. Parents should also know that in law the teacher is responsible for what goes on in the classroom, while the teacher will need assurance that proper insurance arrangements have been made. Caretakers will expect a renegotiation of their terms of employment if the use of the school is varied, and will expect a new formula for the provision of cleaning-staff and caretaking support if the working-day is extended. Even voluntarism has its cost, and if the resource is not forthcoming it is not reasonable to accuse teachers of not being serious about parental involvement.

The Union's booklet *Pupils, Teachers and Parents* closes with a five-point note of advice to parents:

1. If the teacher knows you are interested and want to work with your child, she or he can plan to use your help to teach more effectively. So do not wait until there is a problem — show your interest and give your child a better chance
2. Teachers welcome your support, which helps your

children to get the best out of their time at school.

3 It is the teacher's job to plan a proper educational programme, but *you* can encourage your child to learn with enthusiasm.

4 Parents often do not realize that everyday things, such as talking or singing to little children, or working out the family budget or the week's meals, can help children to practise what they need to learn in school. Your child's teacher will be glad to suggest ways for you to help.

5 Many schools welcome extra help doing simple jobs, such as mending books or displaying children's work. If you have some spare time, this may be a good way to improve the school for all pupils.

This summary of 'advice' to parents, with alternative translations into Urdu, Bengali and Chinese, will appear to some bland and patronizing; the very notion of 'advice' the same readers will find obnoxious. 'Who are these teachers anyway to set out the terms under which parents can participate in the work of the schools? Whose schools are they?' will be a question that readily comes to mind. A major reason for the existence of the National Union of Teachers is to champion the craft of teaching; it is part of a champion's duty to be protective, not only of the craft but of all whom the craft embraces. Sheltered in that embrace are children of parents who may not be able to work with their own children, who have no spare time, who cannot afford participation, who have enough to do in coping with each day as it comes, and are thankful that in their schools their children are being given good care. Perhaps the most important words in the advice say that parental participation must be seen to improve the school 'for *all* pupils' (my emphasis). The benefit of parental participation is clearly proven: the benefit of parental power has not yet been tried.

Parents are, however, but a sub-section of the community and community support for a school is diminished if it is not seen to include representation of that majority who do not have children of school age. The full community of voting age is represented by the local councils and elected authorities. Parents do have, for a time, a direct interest in a school, but cannot provide that corporate accountability which is the strength of local government. 'In this country the autonomous association has been the foundation of our intellectual, religious and political freedom. We tend to forget that local government is also a cornerstone of freedom, as every dictator realizes when, on getting into power, he abolishes it'.[26]

Schools need to be assured that they operate with the strength of the community within and about them: that strength, in the last hundred years or so, has been in the vision, conviction and commitment of hundreds of pioneers in British civic life through the organ of local government. This strength cannot be replaced by the addition of two or three parents to the governing body of a school; you do not strengthen a community by replacing the altruism of constitutional democracy with that kind of anarchism that is the by-product of consumer choice. The devolution of power to schools and parents currently being implemented by a Conservative government with a majority of over a hundred in the House of Commons is not intended to enhance democratic localism or community power; it is a tactic used to continue the New Right's crusade of crippling the effectiveness of local government by diminishing its influence, heaping on it threats and penalties, and stripping it of powers, and in the process it consolidates control and power at the centre.

The scenario of a National Curriculum 5–16, National Testing at 7, 11, 14, and 16, control of teacher education programmes through the Council for Accreditation of Teacher Education (CATE), revenue and expenditure limitations on local authorities, these put into perspective the blandishment to the people in selling them a bogus prospectus, that parental power (in sharing the management of the community's school) and parental choice (giving parents the opportunity to bypass it!) will solve the problems the community has in encouraging children to learn.

References

1 Scruton, R. (1980) *The Meaning of Conservatism*, London, Penguin.
2 *Education Act 1944*, HMSO, London.
3 *Education Act 1944*, HMSO, London.
4 *Lancashire Evening Post*, 12 August 1987.
5 Hall, S. (1983) 'Education in crisis' in Wolpe, A.M. and Donald, J. (Eds) *Is There Anyone Here from Education?*, London, Pluto Press.
6 *The Omega File: Education Policy*, 1983–84, London, Adam Smith Institute.
7 Conservative Manifesto (1987) *The Next Moves Forward*, London, Conservative Central Office.
8 Musgrove, F. and Taylor, P.H. (1969) *Society and the Teacher's Role*, London, Routledge and Kegan Paul.

9 *Children and their Primary Schools: The Plowden Report* (1967) London, HMSO.
10 Department of Education and Science (1978) *Primary Education in England: A Survey by HM Inspectors of Schools*, London, HMSO.
11 Sallis, J. (1987) The National Curriculum Primary Questions. Report of National Primary Conference, Leamington Spa, Scholastic Publications Ltd.
12 *Ibid.*
13 National Union of Teachers (1983) *Home/School Relations*, London, NUT.
14 National Union of Teachers (1987) *Pupils, Teachers and Parents*, London, NUT.
15 *Ibid.*
16 Hargreaves, D. (1986) in Ranson, S. and Tomlinson, J. (Eds) *The Changing Government of Education*, London, Allen and Unwin.
17 *Ibid.*
18 Midwinter, E. (1975) *Education and the Community*, London, Allen and Unwin.
19 Densmore, K. (1987) in Popkewitz, T.S. (Ed) *Critical Studies in Teacher Education*, Lewes, Falmer Press.
20 Sarason, S.B. (1982) *The Culture of the School and the Problem of Change*, Boston, Allyn and Bacon Inc.
21 Nicholas, E.J. (1983) *Issues in Education: A Comparative Analysis*, London, Harper and Row.
22 Smith, B.C. (1985) *Decentralization: The Territorial Dimension of the State*, London, Allen and Unwin.
23 *Ibid.*
24 *Education*, Vol. 170, No. 6, 7 August 1987.
25 National Union of Teachers (1987) *Pupils, Teachers and Parents*, London, NUT.
26 Ree, H. (Ed) (1984) *The Henry Morris Collection*, Cambridge, Cambridge University Press.

Bibliography

Ahier, J. and Flude, M. (Ed) (1983) *Contemporary Education Policy*, London, Croom Helm.

Barrow, R. (1978) *Radical Education: A Critique of Freeschooling and Deschooling*, London, Martin Robertson.

Cave, R.G. (1970) *Partnership for Change: Parents and School*, London, Ward Lock International.

Conservative Party Manifesto (1987) *The Next Moves Forward*, London, Conservative Central Office.

Department of Education and Science (1978) *Primary Education in England: A Survey by H.M. Inspectors of Schools*, London, HMSO.

Department of Education and Science (1984) *Parental Influence at School*, London, HMSO.

Department of Education and Science (1987) *National Curriculum 5–16*

Draft Consultative Document, London, HMSO.
FREEMAN, D. (1983) *Choosing the Right School: A Parent's Guide*, London, Routledge and Kegan Paul.
HAIGH, G. (1975) *The School and the Parent*, London, Pitman Educational.
LAWRENCE, J. (1984) *How to Help Your Child Succeed at School: An Alphabet for Parents*. Shepton Mallett, England, Open Books.
LEVITAS, R. (Ed) (1986) *The Ideology of the New Right*, Cambridge, Polity Press.
MIDWINTER, E. (1975) *Education and the Community*, London, Allen and Unwin.
MUSGROVE, F. and TAYLOR, P.H. (1969) *Society and the Teacher's Role*, London, Routledge and Kegan Paul.
NATIONAL UNION OF TEACHERS (1978) *Partnership in Education: The NUT Commentary on the Taylor Report*, London, NUT.
NATIONAL UNION OF TEACHERS (1983) *Home/School Relations*, London, NUT.
NATIONAL UNION OF TEACHERS (1987) *Pupils, Teachers and Parents*, London, NUT.
NICHOLAS, E.J. (1983) *Issues in Education: A Comparative Analysis*, London, Harper and Row.
THE OMEGA FILE, (1985) *Education Policy*, London, Adam Smith Institute.
POPKEWITZ, T.S. (Ed.) (1987) *Critical Studies in Teacher Education: Its Folklore, Theory and Practice*, Lewes, Falmer Press.
RANSON, S. and TOMLINSON, J. (Ed) (1986) *The Changing Government of Education*, London, Allen and Unwin.
REE, H. (Ed) (1984) *The Henry Morris Collection*, Cambridge, Oxford University Press.
SARASON, S.B. (1982) *The Culture of the School and the Problem of Change*, Boston, Allyn and Bacon Inc.
SAUNDERS, P. (1980) *Urban Politics: A Sociological Interpretation*, Harmondsworth, Penguin.
SCRUTON, R. (1980) *The Meaning of Conservatism*, Harmondsworth, Penguin.
SMITH, B.C. (1985) *Decentralization: The Territorial Dimension of the State*, London, Allen and Unwin.
TAYLOR, B. (1983) *A Parent's Guide to Education*, London, Consumers Association.
WOLPE, A.M. and DONALD, J. (Eds) (1983) *Is There Anyone Here from Education?*, London, Pluto Press.
WRAGG, E.C. (1986) *Education: An Action Guide for Parents*, London, BBC Publications.

9 *Parents and the Left: Rethinking the Relationship*

David Reynolds

> He still conceives of the mass of men as persons who ought to be decently treated, not as persons who ought freely to organize their own life.
>
> (said of Sidney Webb, 1907)

The Rise of the Radical Right

Few educational policies have been so consistently advocated by right wing educationists in Britain as that of increased parental power. If we look back to the first flowerings of what is now labelled 'radical right' educational thinking as seen in the *Black Papers* of the early 1970s,[1] increased parental and consumer choice and increased parental power were both acknowledged as central policy planks in this pressure group's recommended programme of educational reconstruction. Politicians such as Sir Rhodes Boyson[2] and academics such as Antony Flew[3] consistently argued for 'consumer control' throughout the period of the 1970s and by the end of the decade after James Callaghan's 'Ruskin Speech' of 1976, it was clear that for both the Labour and Conservative parties, the increasing of parental rights and power was central to their educational policy.

Following on from the Taylor Report[4] of 1977, the Education Bill of 1979 which fell with the Labour government's election defeat in that same year would have introduced compulsory parental membership of governing bodies, a practice that was already becoming widespread with the co-option of parents' representatives onto secondary school governing bodies within many LEAs. The Conservative Education Act of 1980 of course went further than these proposals and gave parents rights to express a preference as to where their children were to be educated, rights that were to be enforced by an elaborate system of appeals to be administered by each LEA that was brought into play if the parents' wishes were not met.

These somewhat limited moves towards increasing parental power — moves which the Labour Party would certainly not have reversed had it won power in the 1983 election — were subsequently widely argued by the radical right to have been insufficiently radical.[5] By the early 1980s, the early numerically small group of right-wing educationists had been joined by a much larger number in 'think tanks' like the Centre for Policy Studies, the Social Affairs Unit, the National Council for Educational Standards, the Hillgate Group, Policy Research Associates, the Education Research Centre, and the Institute of Economic Affairs, all of whom argued (although with varying emphases) for massive and wholesale transfer of educational power to educational 'consumers' (i.e.parents) and away from educational 'producers' (i.e. the teachers, LEA administrators and members of what was regarded as an educational 'establishment' that had enjoyed excessive intellectual hegemony since the mid 1950s).

For members of these new pressure groups, such as Stuart Sexton, Roger Scruton, Denis O'Keefe, Caroline Cox, John Marks and Digby Anderson, there was to be an educational market in which parents would choose from a variety of competing schools. The 'quality control' that market-based educational policies would ensure would for these right-wing thinkers generate a large number of potential educational benefits:

(i) schools would be more accountable and their quality would improve since good schools would expand and poor schools contract in numbers;

(ii) schools which had moved towards an emphasis upon a more progressive curriculum orientation would be held back by parental control to a more traditional curriculum pattern, without the peace studies, gay rights studies, anti-racism initiatives and anti-sexism orientation that seemed to the Right to be highly prevalent within certain educational authorities like the ILEA;

(iii) schools would also become more relevant to today's contemporary societies, with parental power ensuring that a more vocational orientation pervaded schools in terms both of the content of the curriculum and the increased orientation of pupils towards destinations in industry and commerce;

(iv) increased parental power would lead to a by-passing of the local education authorities, since schools would be in a market where they had to respond to parental, not bureaucratic, wishes.

It would, though, be an important error to over-emphasize the degree of ideological homogeneity amongst the various right wing thinkers concerning the precise forms of education that they would have wanted. Using the labels of the 'old humanists' and of 'the industrial trainers' widely employed in writing on this area,[6] it is clear that different groups and individuals have had widely different policy concerns and ideal practices. The old humanists have seen schools as too 'progressive' in their new modular curriculum orientation for example, yet the industrial trainers have welcomed this further breakdown of subject barriers and an increased concentration upon novel 'skills-based' education instead of 'knowledge-based' education. The old humanists may well have wanted a much greater level of state control to protect and preserve aspects of the traditional, academic and bourgeois curriculum than the industrial trainers, who shared a greater commitment to the market forces or consumer choice that may have damaged the status of subjects close to the hearts of the old humanists.[7]

What *have* united the different radical right groupings, though, are two factors — their reactive agreement on the defects of the old liberal and 'producer-led' policies on education of the 1950s and 1960s, and their linked common agreement in certain key areas such as their shared enthusiasm for parental power. Both groups saw the old educational system as reflecting producer interests in its concern to increase the personnel and resource inputs into the system at the same time as it retained for itself any monitoring and evaluation capacity necessary for quality control. Teachers and Headteachers were regarded by both right-wing groups as out of control, unaccountable, and as uninvolved in the kinds of self-monitoring procedures common to other professions.

Parental power exercised through a right to choose their children's schools would improve the quality of educational institutions by forcing schools of poor quality (as judged by parents) to either improve or simply die as their pupil numbers transferred elsewhere. Although, then, the commitment to parental power may have been a genuine one, it seems likely that the attraction of the policy has also been that it is an ideological device for uniting potentially disparate policies and groups. Although 'old humanists', 'industrial trainers' and 'radical right populists' may have fundamental policy disagreements between themselves on issues like the form of the curriculum or the necessity of central government power, all could unite in distrust of teachers and other educational producers and all could unite in agreement with increased parental consumer power.

Legislating for Parental Power

Because of the ways in which terms like parent power were subsequently sloganized and overused in the political sphere by the Prime Minister, Mrs Thatcher, by the Conservative party in the 1987 election campaign and by Kenneth Baker, the Minister for Education and Science in many public statements during and since the 1987 election, policies have been encouraged which have gone much further than those more modest increases in parental power adopted in the 1980[8] and 1986[9] Education Acts.

The new Education Act 1988[10] and associated educational policies aim to change fundamentally the balance of power in the educational system. They are to:

(i) increase the variety of choices of school in the educational market by further expansion of the Assisted Places scheme, the setting up of twenty city technical colleges and the encouragement of schools to 'opt out' of direct LEA control;
(ii) increase the amount of information available to consumers in the exercise of their choice by the publication of various forms of assessment data on the progress in basic subjects of individual pupils and of schools;
(iii) improve school quality and encourage the growth of high performing schools by removing the limits on their pupil enrolment that had been set by some LEAs.[11]

Transferring power to parents away from the local or national 'state' has one further latent function other than acting as a mechanism of quality control — it also makes more pragmatically possible the increased privatization of the financing of the educational service. Early attempts to privatize certain school services like cleaning and catering have been followed by more far-reaching and fundamental privatization as in the recent permission given to schools to charge for individual music tuition and extra sports tuition in areas such as swimming. Although this is not an expressed or overt reason ever given for parental power, many have quite sensibly argued that the policy encourages parents to bear an increased share of the cost of the service. The attempt by the state to unburden itself of financial responsibiity at a time of mounting financial stringency is to be aided by transferring power *and* subsequently greatly increased financial responsibility jointly to parents and schools.[12]

It is important to realize, however, that the rhetoric of increased parental power sits uneasily with the many other activities of the government that have involved centralizing tendencies. Although parents have a choice of school, all schools will be required by central government first to have a core set of national curriculum subjects. Furthermore, the *criteria* of parental choice are centrally determined, since parents only have information upon a very restricted range of academic criteria about each individual school. Also, the actual curriculum *content* within the new GCSE examination has been drawn up to meet nationally agreed criteria influenced by central government wishes. Since the *goals* of the educational process have become even more clearly defined by central government, parents now have only the freedom to determine the *means* to reach these predetermined goals. Paradoxically, there may well have been more scope for parental power when the educational system was more autonomous, as in the 1970s for example, than at the present time when parental power is in any event said to be markedly increasing.[13]

Furthermore, it is not difficult to discern the links between the recent Conservative policies on parental power and their broader economic and social philosophy in general. Through increasing parental power, individuals will do more for the education of their children, as individuals will in all areas where the state is withdrawing its support. Individual parental financial provision — as in the Assisted Places scheme — is to be encouraged. Differentiation between institutions in the educational system is paralleled by the same differentiation and choice in other welfare areas, all apparently to reduce the possibility of dull uniformity but all in reality offering increasingly differentiated quality. Educational experience is no longer to be made more uniform for children from different social groups or academic categories; it is to be differentiated into experiences that convey highly differentiated status, life chances and rewards, as is the aim of policy in the economic sphere of society.[14]

It is also not a difficult task to work out the likely effects of the range of government policies that have increased parental power. Historically, educational policies have systematically sought to *reduce* the impact of parents upon the life chances of their children — the driving force behind the introduction of schools lay in the fact that society was becoming so advanced in its knowledge base that many parents themselves could not communicate that knowledge successfully to their children. Equality of opportunity, 'a fair chance in life' or 'equal life chances' were all policies based on breaking the link between social class background and that of occupational destination by ensuring that schools actually *replaced* parental influence on their children.

Policies that will now allow parents to choose from a range of differentiated school provision clearly maximize inequalities that the educational system has historically been concerned to minimize. Financial capital is unequally distributed among parents, which permits some to purchase a higher quality independent school education or a higher quality state school experience for their children. Cultural capital, the knowledge of which schools are 'good', and the ability and professional contacts to manipulate and 'play' the educational system to their children's advantage are also possessed more by some parents than by others. If parents have uniformly increased power but are differentially able to exercise that power to enhance their children's life chances, the results of the exercise of parental power will be to change the educational system from one which sought to liberate children from their parents' social class by restraining the influence of their parents into one which confirms children within their parental social class by maximizing their parents' influence.

Lame Labourism

Any survey of responses from the Labour party and from the educational left to the increasing dominance by the educational right of the national discourse within which educational policy generally is deliberated makes depressing reading. In part, the arguments of the educational right have been allowed to flourish because of the manifest 'inefficacy of remedy' that was shown by those educational policies that had been attempted in the 1960s and into the mid 1970s.[15] Expenditure on education was greatly increased as a proportion of Gross National Product (GNP), yet overall academic and social outcomes from educational systems remained disappointing to many commentators in both industrialized and Third World countries.[16] The length of time spent at school was also increased by the raising of the school leaving age and produced a chorus of disappointed hopes. Curriculum projects like those in Nuffield science and mathematics had a very disappointing initial take-up and disappointing effects upon children's academic development once they were adopted.[17] The use of educational technology as in the introduction of language laboratories into the primary school also generated unfulfilled expectations.[18] In virtually all educational policy areas, the collapse of the educational dream of the 1960s led to a lack of self-confidence, an inability to answer right-wing criticism and a damaging intellectual paralysis on the part of the educationists who had originally backed the reforms. It was not just the various individual policies that failed to deliver the radical faith, what crashed in these programmes of educational reform was also an entire ideological world-view about the relative power to be afforded to the educational *producers* in the system and the relative lack of power to be held by the *consumers* of the educational system. Put simply, what crashed in the 1970s was the belief that professional educationists and the persons within the system itself could still deliver the hoped for educational goals without the need for either state or parental accountability.

The view that the system should to a high degree control itself and that parents should have little power as consumers is a product of two primary elements of the left's commitment *to* educational professionals having power for a variety of reasons and of the left's commitment *against* giving power to groups of parents. To look at the former factor first, it does not need exceptional perception to note the close correspondence between Labour party policy on education and the needs and desires of educational producers in the teacher unions over the last thirty years.[19]

In most accounts, the teacher unions in particular and teachers in general have for a long time sought to free themselves from the strong state control typified by the payment by results codes of the late nineteenth century. The desire for greater autonomy and self-determination in the key areas of curriculum and assessment received a further boost with the abolition of the 11+, abolition that was to make possible the development of a wide variety of new curricula in primary schooling. So great was teacher desire to retain control of the 'secret garden' of the curriculum that on the Schools Council, the body involved in the promotion of curriculum reform and development in the 1960s and 1970s, teachers' representatives had what most commentators have labelled as a right of veto over developments of which they disapproved.[20]

Because of the influence of the National Union of Teachers on policy-making, the policies on education offered by the Labour Party in the 1960s, 1970s and up to the 1987 General Election campaign were therefore heavily resource based, involving in 1987 for example commitments to universal nursery education, smaller class sizes, maintenance allowances for pupils aged 16–19, greater spending on books and equipment, more in-service provision and other resource and personnel inputs.[21] All these policies would of course have directly benefited teachers; the professionals who have — directly through membership of the National Union of Teachers and indirectly through local party membership — had influence within the Labour party. Policy was about increasing inputs into the system, not about increased professional accountability nor increased parental or State control of the quality of the processes and the outcomes of the system.

In addition to policies which reflected a commitment *to* professionals within the educational service, there has been a historical desire within the Labour party to *decrease* parental influence over children in the interests of achieving such goals as equality of opportunity. The influences which moulded this desire seem to be as follows:

(i) a belief in child-centred education and in the goodness of the child came from the progressive education movement who saw parents as potentially perverting influences upon children's development. Schools were therefore to set children *free* from parental wishes, not collaborate in children's enslavement;[22]

(ii) a belief that family and parental factors caused problems like delinquency, truancy and low academic achievement was often evident in Labour policy thinking. The wide variety of studies conducted within a socio-psychological paradigm led to a view that schools could compensate for the influence of the family and that the school should be virtually *in loco parentis*, replacing the influence of families that were feckless and communities that were simply seas of social problems;[23]

(iii) in certain areas where the dominance of Labour's ideology was strongest, the school's mission was seen as only attainable by completely cutting off of the child from *any* residual family influence. Jackson and Marsden's[24] unhappy experience at their grammar school as it tried to eradicate the dress, speech, values and cultural styles of their background, together with the Welsh grammar schools that would only allow an English speaking school environment in completely Welsh speaking areas,[25] are but two practical examples of the results of a philosophy which saw the chances of social advancement of poorer children as consequential upon a virtual eradication of the influence of their parents and their communities. Although the price paid for social mobility may have been an individual's isolation from his or her community — and therefore ultimately an individual's alienation from himself or herself — this was a price which, for the Labour Party, had to be paid to give individuals the chance of upward mobility in the class system;

(iv) a belief also existed that parental power should be reduced because substantial inequalities between children would result if parents exercised that power. Many on the left opposed independent schools because parents could purchase advantage for their children by means of it.[26] Many saw middle class parents — with their professional contacts and knowledge about the system — as able to manipulate the state educational system if they were given the opportunity of doing this by their direct involvement in educational decision making. Keeping power from parents was therefore entirely compatible with the socialist objective of increasing equality of opportunity for children from more disadvantaged homes.

The faith in educational producers that we have noted above, together with the desire to reduce the influence of the family upon children in the causes of greater equality of opportunity or lower rates of pupil low achievement, delinquency and truancy, merged with a third factor in generating a left-wing ideology which gave parents little power over salient aspects of the education of their children. This third factor was the dominance within Labour's thinking of the philosophy of Fabianism, in which social advance was seen as coming not from the ordinary members of society and their efforts, but primarily from elite groups who were to impose excellence on people, if necessary, in spite of the expressed wishes of people themselves.[27]

There is not the space here for a detailed historical analysis of the reasons why the ideology of the Labour Party has in the past owed so much to that of the Fabians, and in particular to Sidney and Beatrice Webb. Simply, Fabianism was named after the Roman General, Fabius Cunctator — a general who apparently was never defeated in battle but who also in fact never had a clear victory either! Instead of the philosophy of the Independent Labour Party with its emphasis upon community control, democratic welfare arrangements and political leaders who were also 'followers' of democratically agreed policies, the Labour party when founded in 1918 approved a document entitled *Labour and the New Social Order* which rejected socialism in favour of Fabianism. This new ideology saw socialism as close to do-gooding, since the Fabians envisaged a society with a strong degree of central, bureaucratic control to impose elite determined good by means of professionalized welfare. At heart, the Fabians' leaders were bureaucrats, not democrats — one authority once described Fabianism rather neatly as the ideology of the diploma holding classes. Another said of the Webbs that they believed all that was necessary for human progress were good intentions and a sound filing system![28]

Out of the dominance of Fabianism on Labour Party thinking came a distinctive world view about the organization of State Welfare that was typified by the Labour programme of the 1960s and 1970s. Town planning professionals generated major changes to patterns of working class communities through programmes of urban renewal. The National Health Service was reorganized in ways that reinforced the pre-eminence of the professional power of doctors and dentists. Crucially for our purposes here, the education service was expanded and reorganized as part of the Fabian enterprise. Numbers of professionals were increased. Administrative reorganization, based upon the best empirical evidence collected by educationists like Halsey, Burgess and Young, led to comprehensive reorganization and to other programmes of reform. The Fabian ideology whereby professionals did 'good' to people in ways which they decided blended with the Labour government's commitment to teachers and further blended with Labour's distrust of parental influence to generate the conditions for social engineering that was to prove so disappointing and which was to provide the radical right with its chance of intellectual hegemony.[29]

Labour Isn't Learning

It will be clear from the section above that the range of policies formerly espoused by Labour are not notable for their concern with increasing the accountability of the system either to the state or locally to parents as consumers of education. In spite of the recent Labour Party's additions to its policy of a proposed General Teaching Council to increase professional accountability, education advice centres and school opinion surveys of parents, its policy would, if implemented, represent only a marginal accretion of power to parents.[30]

Accepting that socialist educational goals involve encouraging the development in children of educational *and* social capacities, together with as great an equality of opportunity as possible in both educational and social achievement, it would seem highly unlikely that the range of policies outlined by Labour either in the past or now would realize such goals. The policies continue to emphasize the social and material determinants of learning, together with the need for organizational improvements, and such structural reform as the abolition of selection, yet the precise ways in which *schools* are to improve their internal organizational quality are still very unclear. The policy leverage upon the system is to be the same mixture of slight legislative pressure and very modest increases in parental power, yet there is no evidence that this leverage could improve the nature of internal processes of schools any more than in the past.[31] Although the teaching profession is to be better paid, appraised formatively, better trained, involved more in school management and subject to the oversight of a professional watchdog, the General Teaching Council,[32] it is doubtful if these initiatives will be enough to ensure internal school processes that advance the realization of socialist educational goals. School quality — simply — is highly unlikely to be affected by these policies, since the policies are sociologically and educationally naive in the assumption that *formal* legislative organizational change will necessarily lead to transformations and improvements in the quality of the processes of schooling or in the *informal* world of the school.[33]

The Tory government has of course direct market-based solutions to the problem of school quality that are a combination of parental power and parental choice which, by using market forces, will eradicate 'poor' schools. The variability in the quality of schools since comprehensivization has probably greatly increased, since selection by ability probably generated more homogeneous social class groupings in different schools than does the current selection by catchment area.

Conservative educational policy traded on the widespread public perception that many schools existed that 'weren't working' (to use their 1979 election slogan) and that there was large variability in quality. It seems that their educational policies may well have been particularly popular amongst the skilled working class, since it was this group that was frequently finding its able children in comprehensive schools with disadvantaged catchment areas and since it was this group that may well have accurately perceived that their children might, under a market-based choice system, have been able to attend better quality comprehensive schools. Until Labour can generate a home market-based solution to deal with the issue of school quality, it seems highly likely that the Conservatives' market-based remedies will enable them to be identified as the Party concerned with educational standards. The intellectual hegemony of the right will continue as long as Labour appears to be unable to deal with low quality schooling.

Towards New Socialist Educational Policies

The discussion above indicates that it will be a hard task to counter the dominance in educational discourse that the radical right has succeeded in attaining. Concern about school excellence and quality — once an issue on which socialists had such clear policies as comprehensivization — has been allowed to become an issue exploited by the right, whilst the old policies of the left on this issue have not been radically rethought as their deficiencies have been exposed. Distrust of parental power, the elitist 'top–down' philosophy of Fabianism and a reluctance to abandon union-linked producer-led policies are all responsible for this state of affairs.

Socialist thinking about education has, of course, very different goals from those of the radical right and to generate sets of policies that stand a chance of success in socialist terms whilst also being able to wrest control of national educational discourse from the radical right is a very difficult task. Thatcherism has been able to exploit a strong historical British tradition of dislike of state bureaucracy and portray itself as a populist creed that sets people free to determine their own economic, social and educational lives. The problem for socialist thinkers about education is to make the notion of parental rights in education and the concommitant respect for the educational rights of others as politically attractive as the Thatcherite notion of making individual parental rights in education *independent* of their potential damaging effect upon the educational rights of others.

The following policy planks would seem to be necessary for an effective socialist policy:

(i) individual children have a right of access to high quality education, but that right must not be exercised to the detriment of other children's rights to the same. As far as possible, then, all children would attend common schools, the catchment areas of which should generate the balanced pupil intake that the social and academic development of the children requires;

(ii) schools should be accountable to parents *legally*, with all children entitled to the same statement of their educational and social needs and of the school's response to these needs that children with special educational needs are currently legally entitled to. The curriculum and organization of the school to meet each child's needs are, then, legally prescribed and schools can be prosecuted by parents for failure to meet their legislative commitments;

(iii) legislative parental rights to an education of defined standard would be supplemented by legislation on equal opportunities, racial discrimination and special educational needs to ensure that the exercise of parental rights by certain categories of parents does not adversely affect other groups of children;

(iv) because of the increased pressure on schools to ensure the availability of high quality education to all, major resources and supporting initiatives would need to be targeted at the schools and the teaching profession, probably using local education authorities or smaller educational districts as the facilitators;

(v) to ensure that legislation is followed in practice in the schools even though parents may not take up their rights, certain supra-school bodies such as the LEAs or specially created educational districts would need to exercise a monitoring role to ensure that schools met national standards. While in the long term it is to be hoped that this type of outside school involvement might 'wither away' as parents begin to take up their power, in the short to medium term it would undoubtedly be necessary to ensure the accountability of the system to legislative principles and to ensure that parental power was not being exercised to the detriment of some children;

(vi) it is important to add that collectivities of parents as organized in the community should have rights and responsibilities in relation to the educational system that are separate from but additional to those possessed by their individual members. Socialists have always seen that communities are more than the sum of their parts and have a need for a position midway between the citizen and the State, but the precise way in which community rights and powers would overlap with individual parental rights is an area that will repay further attention.

This view of a future socialist policy in education accepts that the radical right has succeeded in changing the entire basis for discussion and analysis of educational issues in Britain. Consumer-led educational policies are clearly so popular that a return to producer-led policy is both politically impracticable as well as unsound. Socialists must accept that increased democratization of educational decision-making is a genuine political commitment linked to a more democratic society, and socialists must, therefore, go on to assert the importance of substantially increased parental power rather than make an attempt to reduce it. Arguably these proposals will lead to a substantial improvement in school quality, an improvement not achieved in the past.

There are probably at least two areas in the policy recommended that educationists may cavil at. Firstly, giving parents defined rights to a high quality educational experience for their children may advantage those parents (probably of able, white, middle-class pupils) who actually use their legal power. This is why it is important that there are 'end stop' policies in favour of children who are disadvantaged by race, sex and ability level that would prevent or at least ameliorate their disadvantaged state and prevent it worsening. Secondly, the proposed policies would undoubtedly put immense pressure upon teachers and would reduce their professional autonomy even more than the measures on parental power exercised through the market-based policies that have been introduced by the Conservative government. It would seem that there is no alternative to the reduction of teacher professional autonomy if the goals of a socialist educational policy are to be achieved, especially in the absence of any evidence that the profession itself is capable of delivering them.

In conclusion, it can be seen that any socialist educational policy has to be one which underwrites individual parental power, but is also concerned with restraint on that power. It is about both parental *and* local state enforcement of the quality of education in schools. It is about 'squeezing' schools by using state legislation from the top and giving local accountability to consumers at the bottom, yet is also about a wide range of enabling, supportive initiatives that will help schools move towards greater professionalism and higher standards. It extends Conservative policy on parent power by taking that power into the very heart of schooling, yet the above programme also constrains parent power in ways not proposed in current legislation. It is put forward as a programme that may be educationally effective in generating a better quality of schooling, be politically popular and may begin, when further developed and articulated, to start the process of restoring the link between democratic parental rights and educational quality to the central place that it originally held in early twentieth century socialist educational thinking.

Notes

1 Cox, C.B. and Dyson, A.E. (Eds) (1969, 1970 and 1975) *Black Paper 1, Black Paper 2 and Black Paper 3*, London, Critical Quarterly Society.
2 Boyson, R. (1974) *Oversubscribed*, London, Ward Lock.
3 Flew, A.G.N. (1976) *Sociology, Equality and Education*, London, Macmillan.
4 *Taylor Report* (1977) *A New Partnership for our Schools*, London, HMSO.
5 Examples of writings in this genre are Anderson, D. (1981) *The Pied Pipers of Education*, London, Social Affairs Unit; Cox, C. (Ed) (1986) *Whose Schools? A Radical Manifesto*, London, Hillgate Group; O'Keeffe, D. (Ed) (1986) *The Wayward Curriculum*, London, Social Affairs Unit; Scruton, R., Ellis-Jones, A. and O'Keeffe, D. (1985) *Education and Indoctrination*, London, Education Research Centre.
6 Dale, R. (1983) 'Thatcherism and education' in Ahier, J. and Flude, M. (Eds) *Contemporary Education Policy*, London, Croom Helm.
7 These themes are further developed in Ball, S. (1987) *Comprehensive Schooling Effectiveness and Control: An Analysis of Educational Discourses.* Unpublished mss, Kings College, London.
8 HM Government (1980) *Education Act*, London, HMSO.
9 HM Government (1986) *Education Act*, London, HMSO.
10 HM Government (1988) *Education Reform Act*, London, HMSO.
11 Fuller details and analysis of policy changes are to be found in Simon, B. (1988) *Bending the Rules*, London, Lawrence and Wishart; Hargreaves, A. and Reynolds, D. (Eds) (1988) *Education Policies:*

Controversies and Critiques, Lewes, Falmer Press; REYNOLDS, D. (1988) 'Changing comprehensive schools' in *Children and Society*, Spring, pp. 68–77; QUICKE, J. (1988) 'The new right and education' in *British Journal of Educational Studies*, Vol. 36, No. 1, pp. 5–20.

12 Further elaboration of this theme is to be found in HARGREAVES, A. and REYNOLDS, D. (1988) 'Decomprehensivization' in HARGREAVES, A. and REYNOLDS, D. (Eds), *op. cit.* and in OFFE, C. (1984) *Contradictions of the Welfare State*, London, Hutchinson.

13 See REYNOLDS, D. (1984) 'Relative autonomy reconstructed' in BARTON, L. and WALKER, S. (Eds) *Social Crisis and Educational Research*, London, Croom Helm.

14 See Simon, B. (1988) *op. cit.* and Hargreaves and Reynolds (1988), *op. cit.* for further elaboration on this theme.

15 Empirical evidence on this theme is summarised in RUTTER, M. and MADGE, N. (1976), *Cycles of Disadvantage*, London, Heinemann.

16 See REYNOLDS, D. (1982) 'The search for effective schools' in *School Organization*, Vol. 2, No. 3, pp. 215–237.

17 See KELLY, P. (1980) 'From innovation to adaptability — the changing perspective of curriculum development' in GALTON, M. (Ed) *Curriculum Change*, Leicester, Leicester University Press.

18 See BURSTALL, C. (1970) 'French in the primary school: some early findings' in *Journal of Curriculum Studies* Vol. 2, No. 1, pp. 48–58.

19 Details are to be found in LODGE, P. and BLACKSTONE, T. (1982) *Educational Policy and Educational Inequality*, Oxford, Martin Robertson.

20 See FINN, D. *et al* (1977) 'Social democracy, education and the crisis' in *On Ideology: Working Papers in Cultural Studies 10*, Birmingham, Centre for Contemporary Cultural Studies.

21 See RADICE, G. (1987) *Equality and Quality* (Fabian Tract 514), London, Fabian Society, and Labour Party (1987) *Labour's Charter for Pupils and Parents*, London, The Labour Party.

22 This belief of the progressive movement underlay much of the enthusiasm for less structured primary schooling and is reflected in the Plowden Report (1967) *Children and their Primary Schools*, London, HMSO.

23 See examples of this in the voluminous literature on the relationship between family background and juvenile delinquency reviewed in CLARKE, A. (1980) 'Social democratic delinquents and Fabian families' in NATIONAL DEVIANCY CONFERENCE, *Permissiveness and Control*, London, Macmillan.

24 JACKSON, B. AND MARSDEN, D. (1962) *Education and the Working Class*, London, Routledge and Kegan Paul.

25 THOMAS, N. (1967) *The Welsh Extremist*, Llandybie, Christopher Davies.

26 As expressed by many speakers in the composite motion moved by the Socialist Education Association at Annual Conference in 1986 (*The Guardian*, 20 September).

27 Fuller analyses can be found in HOBSBAWM, E.J. (1976) 'The Fabians reconsidered' in HOBSBAWM, E.J. (Ed) *Labouring Men*, London, Weidenfeld and Nicolson, and in SAVILLE, J. (1967) 'Labourism and the Labour government' in MILIBAND, R. and SAVILLE, J., *The Socialist Register, 1967*, London, Merlin Press.

28 Quoted in WILDING, P. (1982) *Professional Power and Social Welfare*, London, Routledge and Kegan Paul.
29 For contemporary treatments of this theme see WILBY, P. (1977) 'The educational gods that failed' in *New Society*, 22 September.
30 As outlined in *Parents and Partnership*, The Labour Party, May 1988.
31 See REYNOLDS, D., SULLIVAN, M. and MURGATROYD, S. (1987) *The Comprehensive Experiment*, Lewes, Falmer Press.
32 See note 26 above.
33 See REYNOLDS, D. (1988) 'Better schools?' in HARGREAVES, A. and REYNOLDS, D. (Eds) (1988) *op. cit.* for further elaboration of this theme.

10 *Community Education and Parent Involvement: a Partnership in Need of a Theory*

Joyce S. Watt

Introduction

Any comprehensive analysis of parent involvement in schooling must examine the role of community education. As its starting point, this chapter suggests that community education in the 1980s still lacks coherent theory and that this is one of the reasons why, despite its obvious success in individual projects and programmes, community education has failed to make a major impact on schools, even community schools.

Community education and schooling have tended to develop in parallel rather than within an integrated planned relationship and the result has been that the major processes of schooling, including parent involvement, have remained largely apart from the influence which community education might have brought to bear on them. For those who believe in what community education has to offer, that must be a matter for regret. Looking to the theme of the present volume, it is a matter of particular regret that community education has not been able to develop within schools a climate of cooperation, expertise and experience in parent involvement capable of dealing with recent government legislation on school management.

Perhaps we have looked for too much too quickly. Community education is still relatively new and its relative failure to effect change in schools has also to be explained, at least in part, against the traditionalism and conservatism of schools themselves. This chapter, however, is about community education. It offers no easy answers, only a brief exploration of some of the concepts likely to be involved if community education is ever to have a major influence on our schools.

The Need for Theory

There is a measure of predictability in the writing of those who have tackled the field of community education from an academic standpoint over the last twenty years. Almost invariably they will start with the search for definitions and conceptual clarity and, not surprisingly, will conclude for 'community education' as Peters[1] did for 'education' itself, that the idea is so complex and dynamic that it defies any attempt to limit it by definitional boundaries. I do not propose in a brief paper to repeat the weary argument from Hillery's[2] identification of ninety-four definitions of 'community' to the present debate: I confine myself to the oft repeated but ever-contemporary conclusion that community education is a concept 'particularly rich in anomalies and contradictions'.[3]

Lack of definition in itself may be no great weakness: what is a fundamental problem is the lack of coherent theories of community education out of which some consistency of purpose and approach, however temporary, may be derived. The practitioners' impatience with esoteric theory may well be understandable in a field rife with the practical issues of social and educational inequality but, in the end, if its theory is neglected, community education as a movement will suffer badly. Looking at community education as it had developed to the late 1970s Batten deplored the fact that 'community education projects are at best piecemeal and pragmatic responses to externally defined local problems'.[4] And Martin, surveying the contemporary scene, seems to see little progress. Community education, as he views it, is 'unreflective pragmatism'.[5]

Pragmatism may provide short-term answers to specific problems: it is unlikely to further the long-term cause of community education particularly if it allows the movement, by default, to be blown by the winds of expediency or mere fashion. The dangers have been evident for some time. The use of the word 'community' itself has given a spurious legitimacy to widely varying concepts: 'community care' and 'community orders' are obvious examples and most recently we have had the 'community charge' the controversial replacement for local rates which a far from naive electorate immediately dubbed the 'poll tax'. 'Community' as Cowburn asserts can be one of the most potent legitimation symbols of our time.[6] 'Community education', on the same argument, can also be used to deflect public concern over the resources available to education. Self-help groups and voluntary effort, educationally totally worthwhile in their own right, can too often be seen as cheap alternatives to governments intent on reducing public expenditure. On a cynical but perhaps realistic view of the late 1980s, community education may even be 'a euphemism for cost-cutting'.[7]

For community education as a whole, the greatest danger may lie in it becoming directed mainly towards one particular section of the population and, even worse, becoming entrenched in one particular ideological stance in its work with that group. The obvious example is the identification of community work with disadvantaged inner city areas. Fletcher regretted what he saw as the over-identification of community education with these areas and the people who lived there:

> community education is all too rapidly becoming a type of education appropriate to a type of people as distinct from 'derived from a theory' and so a full educational perspective.[8]

Some have been loudly critical of its lack of radicalism in inner cities, but others have recognized that community education has probably been supported to the extent that it has taken a reformist stance and tried to being social groups together to give life to social democracy. O'Hagan, however, argues that the assumptions behind this reformist model need to be challenged, that the aims of community education in inner cities are not necessarily to re-establish cohesion within a disintegrating society nor necessarily to minimize interpersonal conflict.[9] Cowburn from his more radical perspective dismisses community education on the reformist model as simply 'a palliative for inner city decay'.[10]

What we seem to have then, is a movement which, in general terms, is reactive to particular circumstances rather than pro-active according to an identifiable theory of community education. It is linked (legitimately or otherwise) in the public mind with disadvantaged groups and areas, but even there its aims and purposes are in dispute.

While sheer pragmatism may be regrettable, the lack of consensus on aims and purposes is inevitable. It is as naive to expect that there should be one theory of community education as it is to assume that there should be one theory of education operating in schools.

O'Hagan in a recent analysis[11] has shown that not only do different models of community education have different aims, their ideological stances make them mutually exclusive.

What matters, then, is not that there should be consensus in community education but that practice should be understandable within an identifiable theoretical framework and that that framework can, if necessary, be made explicit. How then does this relate to community education in schools?

Community Education and Schools

Principles of Community Schooling

Community education, of course, transcends schools, but a community education process which bypasses schools is inconceivable: they are 'a necessary rather than a sufficient reason for community education'.[12] Indeed in practical terms, Cowburn, in the English context, claims that 'most of community education's metaphorical eggs have been placed in the baskets of community schools'.[13]

The idea of the community school has, of course, been a major educational theme since the 1970s. In Scotland, as elsewhere, policy-makers argued that the idea was not to be identified solely with those few purpose-built 'designated' schools which could boast special facilities:

> The implementation of practical schemes linking school and community — any school and any community — is what the Scottish Council for Community Education has in mind in encouraging the development of the community school principle in Scotland . . . To single out certain schools for whatever reason, particularly if they were favoured in the allocation of resources, would imply the coexistence of inferior non-community schools.[14]

Community education rather was to be exemplified by a process based on a pervasive set of principles which would redefine the relationship between communities and schools:

> Community education is a process of commitment to the education and leisure of all ages through local participation in setting priorities, sharing resources and the study of circumstances. Thus, the community and its educational

> provision qualify and enhance each other.[15]

In that sense then, certainly any school could be a community school.

What then is community education in a community school? Is there a theoretical model? Certainly there appears to be no blueprint. As Rennie argues in the context of community primary schools, and other writers have echoed for secondary schools:

> Nobody would wish to see community primary schools conforming to any set pattern. Such an idea is inimical to the whole concept of community education . . . above all they will differ according to the very communities they serve.[16]

But is this not coming close to the pragmatism of community education generally which contemporary writers reject? The answer for some lies in the search for common principles or objectives which would exemplify community education in community schools, a search which for some at least has not yet been successful. Rennie, for example, while arguing the case for diversity equally acknowledged that there is a widespread need to clarify the objectives of community schools.[17]

Many writers on community schools have in fact attempted to identify these principles. Watts,[18] for example, in his analysis of the 'open school' identifies five principles of community education out of which the open school could develop. These are: shared facilities between school and community; learning based on the local area; freedom from the institutional base; shared management; and user control. At around the same time we ourselves in a study of community schools in the Grampian Region of Scotland identified six principles which seemed to underpin their practice. These were: mutually supportive relationships between school and community; shared facilities; a community-oriented curriculum; lifelong education; community involvement in decision-making and management of schools; and community development.[19] More recently Martin has identified six principles of community education in schools: the comprehensive ideal based on public ownership; open access and use; a proactive programme; a partnership which does not accept the need for professional control; a dynamic questioning approach to the curriculum; empowerment — the sharing of power.[20]

The lists (and there are many other similar lists) have common elements although they also differ significantly. Does this mean then that a common theory of community education in schools is emerging? It is my argument that it does not: that while common principles may be emerging, these principles are capable of very different (sometimes opposing) interpretations in action simply because they have not been derived from any coherent theory of community education in schools. We return to our study of community schools in the Grampian Region.

Like many others in the 1970s, the Region's education committee was inspired by the notion of the community school. The vision of breaking down the barriers between school and community seemed exciting and challenging, a new revolution in schooling. The number of purpose-built community schools was small, but the spirit of the community school it was argued, and as we have seen above, was not dependent on bricks and mortar; any school could be a community school.

So far the story is a familiar one. What may not be so familiar, however, is the story of the management structure of Grampian's designated community schools. In Scotland, community education is a service entirely separate from the teaching profession. It has its own training (based in colleges of education but largely quite separate from teacher-training) and its own career structure; only a very small proportion of community education staff are based in schools. In the 1970s a decision was taken by Grampian Region's education committee that purpose-built community schools should have a dual management structure which would place responsibility for the management of these schools jointly with headteachers and senior community education staff. It is a system unique in Scotland; Lothian, the only other Region which has developed the community school idea on any scale has always retained a single management structure under the headteacher.

It was a major if not surprising finding of our research study[21] that in the late 1970s Grampian's community schools lacked a sense of purpose and direction; worse, because of their dual management structure they were often torn in two different sometimes opposing directions. It is dangerous to polarize the two viewpoints and certainly misleading to identify them wholly with the two different professional groups: nevertheless there was a discernible trend for the two groups to interpret the 'principles' of community education in schools quite differently. There was agreement on the principles as such — the sharing of facilities, a community oriented curriculum, life-long education, etc; it was in the interpretation of these principles that the clear differences emerged. The examples were legion: the 'sharing of facilities' on one interpretation meant that the community could use the 'school' premises when they were not required by school students as long as 'school' standards and expectations were upheld; on the other model, community groups had the right to negotiate on equal terms with school groups for the use of premises and to negotiate their own rules. 'Lifelong education' similarly was interpreted on one model largely as access to school classes and to adult education groups; on the alternative model it included the negotiation of learning and teaching and of the curriculum itself in both formal classes and informal community-based groups. The same differences of interpretation were there if one examined the other principles — decision-making, community development, etc in action. One interpretation of community education was that it was a process of slow evolutionary change through consensus and based largely on professional norms; the other was more radical, based on the assumption that change would be effective only if the basis of control in education changed, however slightly, and if traditional authorities were challenged.

It has to be said, of course, that neither interpretation is radical in any fundamental sense. According to Cowburn[22] who takes the perspective of the radical left, it is its lack of radicalism which has been the inherent failure of community education generally. It is a criticism of community education we have already noted in relation to inner city areas. 'Educational change' Cowburn argues, 'is primarily the result of class struggle in the educational arena';[23] community education, by denying the centrality of class conflict preserves the most crucial social and economic relationships and is thus largely irrelevant. 'Its message tells us that conflict is pathological and harmony the norm.'[24] For Cowburn, community education has become 'the new decoration of schools'.[25] Its paradox, he asserts, is that it claims to want to change schools but does not challenge the nature of teacher professionalism.

However, although community education in schools may not be radical in Cowburn's sense, it is clear on our evidence that different, if not necessarily coherent, interpretations of community education are coexisting in our schools. The acceptance of common principles may belie the fact that the interpretation of those principles is very different, based as they are on different aims and in the long run irreconcilable ideological stances. The practical reality is that there exists in many schools an uneasy coexistence of two very different interpretations of community education. Sometimes the differences are articulated and explicit; often they are not. The situation is particularly unfortunate if the term 'community education' comes to be associated primarily with the more radical interpretation since it then comes to be seen as something 'added on' to schooling rather than a distinctive theory of education in the practice of schooling. In our study, of course, the difference was exacerbated by the identification of two models of community education with two different professions and it led us to question whether the 'community education' we were seeing in practice was in any sense a redefinition of schooling or simply a supplement to it. Vallely and Peacock[26] in their study of Lothian schools identified a similar pattern even under a single management structure: the 'school plus' and the 'dynamic' models they claimed, were clearly there. And in the late 1980s it is probably true that not only do the two interpretations of community education still coexist uneasily but that in most schools the 'school plus' model dominates. Fletcher[27] is still arguing that 'community' must not be something added to education but an indication that education can and does change; Richards[28] is still despairing that adult education in schools is merely 'schooling for adults' and Cunningham, in contemplating the prospect of devolved financial management to schools, makes a plea that:

> . . . the financial arrangements must promote and sustain unified management structures, to enable community schools to be one and not two enterprises.[29]

If it is true that different interpretations of community education coexist uneasily in most schools and that the 'school plus' model of the community school dominates, then the implication for parent involvement over the next few years as new legislation on school management is enacted, may be serious. For parent involvement too, is open to widely different interpretations ranging from the tokenism of parents' evenings or practical help in classrooms through to the radicalism of parent control over school policy. *Ad hoc* pragmatic responses, or practices based on different ideological stances within the same school are not good enough: parent involvement in schools, to be effective, should be a reflection of a coherent integrated theory of community education.

It is my conclusion, however, that to date that is what we lack. It is the unsuccessful quest for coherent theories of community education in schools which has led to different sometimes irreconcilable interpretations of the principles of community education. Consequently community education has become largely a supplement to ordinary schooling rather than a distinctive approach to the education of all ages. Parent involvement is one of many dimensions of schooling which has suffered. I would argue that the contribution of community education to parent involvement is vital if that involvement is to be productive: it is the corollary of that argument that it is unlikely to be productive unless we search more avidly for coherent theories of community education in schools. I have no simple answer: only an argument to suggest direction for the search. It is based on two key concepts, 'the social individual' and 'negotiation' and their relationship with the central process of education, 'learning'.

The Social Individual, Negotiation, and Learning

Schools traditionally have tried to promote both individual achievement and corporate responsibility but their emphasis has been largely on the individual. Taking their lead historically from the world of psychology and child development, schools have looked first to the individual child or young person with his peculiar idiosyncrasies: academic success or failure has been seen as a measure of individual achievement and the individual family's relative ability or willingness to identify with schools. For those from disadvantaged backgrounds, educational success has been seen to be about getting out and getting on. The emphasis on individualism has been carried through to much of adult education where educational opportunities have been seen primarily as a chance to find a sense of individual achievement be it in the world of leisure or employment. This emphasis of adult education does not, of course, go unchallenged.[30]

Community education has of course been more ambivalent but even here some official viewpoints put the individual near the centre: the Scottish Council for Community Education, for example, in its first discussion paper defined community education as 'the total effect on the community of successful efforts to meet the learning needs of individuals'.[31] What is rejected, however, is the pursuit of individuality through unbridled competition. Batten in a discussion of the link between knowledge and control argues that the only justification for focusing on the individual is:

> if we envisage individuality as being defined through cooperation rather than competition. It represents a brotherhood rather than a jungle-animal view of man.[32]

In other words, those with a more dynamic view of community education would see individuality as being enhanced even determined by its social context: it is the 'social individual' that the education system should aim to produce. For community educators:

> . . . community is not just a descriptive but an evaluative concept, holding up a model of man as intrinsically social rather than man as an individualist who contracts into society out of self-interest.[33]

For them, educational success or failure has to be interpreted in the context of the individual's social setting. School failure, for example, has to be seen not just in terms of the individual child or family but also, if relevant, in the relative disadvantage which those from his social setting, or class, suffer in relation to schools. Educational success on the part of the individual from the disadvantaged background should be translated into a practical social concern to change the condition of those who share his social background.

We turn now to 'negotiation' which I want to discuss very briefly in the context of power and authority in education. In line with the reformist mode of this argument I take authority in the Weberian sense to mean power which is assigned to an individual or group as a result of negotiation and/or consensus. Traditionally in education, authority was bestowed on teachers by virtue of their professionalism: it was an implicit assumption by students, parents and the wider community that authority, and by implication, control was vested in schools and teachers. It is an assumption which most teachers have been happy to share. More recently, of course, the teacher's authority has often been challenged, not least by students, and while for some students the result has often simply been coercion on the part of the more 'powerful' teacher, in more 'open' schools there has been a move towards negotiation and flexibility. As Watts describes it, it has been a move towards replacing 'coercion' with 'contract', a working agreement made between 'reasonable consenting people' not a 'continuous confrontation between warring tribes'.[34] This kind of 'negotiated authority' is implicit in the more dynamic interpretation of community education and it has long been identified with some adult education groups such as those run through the Workers' Educational Association (WEA). Finally we turn to 'learning' and its link with 'the social individual' and 'the negotiation of authority'.

Traditionally school learning has been individually based. Children and students have, of course, been organized in groups and classes but the learning has been individual: collaboration in learning has been minimal. Equally, learning has been largely according to the dictates of teachers: it has been seen as the professional prerogative, indeed responsibility, to control the content and the approach to learning.

There has certainly been a rhetoric of group and peer learning since the 1960s: the Plowden ideology and the comprehensive ideal for primary and secondary education respectively reflected an acceptance of the social and educational value of learning together. It seems on the whole, however, to have been a fairly empty rhetoric. In their comprehensive study of primary schools, for example, Galton, Simon and Croll[35] claimed that there was little genuine collaborative learning. There was learning in groups but the group was simply the setting in which the child learned in his own individual way for his own individual purposes. Similarly Rutter *et al* arguing for a more insightful understanding of what learning in groups for secondary students was all about, made the point:

> Mere contact in pleasant surroundings does little to reduce conflict: single episodes of cooperation have little effect; and verbal agreements or goals are not much help. Rather it is joint working together over time for the same purpose which helps to break down barriers.[36]

If genuine collaborative learning is minimal, the collaborative learning which involves negotiation either within the group or between the group and the teacher is even less common though some teachers would claim that the skill of negotiation is probably one of the most important social skills any of us can have in an age of social mobility and change.[37]

It is important not to overstate the case. Negotiated collaborative learning does happen in schools: it happens as students plan special projects, outings, etc. It is hardly likely, however, to be a common learning strategy in core subject areas. Like other dimensions of the more dynamic interpretation of community education, it tends to be a supplement to, rather than an integral part of, education in schools. It is not difficult to understand why. The kind of approach to learning we are talking about is full of risks and difficult for any of us trained in traditional strategies of classroom organization and learning — even if we are convinced of its validity. But if we want to develop a coherent theory of community education in schools, perhaps this is the direction in which we should be looking.

Parents and Teachers: Towards Collaborative, Negotiated Learning?

Where then does all this take us in relation to the main theme of this book, parent involvement in education? The link is that in the late 1980s we are faced with a situation where the whole relationship between teachers and parents will change because of current legislation on the management and control of schools.[38] Parents and teachers are being forced, not asked, to work together.

The movement towards increased parent involvement in schools of course goes back many years but progress has been fragmentary and slow. There are, certainly, shining examples of schools which have entered into a genuine partnership with parents at every level and have experimented with a wide variety of joint activities. The literature on parent involvement since the 1960s is massive. It remains true, however, that many schools have moved hardly at all, their relationships with parents token and hierarchical. It is also my experience that just as most teachers are happiest with the 'individual' model of student learning so they are most at ease with the individual parent. Just as they are most confident when they can assume their traditional role of authority with parents so they are at their most confused when that authority is challenged.

And yet these very situations which most teachers would seek to avoid, where working with groups of parents and where negotiation at many levels will be required, will be the norm under the new legislation. In the light of the previous discussion it is tempting to suggest that the very skills and experience which parents and teachers will need are those which a theory of community education translated into schools might have produced. But given that it has not happened, the immediate future may well be bleak, particularly for teachers, because clearly parent involvement is here to stay albeit in a form which many parents themselves would not have chosen:

> The fight for control will be a painful as well as rather inarticulate one. But the fact that those who wish to change schools for radical reasons and those who wish to see greater control over schools for conservative ones agree about the

> importance of parents shows that this development is to a large extent inevitable.[39]

It is ironic that the move to give parents and community a greater control over schools is seen as a retrograde step by many who have traditionally fought for this on the arguments of community education. The reason of course is not hard to find. The new legislation is an undisguised move to limit the power of local authorities. It is, in the words of the officers of the Community Education Association '. . . a retrograde movement towards centralist control and a restriction of community power which . . . could terminate the encouraging developments which have been increasing over the years'.[40] It will be a double irony if parents and teachers, by lacking the skills of collaboration and negotiation, are used by a government for its own ends rather than for community purposes.

Take the example of the core curriculum. All political parties are now committed to the concept of a core curriculum: the debate is less about its desirability, more about its interpretation. Some are convinced that the core curriculum will be closely defined and manipulated from the centre:

> (The proposals) are designed to promote a subject-centred approach and to deny any attempt to develop a learner-centred one. The curriculum is determined at the centre by experts, not negotiated and agreed by the learners and tutors. A school can only be justified in terms of the achievement of satisfactory grades in relation to national benchmarks.[41] Parents will be free to choose those schools which teach the national curriculum best.[42]

Others are more optimistic. Skilbeck, for example, claims that 'core curriculum' need not be interpreted narrowly, that it should not be a new version of the subject-based curriculum nor need it mean central control of schools.[43] But if Skilbeck is right, again there are implications for how teachers and parents negotiate and collaborate in a local interpretation of the core curriculum which is to everyone's satisfaction. Most are not ready for it.

What I have argued here is that, ironically, schools in the late 1980s are paying the penalty for not having taken the quest for a theory of community education seriously many years ago, for not developing communities (children, students, parents, teachers) who learned together by negotiation for both individual and common purposes. They are paying the penalty as a system for those who have been slow to embrace the principles of parent involvement.

Skilbeck claims that the government's Technical and Vocational Education Initiative (TVEI) programme was born out of sheer frustration with the pace of change.[44] Perhaps the new radical legislation on parent management of schools has been born out of similar frustration with a system where much parent involvement has been tokenism and where '. . . parents have no direct access to or influence over the making of decisions which affect the authority of schools in which their children are educated'.[45]

As parents and teachers are now forced to work together with parents having unprecedented powers, the process may well be a painful even traumatic one for all concerned. That schools are not ready for this process is hardly the fault of community education alone but it has to carry some of the responsibility. 'Parent involvement' as a concept is dear to the heart of community educators: that it has been used by government as many would see it, for narrow political purposes is in part the consequence of '. . . the failure of community education to really deliver in the area of parental involvement and partnership'.[46]

Conclusion

We have come a long way in this chapter: we began with the need for a theory of community education, we have ended with a discussion of school management. For me, the link is an important one for two reasons. First, to date there has not been a sufficiently strong 'community school' voice at a national level to anticipate or react to present government proposals. As Pickard has said in the context of the debate on Scottish school boards '. . . fragmentation is the government's best defence . . .it is at its most effective with parents' groups which, by their nature, have disparate local origins'.[47] The government's best defence, in education as in the narrower political arena, is 'a divided opposition'.[48]

The second reason is at the level of the school itself. School boards (and their equivalents elsewhere) must learn to work in a spirit that assumes a theory of community education based on negotiated communal learning for a common purpose. That 'common purpose' must be 'the best possible future for all children'. The future, as Wragg says, lies in professional teachers and lay people working in harmony:

> to fashion appropriate learning experiences for the next generation. It is a model for the twenty-first century and if we fail to operate it effectively we should resist the temptation to settle for central direction . . .[49]

The danger of central direction is all too clear. A commitment to a 'community education' approach might, even yet, allow us to avoid the worst scenarios associated with that fate.

Toffler warns us:

> Tomorrow's illiterate will not be the man who can't read — he will be the man who has not learned how to learn.[50]

Perhaps tomorrow's successful schools will be defined as those in which children, students, parents and teachers have learned how to learn together within a coherent theory of community education.

References

1 PETERS, R.S. (1966) *Ethics and Education*, London, Allen and Unwin.
2 HILLERY, G.A. (1955) 'Definitions of community: Areas of agreement', *Rural Sociology*, **20**, pp. 111–23.
3 MARTIN, I. (1987a) 'Community education now: Why community education matters now', *Community Education Network*, **7**, 2, p. 2.
4 BATTEN, E. (1980) 'Community education and ideology: A case for radicalism' in FLETCHER, C. and THOMPSON, N., *Issues in Community Education*, Lewes, Falmer Press, p. 27.
5 MARTIN, I. (1987b) 'Community education now: What it should be about today', *Community Education Network* **6**, 11, p. 2.
6 COWBURN, W. (1986) *Class, Ideology and Community Education*, London, Croom Helm.
7 MARTIN, I. (1987b) *op. cit.*, p. 2.
8 FLETCHER, C. (1980) 'The theory of community education and its relation to adult education', in THOMPSON, J.L. (Ed) *Adult Education for a Change*, London, Hutchinson.
9 O'HAGAN, B. (1987a) 'Community education in Britain: Some myths and their consequences', in ALLEN, G., BASTIANI, J., MARTIN, I. and RICHARDS, K. *Community Education: An Agenda for Educational Reform*, Milton Keynes, Open University.
10 COWBURN, W. (1986) *op. cit.*, p. 132.
11 O'HAGAN, B. (1987b) 'Efficiency, enrichment and empowerment', *Journal of Community Education*, **6**, 1, pp. 2–5.
12 MARTIN, I. (1986) 'Community education now: What it is and why it matters', *Community Education Network*, **6**, 10, p. 2.
13 COWBURN, W. (1988) 'The coming crisis of community education', *Journal of Community Education*, **6**, 4, p. 24.

14 Scottish Community Education Council (1981) *The Community School in Scotland*, Edinburgh, SCEC, p. 5.
15 Fletcher, C. (1980) *op. cit.*, p. 71.
16 Rennie, J. (Ed) (1985) *British Community Primary Schools: Four Case Studies*, Lewes, Falmer Press, p. 15.
17 Rennie, J. (Ed) (1985) *Ibid.*
18 Watts, J. (1980) *Towards an Open School*, London, Longman.
19 Nisbet, J., Hendry, L., Stewart, C. and Watt, J. (1980) *Towards Community Education*, Aberdeen, University Press.
20 Martin, I. (1987c) 'Community education: Towards a theoretical analysis', in Allen, G., Bastiani, J., Martin, I. and Richards, K. (Eds) *Community Education: An Agenda for Educational Reform*, Milton Keynes, Open University.
21 Nisbet *et al* (1980) *op. cit.*
22 Cowburn, W. (1986) *op. cit.*
23 *Ibid*, p. 22.
24 *Ibid*, p. 22.
25 *Ibid*, p. 50.
26 Vallely, M. and Peacock, A. (1982) *Community Schools in Lothian Region*, unpublished report to Lothian Region.
27 Fletcher, C. (1987) 'The meaning of "community" in community education', in Allen, G., Bastiani, J., Martin, I. and Richards, K. (Eds) *Community Education: An Agenda for Educational Reform*, Milton Keynes, Open University.
28 Richards, K. (1986) 'Community education now: A response', *Community Education Network* **6**, 10, p. 2.
29 Cunningham, H. (1988) 'Value for money and human values', *Community Education Network* **8**, 3, p. 1.
30 See, for example, Keddie, N. (1981) 'Adult education: An ideology of individualism' in Thompson, J. (Ed.) *Adult Education for a Change*, London, Hutchinson.
31 Scottish Council for Community Education (1979) *Discussion Paper 1*, Edinburgh, SCCE, p. 3.
32 Batten, E. (1980) *op. cit.*, pp. 30–31.
33 Skrimshire, A. (1981) 'Community schools and the education of the social individual, *Oxford Review of Education* **7**, 1, pp. 53–65.
34 Watts, J. (1980) *op. cit.*, p. 161.
35 Galton, M., Simon, B. and Croll, P. (1980) *Inside the Primary Classroom*, London, Routledge and Kegan Paul.
36 Rutter, M., Maugham, B., Mortimore, P. and Ouston, J. (1979) *Fifteen Thousand Hours: Secondary Schools and their Effects on Children*, London, Open Books.
37 Watts, J. (1981) 'Community-based education' in Simon, B. and Taylor, W. *Education in the Eighties, the Central Issues*, Manchester, Batsford Press.
38 Education Reform Bill 1988, School Boards (Scotland) Bill.
39 Cullingford, C. (Ed) (1985) *Parents, Teachers and Schools*, London, Royce.
40 Wayment, A., Hedderwick, M., Parker, P., Richards, K. and Jenkin-

SON, D. (1987) 'The Baker proposals — A response and a call for action', *Community Education Network* **7**, 10, p. 2.
41 RICHARDS, K. (1987) 'Control not choice', *Community Education Network* **7**, 9, p. 2.
42 RICHARDS, K. *Ibid.*, p. 2.
43 SKILBECK, M. (1986) 'Core curriculum revisited' in ROGERS, R. (Ed.) *Education and Social Class*, Lewes, Falmer Press.
44 SKILBECK, M. *Ibid.*
45 SCOTTISH EDUCATION DEPARTMENT (1987) *School Management and the Role of Parents*, Consultative Paper, August.
46 COWBURN, W. (1988) *op. cit.*, p. 27.
47 PICKARD, W. (1988) Editorial, *Times Educational Supplement (Scotland)* No. 1106, 15th January.
48 PICKARD, W. (1988) *op. cit.*
49 WRAGG, T. (1984) 'Education for the twenty-first century' in HARBER, C., MEIGHAN, R. and ROBERTS, B. (Eds) *Alternative Educational Futures*, London, Holt, Reinhart and Winston.
50 TOFFLER, A. quotes Gerjoy, H. in TOFFLER, A. (1970) *Future Shock: A Study of Mass Bewilderment in the Face of Accelerating Change*, London, Bodley Head.

11 *14–18: Parental Views on TVEI*

Richard Pring and Jill Christie

Changing Conceptions of Secondary Education

We have seen in the last five years the most radical changes in secondary education since the 1944 Education Act, which introduced secondary education for all. Secondary education *then* was seen as essentially tripartite: grammar schools for the most able, technical education for a few, and secondary modern education for the majority. Within twenty years of the 1944 Education Act, this pattern had changed. Technical schools had not flourished, and comprehensive schools were introduced for the full range of ability. But in recent years these organizational changes have been followed by far reaching curriculum changes.

In all these innovations, parental views have rarely been solicited. Rather the changes were first and foremost political matters. Indeed, it is rare for parents to be consulted, despite the statements in the Plowden Report that parental support was the one most significant factor in accounting for pupil achievement. Parents were hardly consulted in the development of the tripartite system; they have not been consulted in subsequent developments. And yet these are, as we have pointed out, radical in the extreme. What, then, have been the most recent changes?

Putting it very crudely, secondary education has traditionally been seen in subject terms — discrete subjects which, aggregated together, constitute a balanced secondary education for all. But, mainly as a result of intervention from the Manpower Services Commission (MSC), such a *dis*integrated conception of education is being challenged. The MSC's Technical and Vocational Education Initiative (TVEI) has raised fundamental questions about the aims of education, about its connection with the world of work, about how students should be assessed, about how teaching should be conducted, and about personal and social development. Indeed, TVEI links with other initiatives (often referred to as prevocational, and represented by such innovations as the Certificate in Prevocational Education and Business and Technician Education Council (BTEC)/City and Guilds of the London Institute (CGLI) foundation courses) in challenging the essentially subject-based approach to curriculum planning. Rather, so it is argued, should the curriculum begin with more fundamental questions about how that which is learned prepares the students for the future — that is, for coping with a less certain and secure world, for acquiring skills and knowledge related to job opportunities, and for developing appropriate attitudes towards industry and further training opportunities.

It is interesting therefore to see how far parents, brought up on a view of the curriculum as an aggregate of subjects, will respond to and support a radically different way of seeing things.

TVEI has, on the whole, been such a radical departure. Under its banner schools have often eschewed the traditional subject-based approach to the organization of learning. Indeed, a major aim has been to transform styles of learning (and thus teaching) — by providing a place for the experience and the activities of the learner, by encouraging cooperative learning, by discouraging sex stereotyping in learning roles, by involving the community much more in the learning experience. All this is a far cry from what most parents will have experienced in their schooling. And, therefore, one might expect a rather negative attitude towards it — certainly not a 'thumbs up' for what, set against traditional criteria and expectations, must seem mysterious, if not miseducative.

Technical Vocational and Educational Initiative (TVEI)

TVEI was announced in November 1982 by David Young (later Lord Young), as Secretary of State for Employment, in a new initiative funded by the MSC to make the curriculum of schools more vocationally and technologically oriented — so that schools might be more relevant to the needs of industry and to the needs of young people who want to find a place in that industry. A lot of reference was made to relevant skills and attitudes, to personal qualities, to equal opportunities, and to generic skills of problem solving.

Local authorities produced schemes of curriculum and organizational development that conformed to broad criteria laid down by the MSC. They then bid for the limited amount of money available. The criteria were that the different schemes should:

(a) provide equal opportunities for all;
(b) provide a four-year curriculum designed as a preparation for adult life in a society liable to rapid change;
(c) encourage initiative, problem-solving, and other aspects of personal development;
(d) contain a vocational element throughout;
(e) relate technical and vocational elements to potential employment opportunities;
(f) plan work experience within the programmes;
(g) establish links with subsequent training and educational opportunities;
(h) include regular careers and educational assessment;
(i) prepare students for one or more nationally recognized qualification;
(j) design courses so that they might usefully be replicated.

Initially there were fourteen schemes, heavily funded by MSC. Later there emerged over 100 schemes, and presently there is TVEI extension to all secondary schools in the country.

TVEI therefore has been an immensely important innovation. It has introduced a very different mode of funding education (different both in terms of central intervention, and in terms of contractual obligation); it has related what is taught much more closely to the needs of industry and commerce; it has questioned how learning should be organized and promoted; and it has pursued a more generous view of how students should be assessed in recording personal achievement in non-academic areas. In all this it is to be contrasted with the proposals for the national curriculum and the national assessments that are being introduced by the Secretary of State for Education and that are claimed to be in response to parental concerns and wishes.

The Enquiry

It was because of the radical departure of TVEI from the normal curriculum that the National Confederation of Parent Teacher Associations (NCPTA) wanted to solicit parents' views.[1] After all, if it were true that parental support is the most significant factor in student success, then parents' knowledge about and appreciation of TVEI could be an important element in its success. How extraordinary that, in the contemporary efforts to be 'relevant', parental opinion is almost always ignored.

> It is rare for parents' opinions to be surveyed in depth but their knowledge, or lack of it, and the opinions that they have formed are of importance and may help to suggest improvements to the TVEI scheme in particular and methods of communication in general.[2]

It had originally been intended to contact parents in two LEAs. But in the event only one LEA survey could be carried out.

The study consisted of questionnaires and interviews. The questionnaires were sent to parents of second, third, and fifth year students — thus parents of those who were not directly involved in TVEI, of those who were making choices of options (that would include TVEI) and of those who had been taking TVEI for two years. But possibly it was the interviews that gave richest and most interesting information.

The interviews were carried out mainly by eight third year BEd students who were well briefed and trained beforehand. Each student did ten interviews and the rest were done by the writers of this chapter.

One hundred families were chosen from one scheme, and ninety of them were interviewed in their homes for, on average, one hour each. Of these sixty were carried out with parents of fifth formers and thirty with parents of second and third years. Initially, about 250 parents were sent request forms asking if they would be willing to be interviewed, which required to be ticked and returned on the basis of equal numbers from the five high schools. Only sixty positive replies were received and it therefore became necessary to contact more parents by phone. This form of contact obviously produces a bias in socio-economic terms. But this was considered to be unavoidable in the circumstances. And the disadvantages were far outweighed in our opinion by the facility such an approach offers in research that has to be conducted quickly and on a very low budget. Actually speaking to people about the research and explaining why their cooperation was important proved very successful in recruiting additional volunteers. Hardly anyone contacted in this way said 'no'. Even so, we approached the research with some trepidation, not knowing how welcome we and the student interviewers would be. In almost every case, however, we found that the parents were happy to talk at length. Indeed, many were delighted to do so because never before had anyone bothered to ask them what they thought of their children's education.

The questions were kept open — they were aimed at soliciting parental views and in no way did we want to put words into parents' mouths. We were seeking to discover their understanding of TVEI and their feelings about the scheme with as few prompts as possible. Some of the questions did not relate specifically to the scheme but raised issues with which it is closely concerned.

The Analysis of the Data

Ninety one-hour interviews which encouraged as free expression as possible cannot easily be synthesized into a brief report. We therefore did two things; firstly, where feasible, we gave a short quantitative analysis of the answers; secondly, we provided as fairly as possible, an account of what seemed to lie behind the numbers. Obviously, this qualitative analysis was no more than a crude synopsis of what parents said, but it nonetheless allowed the reader to obtain a quick overall view of parental opinion. The categories within which responses were quantified emerged from the data itself. This was in keeping with our intention not to impose our own ideas, but rather to listen as open-mindedly as possible to individual responses, letting them take their own shape.

As a result, interviewers were left with the feeling that the interviews themselves were often therapeutic, helping to clarify views and disentangle complicated perceptions. Undoubtedly the student interviewers found the interviews particularly valuable in giving insights into the way parents think. They enjoyed going into homes where they were nearly always greeted warmly.

Summary of Parental Responses

What follows is a summary of how parents responded to particular questions:

Question 1. What do you know about TVEI?

Parents were often diffident where knowledge of TVEI was concerned. Misunderstandings were common. Some thought it was something to do with television. Others were under the misapprehension that TVEI inevitably led to a place in college or that it was for the less able. An initial response was sometimes one of being put off by yet another acronym, when so many that related to education were found already. Interviewers commented that often the first thing parents said was that they knew nothing, then with a little encouragement they went on to describe TVEI as 'helping children to work together', 'getting them to make decisions for themselves', 'getting them out and about'.

Although information had reached most parents in the form of leaflets from the schools, many expressed reluctance to pay attention to this sort of communication. Indeed, one of the conclusions of our report to the NCPTA was that overall, sending pupils home with written information or posting it to parents was not an effective way of disseminating knowledge. The personal approach won hands down. Most parents said that they had come to know about TVEI through descriptions offered by their children. Work experience and residentials seemed to catch the imagination most of all, together with stories about businesses that were being run by pupils at school. All three areas of TVEI just mentioned (work experience, residentials, and small businesses) met with considerable parental approval for being connected with 'real life' and 'employment'. 'Going out of school' was also seen by many as being a 'good thing'.

Question 2. How did you learn about it?

Although a significant number of parents did say that they had learnt about TVEI through written communication, almost half added that they felt the information had been inadequate either because it was unclear or because there had not been enough of it.

A picture of schools operating very differently emerged, with some parents saying they had received no information about TVEI in advance of options in the third year, others (of the older children) saying they had received none since. Personal talks with teachers and special presentations of TVEI were commented upon warmly by a few. Again, we felt that this sort of communication, time consuming though it might be, paid great dividends in terms of parental enlightenment and goodwill.

A small but vociferous number of parents complained about handouts or talks that were laden with jargon — some seemed to feel that they were being 'got at' in this context. Pitching any sort of communication at the right level emerged as an art worthy of careful consideration. Perhaps the golden rule should be 'Keep it as simple and direct as possible'. This at any rate was the message that parents seemed to be trying to convey.

Question 3. Do you think it's the right course for your child?

Parents of the lower school pupils had to speculate as to whether they thought TVEI was the right course for their children. Numbers were about equally divided for and against. Quite a proportion of those against the course felt that it was not suitable for the more able or had doubts about its credibility with employers. These parents were particularly concerned about the lack of academic or specific content of TVEI.

The responses of fifth form parents are much clearer with a definite lessening of these anxieties once TVEI was a reality. Two thirds of these parents said TVEI was undoubtedly the right course for their offspring and, when asked why, put personal development at the top of their list of priorities. Obviously, seeing their children gain in confidence; independence and the ability to cope generally in the outside world was important — many pointed out that that these days it was just not enough to have 'bits of paper', employers were looking for much more. One parent, when considering the effect TVEI had had on her son, said 'I think he felt valued', a remark that reflected much of what was said by others. Compared to the emphasis placed on the development of maturity, self-reliance and confidence there was a relative lack of reference to the better equipment and facilities associated with TVEI.

TVEI was also seen as providing positive help towards enhancing pupils' decision-taking, for example, whether to continue in further education or training and to find out what type of jobs interested them. More than half the parents of fifth formers thought that TVEI had provided a better chance of getting a job (although in a separate study only 35 per cent of pupils felt they had a better chance in the job stakes as a result of TVEI).

Question 4. How would you like to see your child's learning programme develop?

The main answers to this question were particularly varied, making a detailed summary difficult. Briefly, parents seemed to be most concerned with standards. They were often worried that, in the attempt to provide a broader curriculum, based on informal teaching methods, these would be diluted. Mention was made of children who lacked facility in writing good English and in simple mathematics. Motivation and discipline were other areas of concern particularly amongst the parents of older children. Real anxiety was expressed by several of these about slack behaviour and lack of respect for teachers. Clearly some were worried about a new style of learning which came perilously close to 'mucking about' in their eyes. One parent described TVEI as a 'life saver' as far as her son was concerned since it had given him the opportunity to do things he was interested in and good at.

Question 5. Do you generally agree with each other about your child's education?

The main purpose of this question was to enable the interviewer openly to pursue and to note down differences between parents should these appear to be emerging. In fact, few parents disagreed or, if they did, they kept it to themselves.

There is evidence to show that most of the parents seemed to feel that a united front was supportive for their child and, in nearly every case, discussion was upheld wherein the child's own wishes and opinions were taken into account.

Question 6. Do you feel you have had some say in what goes on in your child's school?

The responses in their numerical form appeared odd, with well over half the parents saying they didn't feel they had any say, set against a large number who said they felt happy with their communications with the school.

On closer examination however, this apparent anomaly was seen to be based on the fact that many of the parents who felt they had had no say, often added that they knew the doors were open if they needed to be more in touch.

Other more decided contradictions existed in several responses where, for example, an individual would comment 'no, because the school is such a big one' and then add that it was nevertheless 'approachable and easy to contact'. Difficulties within the school most often referred to teachers who hadn't the time to listen. Several felt that what they call open or parents' evenings did not offer any real opportunity for discussion. Parents seemed to feel daunted by these meetings. It would not be hard to deduce from this that some parents feel either uncertain or perhaps a touch guilty when it comes to their role in exercising direct involvement in their child's education.

The parent teacher associations came in for criticism, parents apparently feeling that it was often a 'clique' or a 'closed shop' or merely 'a fund raising body' which did not invite dialogue. Some parents obviously felt inadequate about expressing themselves at PTA meetings and in trying to gain admittance, though this did not necessarily affect their confidence in the school as a whole. One said 'The PTA consists of people seeking influence more than normal parents — I feel out of my depth'. Opinions varied as to the extent PTA membership helped to reduce powerlessness to affect educational decisions: 'They listen and then there's no action'. At the same time as recognizing that many parents do not feel they have a say in their child's school the interviews also revealed that a quarter of the parents were happy to leave their child's education with the school and a number well above this were confident that the school and the teachers were approachable, should they feel so inclined.

Question 7. What changes in school would you like to see?

As a general observation, it seemed that parental views were well in agreement with one of the main aims of TVEI, namely to bring the curriculum closer to the world of work. Apart from this, a considerable number expressed concern, perhaps predictably, about two main areas: discipline and basic standards, in particular the wearing of uniforms and homework. Interestingly, parents of the older children were more anxious about discipline, whilst parents of second and third formers feared that subjects like maths and English were not given enough attention.

This emphasis on basic subjects was significant and often related to fears that they were not being given enough attention because so much else was on offer. What exactly these other 'new' subjects consisted of eluded some parents, who expressed mystification at the crop of new acronyms they were expected to be familiar with. The rare comment, 'a load of rubbish', which the interviewers were met with occasionally, seemed to have its roots in the simple frustration of not understanding. However, often those parents who mentioned basics and practical subjects felt that towards the end of secondary education there should be a move to integrate school with work.

Improving the quality of teaching and facilities often appeared as linked under a broad requirement for more crispness and professionalism in the way schools and also individual teachers presented themselves. Parents were also concerned that schools were dingy and uncared for places which could do with a clean-up and a lick of paint.

Fifth form parents quite often felt that communications between pupils and teachers had deteriorated, mentioning size of secondary schools as being to blame; some looked back at their children's primary school with nostalgia.

Question 8. Compared with your own education, what do you think about the kind of education your child is receiving?

Clearly, the majority of parents looked on education today favourably. Three parents of fifth formers stood out for the way they elaborated on their perceptions of 'independent' learning. They described a process whereby their children had 'learnt how to learn' and went on to evaluate their children's education well beyond looking merely at the 'products' of learning. In so doing they were, of course, very much in tune with a core concept of TVEI. Others qualified favourable comments by saying things like 'There are better opportunities for children these days but there were better standards in my day'. Discipline came up as a serious cause for worry again, but positive remarks about what schools offered today, particularly in terms of scope and relevance, took precedence.

Question 9. Do you agree with your child about what's most useful for him or her to be doing at school?

This was not a very fruitful question, perhaps because parents are keen to present a united front when being interviewed. What did emerge was that most parents felt their children had a right to make their own decisions and if necessary learn from their own mistakes.

A small but significant number said that they did not know enough about their chlldren's education either to agree or to disagree. They would like to know more. The oft-mentioned problem with new course names cropped up again with one parent saying 'teachers can't explain GCSE to kids who then can't explain to their parents'.

Question 10. What would you most like your child to have learnt by the time he or she leaves school?

Most parents put personal development along with mastery of the basic skills as top priorities for their children. The shift away from viewing academic qualifications as the most valuable outcome of education was very obvious and the most significant outcome of the question. Frequently, parents wanted to convey that they recognized the world as a different place in which to find a firm footing and that self confidence, being able to communicate and being able to 'stand on your own feet' were of prime importance. Independence, both of mind and in terms of practical skills was much prized. Few comments were concerned merely with curriculum content.

Generally, it appeared that parents took a very broad view of what they hoped their children would have gained at 16, much of it was not directly connected with learning in the classroom. The ideal image presented was of a young person who was aware of what lay beyond school, was realistic and able to use his or her talents and education to practical advantage whilst not being too daunted by adults. Here their views came very clearly into line with important TVEI objectives.

What we do not gain from the answers is an insight into the *extent* to which parents rely on schools for the development of their children's character, nor how they perceive their own role and influence. When education and the relationships within schools are changing so fast this would seem to be a rich area for further investigation.

Conclusion

The project we have described was small indeed. But it is noteworthy because it was the first, and probably the only time, that parents' views have been solicited on this major project that claims to be transforming the shape and purpose of secondary education. And the parents valued being consulted — valued the opportunity to talk to interested people about their children's education.

The questions were open, encouraging the parents to give their views on a range of issues that impinged upon these new developments. Many valued this increased concern for personal development, remarking on the importance of personal qualities in the preparation of their offspring for the future, particularly employment. They valued the increased interest, commitment, engagement that they had witnessed in their classroom. But clearly much needs to be done to improve the communication between schools and parents, especially where new approaches to the curriculum are being introduced — with their own distinctive jargon and acronyms and with a philosophy and a teaching style that are unlike what the parents have experienced.

Our conclusion on such a small sample of parents in one authority can be only tentative. But they point to the need for a much more thorough survey of parents' views. Otherwise how can schools claim to be taking parents seriously? And how ever can they begin to educate parents which is essential if school reforms are to receive their support?

References

1 NATIONAL CONFEDERATION OF PARENT TEACHER ASSOCIATIONS (1987) *Parental Perceptions of TVEI*, London, NCPTA.

2 *Ibid.*

Postscript: Themes, Issues and Assumptions

Flora Macleod

It is the purpose of this chapter to draw together the main themes, issues and assumptions raised and to examine them for consistent and underlying patterns. More specifically this section will make an initial attempt to address the following questions: What is the nature of the problems of equalizing educational opportunities and increasing accountability as seen by the various authors? How do the problems manifest themselves? What solutions do they offer to alleviate the problems as they identify them? To what extent do the contributors contradict or agree with one another? What areas of ignorance emerge from the chapters from which a research agenda can be drawn up?

Equalizing Educational Opportunities

A number of authors point to the need to balance individual freedom with the freedom of others and to set these in the context of the needs of society. But what are the educational rights and responsibilities of individual families? The state provides a safety net of structures to support families but retains the right to intervene if they neglect their share of the responsibility. In keeping with this the 1944 Education Act legislated that the state provides education and insists that the family keep its side of the bargain by dutifully sending its children to school regularly or educating them otherwise.[1]

The state thus helps people to help themselves toward a particular way of life as defined by the state and in line with the prevailing value system. But it has been implied in this book that these standards are set by the liberal minded middle classes causing remedial intervention to involve the control of certain groups and families more than others.

The present government advocates self-determination. This is made manifest in their recent legislation aimed at increasing parent power in the education system. Parents are taken to have the right to make decisions about the kind of education their children will receive and who will provide the programme. But this inevitably is limited to what is available to them free of charge. It has been asserted (for example, Wragg, chapter 6) that enhancing the rights of parents as a group does not necessarily mean enhancing the rights of individuals — in fact the reverse is likely to be true for the less articulate, the less persistent and the less knowledgeable. So it would seem that unless parents have the will, the money and the time to do otherwise, they are restricted to what the state has provided for them in their local area.

Increasing parent power may thus be seen as a policy which flies in the face of a desire to equalize opportunities. This is a recurring argument in the book (see Reynolds, chapter 9, in particular for a detailed analysis). Even Flew (chapter 5) who argues strongly for power to the parents would accept inequality of outcome as an inevitable consequence of schooling, but he would not agree that such an effect is undesirable provided unfair advantages were removed. Flew, and Murphy (chapter 1) are among those for whom equality of outcome is not a value in the same way as equality of consideration is as it is not an absolute position on any scale of achievement. Rather it involves comparisons between people. Equality of consideration refers to fair treatment of all pupils. Equality of outcome implies unfair treatment or deliberate rigging as the ideal of equality of opportunity of necessity results in inequality of outcome. To Flew those who value equality of outcome must do so at the cost of mediocrity because they not only fail to distinguish between opportunity and outcome but also fail to distinguish chance (probability) of achievement from chance (opportunity) of achievement. To help clarify our understanding of why the argument cannot go straight through from set inequalities of outcome to set inequalities of opportunity, Murphy examines the nature of the ideal of equality of opportunity. Although he acknowledges that equality of opportunity is a principle of social injustice he does not accept that the influence of the home on opportunities in school should be discussed in the context of a social injustice. He bases this on the fact that many analysts insist upon concluding directly from set inequalities of outcome to set inequalities of opportunity.

Given the present context the nub of the debate would seem to rest on the answer to the question of whether the greatly inc role of the family in making decisions about the education of its children involves giving some children an unfair advantage over others. If one reflects on the issues raised in the early part of chapter 3 the relative fairness or unfairness of the parental influence applies within families as well as between families. Anderson reminds us that nineteenth century values are currently being readopted and emphasized by the present government in their policies concerning the family, and that the family is still, on the whole, very conservative. Despite historical changes which have affected women's position in British society the stress in families is still very much on the division of labour between public and private lives where men become associated with the public sphere (the world of work) and the attached values and women with the private sphere (domesticity) and the attached values, although this is complicated by class considerations. Might one undesirable effect of the new legislation be parents taking decisions for their female offspring that will reduce the options available to them in later life? Is the government collaborating with families to girls' disadvantage by passing laws which enhance parental power?

Parents are not the only ones to have a stake in the education of future citizens. Golby (chapter 7) and Morgan (chapter 8) believe that it is inappropriate to designate to the parent the status of sole 'consumer' as the child and the wider community are equally important. The present government either assumes or does not stop to consider whether the economic, social and cultural needs of the local community, society and the immediate and future needs of children are being met by the notion of market forces.

Several of the chapters remind us that the nurturing and empowerment of future citizens is an essential aim of education. Teachers, it is argued, must be clear what social values they are trying to inculcate even if they do not correspond with those of the families represented in the school (for example, Anderson, chapter 3). Parents' prejudices should not go unchallenged even if the parents disapprove of what the school is teaching. Inevitably some parents will hold prejudices which society in general, and teachers in particular, could not endorse such as sex or race stereotyping.

If it is accepted that education involves making individuals into good members of society who are respectful and tolerant of others, even those they do not agree with, then the emphasis will be on the rights of society to make decisions on behalf of individuals and families. One does not wish, of course, to overstate this point as in many cases it is likely that the value system of the family and the value system of society are neither incompatible nor mutually exclusive. However, there are cases where it is commonly believed that society and the family hold values which need to be dismantled and disposed of in the interest of individual member's personal identities and freedoms. One example of this has been hinted at above and is elaborated on in Anderson's chapter. She argues that women cannot easily be accommodated within a conceptual system that is predominantly patriarchal. It follows that informed intellectual debate coupled with deliberately planned action within our schools insisting on female equality and status is essential if this state of affairs is not to be perpetuated. In short, implicit in Anderson's chapter is the question of whether it is possible to attempt to achieve equality in education without also striving for equality through education.

But would deliberate and planned intervention in the socialization processes aimed at the needs of tomorrow's society be incompatible with the 'free' development of individual children and the principles of a child-centred education? It would seem not. Child-centred theories do recognize that the child has to live within society. For instance Dewey[2] maintained that education for society also allows free development of individual children. And Raven (chapter 4) reminds us that there is no such thing as a value-free education, therefore informed and explicit action has to be the only way of handling the preparation of our future citizens to become responsible members of society.

Raven is a strong supporter of child-centred education and would appear to have some sympathy with deschoolers such as Reimer[3] and Illich.[4] He argues that school as it is currently conceived inadvertently prevents proper education from taking place by forcing an unwanted pattern of learning on children and by so doing kills their natural curiosity and motivation. Children are prevented from thinking by being kept busy. Raven has doubtless put his finger on a real problem within the education system — a problem which he believes results in the disastrous miseducation of many children. He points to the other educating forces within society and the family in particular which he views as far more effective than schools in fostering children's talents and competencies and, of providing a suitable basis on which to model schooling.

His ideas on how to radically change the situation have more in common with Goodman[5] than Reimer and Illich. He argues for decentralization and the introduction of small units where children can follow their own interest and talents and where the school is part of the community and the community part of the school. At the same time he acknowledges that catering for a diversity of talents is by no means easy until people take seriously and respect other peoples' value systems which have little in common with their own. Democratic leadership, he believes, is not about putting policies into effect which satisfy the consensus view, rather it is about judging what is in 'the best interest' of the people and acting accordingly. To prevent the shortcomings of a 'top–down' system, such as the Fabian ideology (chapter 9), he sees the need to set up structures to hold managers accountable. He would like to see the introduction of political education to the curriculum which would encourage children to be independent thinkers and reach decisions based on knowledge and understanding of the basic issues and principles which govern our society not negative critical thinkers or unthinking accepters of the status quo. Implicit in his pronouncements is a view of equality as a principle of social justice which is not taken to mean equality of treatment — a view also upheld by other authors in this book such as Murphy and Flew. Education must be differentiated in nature in order to meet the needs of the individual and society.

Equal opportunities is thus a nebulous concept in an education system which must by its very nature cater for diversity. People from different political persuasions place different emphasis on the individual, the community and society. The pendulum at the moment has swung towards the individual, his/her family and his/her rights. Several contributors feel that this current trend towards self-determination in a market economy and its related values will result in the increased alienation of certain groups and families. In a consumer model of education, such as the one advocated by right-wing thinkers like Flew, schools and teachers are construed in the same way as the 'supply' of any commodity to satisfy the 'demand' for it. To maintain equilibrium in this type of society children must compete for the most prestigious qualifications which are usually academic in nature. This could well result in a 'caste system' where the academically indifferent (see Murphy, chapter 1) and those who just cannot achieve academic success will be left struggling at the bottom of the heap.

Golby (chapter 7) thinks that individualism has been over-emphasized by the present government. In his view most achievements are the result of team work not uncoordinated individual competition. In a similar vein Watt (chapter 10) sees the pursuit of individuality through unbridled competition as morally spurious. As an alternative she grapples with the concept 'social individual' where individuality is envisaged as being defined through cooperation rather than competition. This seems to be something akin to Hargreaves's 'social solidarity'[6] which was aimed at reducing alienation from society via community studies and practical activities of relevance to one's future. For instance, the provision of a vocational approach to subjects such as TVEI (see chapter 11) goes some way to prepare future well adjusted citizens. It would, of course, be incorrect to assume that the concepts 'cooperation' and 'competition' are antithetic; teams need cooperation to compete effectively and individuals need to cooperate with an opponent to compete at all. Nevertheless it is commonly alleged in the popular press and elsewhere that many young people emerge from school feeling no responsibility for the well-being of their immediate community far less society in general. It is a real fear, therefore, that any reduction in the nurturing of our future citizens in a free-for-all market place might lead to a marked lowering of standards essential to a democratic society.

Individual freedom is central to the equal opportunities debate. It has been argued by authors in this book and elsewhere [7] that freedom from constraints is not sufficient to assume that justice is being done or that people can exercise this freedom. For instance the Sex Discrimination Act and the Race Relations Acts have done nothing in and of themselves to break down existing prejudices or to inform those involved of the implications for them of the lifting of previously held restrictions. Additionally there could be all sorts of bribes and inducements subtle and overt which force an individual to act one way as opposed to another. This is made particularly explicit in chapter 3 where Anderson presents evidence to show that the pressures on girls and women to conform to the sex stereotype are enormous. Similarly implicit in chapters 1 and 2 is the argument that some cultural and subcultural groups are less free to opt for an academic education while others are less free to choose alternatives to it. There is, in short, a strongly held view that people make choices which conform very closely to society's view of them.

None is free from restraint of any sort. However, one can to a greater or lesser extent choose one's own constraints, and the extent to which these choices are made correlates with the extent to which one is self-governed rather than ruled by others. But how can one achieve a greater level of self-realization or become one's own person? Isaacsen[8] uses Berlin's[9] distinction between positive and negative freedom to help shed light on this question. Negative freedom is defined as the absence, or reduction to a minimum, of deliberate interference of others in the areas in which one might wish to act. Positive freedom, on the other hand, is seen as pertaining to self-awareness — an ability to answer the question 'by whom am I ruled?'. The desire for positive freedom is seen as arising from the desire to be in charge of one's own life. As freedom is never absolute nor context free, positive and negative freedoms may be in conflict with one another. One could argue, for example, that the only way to achieve equality of consideration for girls in their career choices would be to limit their freedom to opt out of maths and physics by making these subjects compulsory. This reduction of negative freedom in the short term would according to this argument enable them to exercise more positive freedom in later life through wider career choices. Equally, implicit in the egalitarian policy of raising the school leaving age to 16 was the desire to prevent some pupils from exercising their negative freedoms in the short term in order to increase their positive freedoms in the long term. This would, of course, be an intellectually uncomfortable strategy for some of the contributors to this book (for example, Murphy, chapter 1, Raven, chapter 4) not least because it fails to identify and respect far less nurture children's natural desires and curiosities and take account of the economic, social and cultural needs of society. Such a policy would fall gravely short of the ideal equality of consideration in an attempt to achieve the ideal equality of outcome.

It would also seem from the discussion earlier in this chapter that a balance needs to be achieved between the freedom allocated to a particular individual and maximizing the freedom allocated to people in general. Golby (chapter 7) illustrated this through reference to the policy of channeling tax cuts back to individuals to increase their freedom to spend as they wish. He argues that this concession flies in the face of the desire to provide a wide range of services to meet the basic needs of people regardless of their spending power. Could this be equally true of Flew's desire to introduce education vouchers? It is certainly a system wherein public money is passed back to the parents who are then free to channel it towards the 'education firm' of their choice.[10] He himself has argued elsewhere[11] that it is the state's monopoly of education that is possibly the greatest threat to the freedom of the individual. Flew's ideal is one of variety rather than uniformity; of freedom instead of compulsion.

But not every theory of education and philosophy places the ideals of freedom and equality at its core — many see it as the outcome of education rather than a gift from nature.

Increasing Accountability

The official pronouncements of central government hope that governing bodies and their equivalents north of the border will raise the standards of education and ensure better teacher performance. However this is based on the assumption that these formal committees are adequate tools to give parents greater influence in what happens in school, and on the assumption that increased parent power via these committees actually correlates with greater accountability and better quality schooling. Similarly the market place economy assumes that through parental choice the distribution, size and character of the school will be more effectively determined. Neither Raven (chapter 4) nor Morgan (chapter 8) would accept that the legislation will be effective in achieving these goals. This is partly due to too many centrally predetermined decisions and partly to do with the inadequacy of the machinery. Morgan would go a step further by arguing that the evidence suggests that provided everything is running smoothly parents do not wish to be consulted anyway. This latter point was indeed a finding of Pring's and Christie's interviews with parents (see chapter 11).

Golby (chapter 7) reminds us that parents elected to governing bodies are not so much delegates of the other parents with responsibilities for putting forward views agreed by the other parents and reporting back to them. They are representatives who freely express their own views and have no special responsibilities for maintaining contact with those who have elected them. Indeed as Golby found the elections themselves take various forms from persuasion by the head to self-selection often through apprenticeship in a parent teacher association. Concerns have also been expressed both in this book (Golby, chapter 7) and elsewhere[12] that matters for discussion are more politically orientated than having any real bearing on what happens in the school itself. But will opting out give parents and governing bodies more genuine influence over what happens in school? The answer to this question at the time of writing remains to be seen but it is equally possible that central government, for better or for worse, will be more favourably placed to call the shots in such a scenario.

Reynolds (chapter 9) seems to accept that increased parental consultation is the key route to changing the nature and quality of schools' internal processes for the better. However he provides very little evidence to back up this assertion other than that it appears to be politically popular with the skilled working classes. His views are further complicated by the fact that he does not define what he means by quality in education and whether it is something different to right-wing observers as opposed to left-wing observers. He assumes that it is not. A cynic might argue that good quality education in right-wing terms essentially involves an education which appeals to parents (the consumers). Such a view is unlikely to be shared by left-wing thinkers whose ideals are bound to embrace a more objective view of quality which they would like to see extended to *all* children regardless of their parents' influence or spending power. Before one can broach the issue of accountability one needs to reach some consensus on what is a 'good quality' school. But the answer to this question is likely to be complicated by one's view of whom the school is meant to serve — whether it be society, employers, parents or children — and to whom the school should be accountable. Earlier in this chapter it was noted how the answer to these questions varies according to one's political persuasion. For instance Flew sees parents not HMIs, as being in the best position to monitor what goes on in schools. However this assumes the presence of certain knowledge, skills and self-confidence which are likely to vary both in amount and nature according to one's social standing (see Wragg, chapter 6).

To socialists quality and equality go hand in hand.[13] They seek high educational standards not just for a few but for all pupils. But Flew (chapter 5) would argue that denying excellence for a few is compatible with an equality of outcome ideal; it is about mediocrity which he believes is an anti-education ideal. However what is unclear from Flew's analysis is whether excellence for some can be achieved without mediocrity for others. The unevenness of knowledge, affluence and so on, referred to by Wragg and Morgan in particular when one transfers power to parents, could result in the already advantaged benefiting and the less fortunate being consigned by the operation of the market to less good schools.

In Flew's scenario safeguards on quality will be at the discretion of parents who through a policy of open enrolment will close less good schools (inefficient/ineffective producers unable to attract clients) with resources going to those the consumers favour. Any reference to future growth points either demographic or educational will be discounted as irrelevant to the decision of school closure. The local education authorities' role in shaping and providing future citizens and related services will be greatly reduced. Doubtless Flew has great faith in parents' judgment. He believes they have, and feel, the greatest interest in doing that which is for the real benefit of their children. He sees the voucher system as only one possible way of realizing the ideal of an independent education for all children. But Reynolds fears that this transfer in power will be subsequently followed by increased financial responsibility with parents bearing the brunt.

The fact is that the legislation is on the statute books. It is meant to have far reaching effects some of which have been the subject of speculation in this volume. Policies and legislation have rarely waited upon the deliberations of social scientists and this case is no exception. But as Robert Burns had it 'the best laid schemes o' Mice an' Men, gang aft agley'. Policies frequently fail in their purpose and indeed produce unintended and unfortunate effects. It would seem to be in everyone's interest to monitor the processes and products of the Education Reform Act, 1988. We must aspire for the record to be theoretically driven so that sense can be made of it in terms broader than the political. The nightmare is that for such a venture politicians will be uninterested in finding the money and social scientists will prove unable to offer the theory.

Notes

1 While there is the legal obligation that a child receive an adequate education, it is possible for parents in Britain to make their own arrangements for education and so avoid having to send their children to school. Hence the existence of 'Education Otherwise' which is an organization that seeks to provide support for families who wish to take up this option — it is an option which Ian Morgan (chapter 8) sees as rare enough to be eccentric.

2 DEWEY, J. (1916) *Democracy and Education*, New York, Macmillan.

3 REIMER, E. (1971) *School is Dead*, London, Penguin.

4 ILLICH, I.D. (1973) *Deschooling Society*, London, Penguin.

5 GOODMAN, P. (1971) *Compulsory Miseducation*, London, Penguin.

6 HARGREAVES, D. (1986) 'Community and educator' in RANSON, S. and TOMLINSON, J. (Ed.) *The Changing Government of Education*, London, Allen and Unwin.

7 ISAACSON, Z. (1986) 'Freedom and girls' education: a philosophical discussion with particular reference to mathematics' in BARTON, L. (Ed.) *Girls Into Maths Can Go*, London, Holt, Rinehart and Winston.

8 Isaacson, Z. (1986) *op. cit.*
9 Berlin, I. (1969) *Four Essays on Liberty*, Oxford, Oxford University Press.
10 Flew, A. (1987) *Power to the Parents: Reversing Educational Decline*, London, Sherwood Press.
11 Flew, A. (1987) *op. cit.*
12 Sutherland, M. (1988) *Theory of Education*, London, Longman.
13 Hargreaves, D. (1985) *op. cit.*

Notes on Contributors

Beverly Anderson is an educational consultant and trainer. She was formerly a primary school headteacher and a senior lecturer at Oxford Polytechnic. She is currently a member of the National Curriculum Council and the Commission for Racial Equality. She chaired the NAB equal opportunities group and was a member of the Education Reform Group.

Jill Christie taught English in England and India. She has evolved an interest in research as a therapeutic process as well as a scientific one. She prefers to use the personal interview approach.

Antony Flew is Emeritus Professor of Philosophy at the University of Reading and author of, interalia, *Power to the Parents: Reversing Educational Decline* (London, Sherwood, 1987).

Michael Golby is a senior lecturer in education at the University of Exeter. He is a former editor of the European Journal of Curriculum Studies and Director of the Leverhulme Parents as School Governors Project.

Flora Macleod is a lecturer in Education at the University of Exeter. Prior to this she taught in Glasgow and Manchester and was a researcher at the Community Education Development Centre in Coventry. She has published several articles on involving parents in their children's educational development and is currently researching the link between gender and educational participation and achievement. She is also Review Editor of the *British Journal of Educational Psychology*.

Ian Morgan was President of the National Union of Teachers 1987–88. He is an educational consultant in Educational Management. Prior to this he was a Headteacher.

Jim Murphy lectures in the Department of Educational Research at Lancaster University. He is currently researching the relationship between higher education and national prosperity. His previous work includes several papers in the *British Journal of Sociology* and the link between education and inequality.

Richard Pring is Professor of Education at the University of Exeter. He is the author of *Knowledge and Schools* (Open Books, 1976) and *Personal and Social Education in the Curriculum* (Hodder and Stoughton, 1984). In September 1989 he takes up the post of Professor of Education at Oxford University.

John Raven consults in educational evaluation, educational and psychological assessment, staff development, organisational development, and values, attitudes and institutional structures associated with economic and social development.

David Reynolds is a lecturer in education at the University of Wales, College of Cardiff. He has recently published in the areas of school effectiveness and school organisation and his most recent publication is *Educational Policy: Controversies and Critiques* (Falmer Press, 1989).

Joyce Watt is a senior lecturer in the Department of Education at the University of Aberdeen. She is co-author of *Towards Community Education* (Aberdeen University Press, 1981) and has written widely on community aspects of early education.

Ted Wragg is Director of the School of Education at Exeter University. He is the author of *Education: An Action Guide for Parents*, *A Handbook for School Governors* and *Parents in Education*.

Subject Index

Author Index